1997 Supplement to

Arrest,
Search, *and*
Investigation
in
North
Carolina

1997 Supplement to

Arrest, Search, *and* Investigation

in
North Carolina

Second Edition

Robert L. Farb

INSTITUTE *of* GOVERNMENT
The University of North Carolina at Chapel Hill

THE INSTITUTE OF GOVERNMENT of The University of North Carolina at Chapel Hill is devoted to teaching, research, and consultation in state and local government.

Since 1931 the Institute has conducted schools and short courses for city, county, and state officials. Through monographs, guidebooks, bulletins, and periodicals, the research findings of the Institute are made available to public officials throughout the state.

Each day that the General Assembly is in session, the Institute's *Daily Bulletin* reports on the Assembly's activities for members of the legislature and other state and local officials who need to follow the course of legislation.

Over the years the Institute has served as the research agency for numerous study commissions of the state and local governments.

Michael R. Smith, DIRECTOR
Thomas H. Thornburg, ASSOCIATE DIRECTOR FOR PROGRAMS
William A. Campbell, ASSOCIATE DIRECTOR FOR SERVICES
Patricia A. Langelier, ACTING ASSOCIATE DIRECTOR FOR PLANNING AND OPERATIONS
Ann C. Simpson, ASSOCIATE DIRECTOR FOR DEVELOPMENT

FACULTY

Gregory S. Allison	James C. Drennan	Janet Mason
Stephen Allred	Richard D. Ducker	Laurie L. Mesibov
David N. Ammons	Robert L. Farb	Jill D. Moore
A. Fleming Bell, II	Joseph S. Ferrell	David W. Owens
Frayda S. Bluestein	Milton S. Heath, Jr.	John Rubin
Mark F. Botts	Cheryl Daniels Howell	John L. Saxon
Joan G. Brannon	Joseph E. Hunt	John B. Stephens
Anita R. Brown-Graham	Kurt J. Jenne	A. John Vogt
Margaret S. Carlson	Robert P. Joyce	Gordon P. Whitaker
Stevens H. Clarke	David M. Lawrence	Michael L. Williamson
Anne S. Davidson	Charles D. Liner	(on leave)
Anne M. Dellinger	Ben F. Loeb, Jr.	

© 1998

Institute of Government
The University of North Carolina at Chapel Hill

♾ This publication is printed on permanent, acid-free paper in compliance with the North Carolina General Statutes.
Printed in the United States of America
02 01 00 99   5 4 3 2

ISBN 1-56011-312-X

♻ Printed on recycled paper

Contents

Note: *Each chapter includes a detailed Contents for that chapter.*

Preface

This supplement explains new legislation and appellate cases since the publication of the second edition of *Arrest, Search, and Investigation in North Carolina.* (For ease of reading, this supplement will refer to that publication as the "second edition.") This supplement includes federal and state legislation through August 1997; cases of the United States Supreme Court, North Carolina Supreme Court, and North Carolina Court of Appeals through June 1997; and cases of the federal courts of appeals reported through volume 102 of the *Federal Reporter, Third Series.*

A third edition (1996) of LaFave's *Search and Seizure: A Treatise on the Fourth Amendment* has been published since the second edition of *Arrest, Search, and Investigation* went to press. Fortunately only a few topical section numbers have changed in LaFave's third edition. Thus almost all of my second edition references to LaFave's topical section numbers will still lead to the appropriate reference materials in his third edition. (Of course, the page-number references to LaFave's second edition are no longer useful for those referring to his third edition.)

I thank Randolph B. Means, of Thomas and Means, L.L.P., in Charlotte, North Carolina, who has been a police legal adviser since 1979, and John Rubin, a member of the Institute of Government faculty, who read drafts of the text and notes and offered useful comments.

I welcome comments about this supplement's scope, organization, or content. Comments may be sent to me at the Institute of Government, CB# 3330, Knapp Building, The University of North Carolina at Chapel Hill, Chapel Hill, North Carolina 27599-3330.

Robert L. Farb

Chapel Hill
August 1997

How to Use this Book

This book supplements both the chapters and the case summaries section of the second edition of *Arrest, Search, and Investigation in North Carolina*. It has been prepared so the reader is not required to refer to the second edition to understand the material in this book—unless a specific reference is made to the second edition. Headings and page number references to the second edition are provided throughout this book so that the reader may readily find the corresponding topics in the second edition.

The supplementary material to the chapters of the second edition includes new legislation and case law that modify or enlarge the second edition's contents. Footnotes to the new, supplementary material appear at the bottom of the page. Modifications of the second edition's endnotes appear at the end of each chapter supplement.

The case summaries section of this book adds summaries of appellate cases that have been decided since the publication of the second edition.

Supplement to

1 **An Introduction to Constitutional Law and North Carolina Criminal Law and Procedure**

Supplement to

1   **An Introduction to Constitutional Law and North Carolina Criminal Law and Procedure**

Note: Headings and page numbers from the second edition are provided for reference.

Sources of Criminal Law
City and County Ordinances [page 3]
Under the Structured Sentencing Act, which became effective for offenses committed on or after October 1, 1994, a violation of an ordinance is a Class 3 misdemeanor and the maximum punishment is twenty days' imprisonment or a $500 fine.[1] The sentencing judge may impose an active term of imprisonment only if the defendant has a prior criminal record consisting of five or more convictions.[2]

Constitutional and Statutory Restrictions on an Officer's Authority
Statutory Restrictions [page 5]
In 1995 the North Carolina General Assembly enacted legislation that permits law enforcement officers to use wiretapping and eavesdropping devices under limited circumstances. This legislation is discussed in detail in Chapter 3 of this supplement.

Criminal Pretrial and Trial Procedure
Felonies [page 6]
In 1996 the North Carolina General Assembly enacted legislation to give a district court judge the authority to accept a plea of guilty or no contest to a Class H or I felony, if the judge, prosecutor, and defendant all agree to do so.[3] Before this legislative change, all pleas of guilty and no contest to felonies had to be heard in superior court.

Appellate Review [page 7]
In 1995 the North Carolina General Assembly enacted legislation to provide that an appeal from a first-degree murder conviction that resulted in a sentence of life imprisonment must go to the North Carolina Court of Appeals.[4] However, an appeal from a death sentence in such a case will continue to go directly to the North Carolina Supreme Court.

Changes to Chapter 1 Notes
Note: Both note and page numbers from the second edition are provided for reference.

4. [page 8] There is a new edition of the publication that was cited in this note. For the elements of larceny, see Thomas H. Thornburg, ed., *North Carolina Crimes: A Guidebook on the Elements of Crime*, 4th ed. (Chapel Hill, N.C.: Institute of Government, The University of North Carolina at Chapel Hill, 1996), 158.

---

1. *See* N.C. GEN. STAT. § 14-4.
2. *See id.* § 15A-1340.23.
3. *See id.* § 7A-272(c). The legislation applies to offenses committed on or after December 1, 1995.
4. *See id.* § 7A-27(a) and (b). The legislation applies to cases tried on or after December 1, 1995.

Supplement to

2 Law of Arrest and Investigative Stops

Supplement to

2   Law of Arrest and Investigative Stops

Note: Headings and page numbers from the second edition are provided for reference.

Jurisdiction
Limits on Law Enforcement Officers' Jurisdiction

Territorial Jurisdiction

City Law Enforcement Officers [page 16]. In 1995 the North Carolina General Assembly enacted legislation authorizing city law enforcement officers to transport a person in custody to or from any place in North Carolina so that the person can attend a criminal court proceeding. The new law also authorizes officers to arrest the person in custody for any offense he or she commits while being transported.[1]

Company Police Officers [page 16]. The North Carolina Supreme Court in *State v. Pendleton*[2] ruled that the state's delegation of its law enforcement power (through the law authorizing company police officers) to Campbell University, a religious institution, violated the First Amendment's Establishment Clause. The court stressed that its ruling was based on the unique nature of Campbell University as found by the trial court in this case. It is unlikely that the ruling would apply to company police agencies at other religious institutions in North Carolina.

Legal Standards
The Authority to Make an Investigative Stop: Reasonable Suspicion

Appellate Court Cases on Reasonable Suspicion [page 24]

The text of the second edition on pages 24–29 describes several appellate cases on reasonable suspicion. Below is an additional appellate case.

—■ *State v. Watson*

> *At approximately 2:30 A.M. in June 1993, a trooper of the North Carolina Highway Patrol saw a 1971 Ford pickup truck driving on the dividing line of a two-lane highway near a nightclub. After the trooper turned to follow the vehicle, he noticed it weaving back and forth in its lane. After observing this behavior for approximately fifteen seconds, the officer stopped the vehicle.*

The North Carolina Court of Appeals in *State v. Watson*[3] ruled that these facts were sufficient to provide reasonable suspicion to stop the driver of the vehicle for impaired driving. The court noted the trooper's observation of the defendant's driving on the center line and weaving back and forth within his lane for fifteen seconds, and that this activity took place at 2:30 A.M. on a road near a nightclub. The court stated that the totality of circumstances supported reasonable suspicion to stop the vehicle for impaired driving.

---

1. *See* N.C. Gen. Stat. § 15A-402(c).
2. 339 N.C. 379, 451 S.E.2d 274 (1994), *cert. denied*, 115 S. Ct. 2276 (1995). The court relied on Larkin v. Grendel's Den, Inc., 459 U.S. 116, 103 S. Ct. 505, 74 L. Ed. 2d 297 (1982).
3. 122 N.C. App. 596, 472 S.E.2d 28 (1996).

Pretextual Arrest, Investigative Stop, or Search [page 33]

The United States Supreme Court in *Whren v. United States*[4] ruled that stopping a vehicle for a traffic violation, when there is probable cause to believe the traffic violation was committed, does not violate the Fourth Amendment regardless of the officer's motivation for doing so. (In this case, drug officers had stopped a vehicle for traffic violations.)[5] This ruling effectively overrules *State v. Morocco*,[6] a North Carolina Court of Appeals case discussed on pages 33–34 of the second edition. The court of appeals in *Morocco* had adopted a test that asked what a reasonable officer *would* have done in similar circumstances. After the *Whren* case, a court must simply determine what an officer *could* legally do under the Fourth Amendment.

Special Aspects of Stopping Authority
Investigative Stop Based on Reasonable Suspicion

Investigative Techniques Used during an Investigative Stop [page 34]

Ordering Vehicle's Driver and Passengers out of Vehicle after Lawful Stop (new section). In 1977 the United States Supreme Court in *Pennsylvania v. Mimms*[7] ruled that an officer who has lawfully stopped a vehicle may order the driver out of the vehicle without showing any reason to do so under the Fourth Amendment. In 1997 the Court ruled in *Maryland v. Wilson*[8] that an officer may order the passengers out of the vehicle under the same circumstances.

The Arrest Warrant and Other Criminal Process
Criminal Process

Arrest Warrant

Issuance and Contents [page 38]. In 1997 the North Carolina General Assembly enacted legislation that permits a magistrate (or other judicial official) to issue an arrest warrant based on oral testimony given by a sworn law enforcement officer to the magistrate (or other judicial official) by means of an audio and video transmission in which both people can see and hear each other.[9]

---

4. 517 U.S. 806, 116 S. Ct. 1769, 135 L. Ed. 2d 89 (1996). The Court did not discuss whether its ruling would also apply when an officer has only reasonable suspicion to stop a vehicle for a traffic violation (although it likely would so rule). *See, e.g.,* United States v. Dumas, 94 F.3d 286 (7th Cir. 1996) (court noted that any argument that investigative stop based on reasonable suspicion was invalid as mere pretext to search for drugs was foreclosed by *Whren v. United States*). Of course, the court's ruling in no way changes Fourth Amendment law that an officer may make an investigative stop of a vehicle based on reasonable suspicion. *See, e.g.,* Alabama v. White, 496 U.S. 325, 110 S. Ct. 2412, 110 L. Ed. 2d 301 (1990); United States v. Brignoni-Ponce, 422 U.S. 873, 95 S. Ct. 2574, 45 L. Ed. 2d 607 (1975). *See also* United States v. Hudson, 100 F.3d 1409 (9th Cir. 1996) (when probable cause supported arrest under arrest warrant, officer's motive in making arrest was irrelevant under *Whren v. United States*); Holland v. City of Portland, 102 F.3d 6 (1st Cir. 1996) (similar ruling).

5. For a similar North Carolina ruling after *Whren*, when drug officers stopped a vehicle for traffic violations (neither driver nor passenger was wearing a seat belt), see State v. Hamilton, 125 N.C. App. 396, 481 S.E.2d 98 (1997).

6. 99 N.C. App. 421, 393 S.E.2d 545 (1990). The North Carolina Court of Appeals recognized in State v. Hamilton, 125 N.C. App. 396, 481 S.E.2d 98 (1997), that the *Whren* decision effectively overruled *Morocco*.

7. 434 U.S. 106, 98 S. Ct. 330, 54 L. Ed. 2d 331 (1977).

8. 519 U.S. ___, 117 S. Ct. 882, 137 L. Ed. 2d 41 (1997).

9. N.C. Sess. Laws 1997-268. This legislation was effective July 3, 1997, and was codified in G.S. 15A-304. The use of this procedure and the equipment must be approved by the Administrative Office of the Courts.

Arrest without a Warrant or Order for Arrest
Misdemeanor

General Rules [page 42]

In 1995 the North Carolina General Assembly amended G.S. 15A-401 to permit an officer to make a warrantless arrest when the officer has probable cause to believe that a person has committed the following misdemeanors out of the officer's presence: impaired driving (G.S. 20-138.1) and impaired driving in a commercial vehicle (G.S. 20-138.2). For these offenses, an officer no longer needs to justify a warrantless out-of-presence arrest based on evidence that the person would not be apprehended or would cause injury to himself or herself or others or damage to property unless he or she were immediately arrested.

Delay in Making a Warrantless Misdemeanor Arrest [page 43]

The text on page 43 of the second edition states that an officer who wants to make a misdemeanor arrest without a warrant must make the arrest immediately or lose the authority to proceed without a warrant. That statement needs to be clarified. An officer who delays making an immediate arrest for a law enforcement purpose associated with the arrest (for example, when an unruly crowd is impeding the arrest or when the officer must pursue the offender to make the arrest) would still retain the authority to make a warrantless arrest as long as the officer does not become involved in unrelated matters before making the arrest.

The Arrest Procedure
Notice of Authority

Before Entering a Dwelling [page 47]

The text of the second edition states that officers need not give notice before entering a private dwelling when they have reasonable grounds to believe that giving the notice would present a clear danger to human life. The North Carolina Court of Appeals has recognized another circumstance when notice is not required. The court ruled in *Lee v. Greene*[10] that officers were not required to give notice to a fleeing suspect of their authority and purpose under G.S. 15A-401(e) when they followed her into her house while in immediate pursuit to arrest her, because she knew during the entire pursuit that they were State Highway Patrol officers and knew why they had entered her house.

Entrance onto Premises to Arrest [page 48]

The text of the second edition discusses the authority of an officer to enter premises with an arrest warrant or order for arrest. Most commonly, an order for arrest will be issued in connection with a criminal offense (because a case has begun with an indictment or a defendant has failed to appear in court). However, it would also appear that, if the conditions set forth in the second edition are satisfied, an officer may also enter premises to arrest when an order for arrest has been issued in conjunction with proceedings for civil or criminal contempt under Chapter 5A of the General Statutes. Such proceedings include contempt proceedings arising from actions for nonsupport.[11]

---

10. 114 N.C. App. 580, 442 S.E.2d 547 (1993).

11. G.S. 5A-16(b) authorizes, under certain circumstances, the issuance of an order for arrest in conjunction with plenary proceedings for criminal contempt. A judge also has the authority to issue an order for arrest for a person who fails to appear in response to a show cause order for either criminal or civil contempt proceedings.

Completion of Custody of the Arrestee
Taking Fingerprints and Photographs

Adults [page 53]

The text of the second edition states that an arrestee who is charged with a motor vehicle offense may not be fingerprinted or photographed if the authorized penalty does not exceed a fine of $500, six months' imprisonment, or both. The North Carolina General Assembly has modified this provision to reflect the enactment of the Structured Sentencing Act. The law now provides that an arrestee who is charged with a motor vehicle offense may not be fingerprinted or photographed if the offense is a Class 2 or Class 3 misdemeanor.[12]

The text of the second edition states that it is not clear whether the age of sixteen or eighteen constitutes adulthood for the purpose of fingerprinting and photographing, but that the more persuasive view is that an adult is a person sixteen years old or older. A 1996 legislative amendment to G.S. 15A-502 (which specifies the circumstances in which an adult may be photographed and fingerprinted) lends support to the statement that an adult is a person sixteen years old or older. The legislative amendment specifically states that G.S. 15A-502 does not authorize the taking of photographs or fingerprints of a juvenile *alleged to be delinquent* (the emphasized words were added by the legislative amendment).[13] Only a juvenile under sixteen years old may be alleged to be delinquent.[14]

Juveniles [page 53]

The text of the second edition states that it is not clear what age defines a juvenile for the purpose of fingerprinting and photographing, but that the more persuasive view is that a juvenile is a person under sixteen years old. A 1996 legislative amendment to G.S. 15A-502 (which specifies the circumstances when an adult may be photographed and fingerprinted) lends support to the statement that a juvenile is a person under sixteen years old. The legislative amendment specifically states that G.S. 15A-502 does not authorize the taking of photographs or fingerprints of a juvenile *alleged to be delinquent* (the emphasized words were added by the legislative amendment).[15] Only a juvenile under sixteen years old may be alleged to be delinquent.[16]

In 1996 the North Carolina General Assembly enacted legislation to require that a juvenile must be fingerprinted and photographed if adjudicated delinquent of an offense that would be a Class A through E felony if committed by an adult, if the juvenile was ten years old or older at the time the offense was committed.[17] The fingerprints and photographs may be retained and used for future investigative or comparison purposes.

Conducting an Initial Appearance [page 54]

In 1997 the North Carolina General Assembly enacted legislation to allow an initial appearance for an offense other than first-degree murder to be conducted by an audio and video transmission between the magistrate (or other judicial official) and the defendant, in which both people can see and hear each other. If the defendant has counsel,

---

12. N.C. Gen. Stat. § 15A-502(c).
13. 1996 N.C. Sess. Laws (Second Extra Session) ch. 18.
14. See the definition of "delinquent juvenile" in G.S. 7A-517(12).
15. 1996 N.C. Sess. Laws (Second Extra Session) ch. 18.
16. See the definition of "delinquent juvenile" in G.S. 7A-517(12).
17. 1996 N.C. Sess. Laws (Second Extra Session) ch. 18. This legislation was codified in G.S. 7A-603.

the defendant must be allowed to communicate fully and confidentially with counsel during the proceeding.[18]

Considering Pretrial Release Conditions [page 55]

In 1995 the North Carolina General Assembly enacted legislation to provide that only a judge may set conditions of pretrial release for defendants arrested for domestic violence offenses.[19] However, if a judge has not set conditions of pretrial release within forty-eight hours of arrest, then a magistrate must set conditions in accordance with G.S. 15A-534 and -534.1. A domestic violence offense includes (1) assaulting or communicating a threat to a spouse or former spouse or a person with whom the arrestee lives or has lived as if married, (2) domestic criminal trespass, or (3) violation of a domestic violence protective order entered under Chapter 50B of the General Statutes.

Informing a Minor's Parent [and School Principal] of a Criminal Charge [page 55]

In 1994 the North Carolina General Assembly revised the statute requiring an officer to notify a parent or guardian when the officer charges a minor (a person under eighteen years old) with a criminal offense.[20] (This notification requirement does not apply to infractions.) The statute now requires an officer to notify the minor's parent or guardian of the charge as soon as practicable, either in person or by telephone. If the minor has been taken into custody, the officer or his or her immediate supervisor must notify the parent or guardian in writing, within twenty-four hours of the minor's arrest, that the minor is in custody. If the parent or guardian cannot be found, then the officer or immediate supervisor must notify the minor's next-of-kin of the minor's arrest as soon as practicable. This notification requirement does not apply if (1) the minor has been emancipated (by court order or by being married) or (2) the minor has not been taken into custody and has been charged with a motor vehicle moving violation for which fewer than four driver's license points are assessed, except that the parent or guardian must be notified of an offense involving impaired driving.

In 1997 the North Carolina General Assembly amended G.S. 15A-505, effective November 1, 1997, to require a law enforcement officer who charges a student with a felony (excluding a felony under Chapter 20 of the General Statutes) to notify the principal of the student's North Carolina public or private school of the charge.[21] The notification may be made in person or by telephone, and it must be made as soon as practicable but at least within five days of the charge. However, if the student is taken into custody, the officer or the officer's supervisor must notify the principal in writing within five days of the student's arrest. If the principal receives notification under the statute, the district attorney's office must notify the principal of the final disposition of the case at the trial court level, and the notification must be in writing and be made within five days of the disposition.

The requirement that an officer must notify a principal would apply only to students who are sixteen years old or older when they are charged, because G.S. 15A-505 does not apply to students who are charged in juvenile court.[22] The same 1997 legislation that amended this statute imposes a requirement on a juvenile court counselor, not

---

18. N.C. Sess. Laws 1997-268. This legislation was effective July 3, 1997, and was codified in G.S. 15A-511. The use of this procedure and the equipment must be approved by the Administrative Office of the Courts.

19. *See* N.C. Gen. Stat. § 15A-534.1

20. *See id.* § 15A-505.

21. N.C. Sess. Laws 1997-443.

22. Although highly unlikely to occur, the statute could also apply to a student under sixteen years old who was married, otherwise emancipated, or subject to prosecution as an adult under G.S. 7A-524.

a law enforcement officer, to notify a principal when a petition is filed against a juvenile that alleges delinquency for an offense that would be a felony if committed by an adult.

Changes to Chapter 2 Notes

Note: Both note and page numbers from the second edition are provided.

7. [**page 56**] For a discussion of state and local law enforcement agencies in North Carolina, see Michael F. Easley and Jeffrey P. Gray, *Territorial and Subject Matter Jurisdiction of Law Enforcement Agencies in North Carolina* (Raleigh, N.C.: North Carolina Department of Justice, May 1996).

21. [**page 57**] For a discussion of company police in North Carolina, see Michael F. Easley and Jeffrey P. Gray, *Powers and Jurisdiction of Company Police in North Carolina* (Raleigh, N.C.: North Carolina Department of Justice, January 1996).

67. [**page 60**] For a discussion of diplomatic immunity, see *Guidance for Law Enforcement Officers: Personal Rights and Immunities of Foreign Diplomatic and Consular Personnel,* 2d ed. rev. (Washington, D.C.: United States Department of State, Office of Protocol and the Office of Foreign Missions, November 1993).

68. [**page 60**] In 1994 the North Carolina General Assembly added Immigration and Naturalization Service (INS) officers to the list of federal law enforcement officers who are authorized to enforce North Carolina's criminal laws, as explained in the second edition on page 20.

70. [**page 60**] For a discussion of mutual aid agreements between law enforcement agencies, including sample resolutions and mutual assistance agreement forms, see Michael F. Easley and Jeffrey P. Gray, *Mutual Aid Agreements between Law Enforcement Agencies in North Carolina* (Raleigh, N.C.: North Carolina Department of Justice, March 1996).

97. [**page 62**] In Whren v. United States, 517 U.S. 806, 116 S. Ct. 1769, 135 L. Ed. 2d. 89 (1996), the Court ruled that stopping a vehicle for a traffic violation, when there is probable cause to believe the traffic violation was committed, does not violate the Fourth Amendment regardless of the officer's motivation for doing so. The Court did not discuss whether its ruling would also apply when an officer has only reasonable suspicion to stop a vehicle for a traffic violation (although it likely would so rule). Of course, the Court's ruling in no way changes Fourth Amendment law that an officer may make an investigative stop of a vehicle based on reasonable suspicion. *See, e.g.,* Alabama v. White, 496 U.S. 325, 110 S. Ct. 2412, 110 L. Ed. 2d 301 (1990); United States v. Brignoni-Ponce, 422 U.S. 873, 95 S. Ct. 2574, 45 L. Ed. 2d 607 (1975).

127. [**page 63**] The discussion in this note is no longer relevant as a result of the ruling in Whren v. United States, 517 U.S. 806, 116 S. Ct. 1769, 135 L. Ed. 2d. 89 (1996), discussed in the text of Chapter 2 of this supplement.

152. [**page 65**] The North Carolina Court of Appeals in State v. Sanders, 112 N.C. App. 477, 435 S.E.2d 842 (1993), upheld a driver's license check set up by two State Highway Patrol troopers who, following guidelines established by their agency, selected a location and time during daylight hours for the license check. The troopers detained every vehicle that passed through the checkpoint, with the exception of those that came through while the troopers were issuing citations to the operators of other vehicles. The court's opinion did not discuss whether the troopers had received supervisory approval when setting up the license check. *See also* State v. Barnes, 123 N.C. App. 144, 472 S.E.2d 784 (1996) (court upholds license check set up by State Highway Patrol sergeant who was acting as shift supervisor; check substantially complied with a patrol directive and G.S. 20-16.3A); State v. Grooms, 126 N.C. App. 88, 483 S.E.2d 445 (1997) (court upholds license check roadblock by deputy sheriffs that was approved in advance by sheriff).

157. [**page 65**] The ruling in State v. Nobles, 107 N.C. App. 627, 422 S.E.2d 78 (1992), cited in this note, was affirmed by the North Carolina Supreme Court, 333 N.C. 787, 429 S.E.2d 716, *cert. denied,* 510 U.S. 946 (1993).

171. [**page 66**] There is a new edition of a publication cited in this note: Robert L. Farb, ed., *Arrest Warrant and Indictment Forms,* 4th ed. (Chapel Hill, N.C.: Institute of Government, The University of North Carolina at Chapel Hill, 1996).

195. [**page 67**] Since the publication of the second edition, the following states have joined the uniform reciprocal nonresident violator compact: Arizona, Hawaii, Idaho, and Washington. Thus the only states that are not members of the compact are Alaska, California, Michigan, Montana, Oregon, and Wisconsin.

Supplement to

3 Law of Search and Seizure

Supplement to

3   **Law of Search and Seizure**

Note: Headings and page numbers from the second edition are provided for reference.

Observations and Actions That May Not Implicate Fourth Amendment Rights
Abandoned Property and Garbage

Garbage [page 80]

In *State v. Hauser*,[1] a detective made arrangements with the city sanitation department to collect trash at the defendant's residence and give it to him and other detectives. A sanitation worker collected the garbage left at the back of the residence for pickup. The collection was routine except that the sanitation worker prevented the garbage from commingling with other garbage by depositing the defendant's garbage into his own container in the back of the garbage truck instead of into the truck's collection bin.

    The sanitation worker gave the defendant's garbage to the detectives, who found cocaine residue in it. One of the detectives then obtained a search warrant based on the cocaine found in the garbage and information received from four informants. One of the informants stated that the defendant had sold him cocaine at the defendant's residence. In addition, the officers provided facts showing the reliability of the informants' information. The officers executed the search warrant and found more than a pound of cocaine in the defendant's residence. The North Carolina Supreme Court ruled that the search of the defendant's garbage did not violate the Fourth Amendment. The court stated that the location of the defendant's garbage within the home's curtilage did not automatically establish that he possessed a reasonable expectation of privacy in the garbage. The court ruled that the defendant did not retain a reasonable expectation of privacy in his garbage once it left his yard in the usual manner, based on the facts in this case.

Plain-View Sensory Perceptions (Observation, Smell, Sound, Touch, and Taste) [page 80]

The text of the second edition states that some courts, though not all, have recognized the sense of touch within plain-view sensory perceptions. In 1993 the United States Supreme Court, in *Minnesota v. Dickerson*,[2] recognized the sense of touch within plain-view sensory perceptions under the Fourth Amendment. In *Dickerson*, an officer had reasonable suspicion to stop the defendant and to frisk him for weapons. During the

---

    1. 342 N.C. 382, 464 S.E.2d 443 (1995).
    2. 508 U.S. 366, 113 S. Ct. 2130, 124 L. Ed. 2d 334 (1993). North Carolina cases decided since *Minnesota v. Dickerson* include: State v. Beveridge, 112 N.C. App. 688, 436 S.E.2d 912 (1993), *aff'd per curiam*, 336 N.C. 601, 444 S.E.2d 223 (1994) (once officer concluded that cylindrical-shaped rolled-up plastic bag in the defendant's front pocket was not a weapon and it was not immediately apparent that it was an illegal substance, he could not continue the search); State v. Benjamin, 124 N.C. App. 734, 478 S.E.2d 651 (1996) (officer during frisk felt two hard plastic containers customarily used to hold illegal drugs and asked defendant about them; defendant promptly responded that they were "crack"; these and other facts supported seizure of

frisk the officer felt a lump (a small, hard object wrapped in plastic) in the defendant's jacket pocket that the officer knew was not a weapon. However, after concluding that the lump was not a weapon, the officer determined that the lump was cocaine *only* *after* "squeezing, sliding and otherwise manipulating the contents of the defendant's pocket."

The Court ruled that the plain-view doctrine applies by analogy to cases in which an officer discovers contraband through the sense of touch during an otherwise lawful search. [The plain-view doctrine provides that if (1) officers are lawfully in a position in which they view an object, (2) its incriminating character is immediately apparent (that is, they have probable cause to seize it), and (3) the officers have a lawful right of access to the object, they may seize it without a warrant.] However, the Court also ruled that the officer in this case was not justified in seizing the cocaine because the officer exceeded the search for weapons permitted by the Fourth Amendment.[3] Once the officer determined the lump was not a weapon, his continued exploration of the lump until he developed probable cause to believe it was cocaine was an additional search that was not justified by the Fourth Amendment. Thus the officer's action would have been permissible in this case only if he had developed probable cause to believe the lump was cocaine at the time he determined the lump was not a weapon.

Use of Special Devices

Wiretapping and Eavesdropping—Federal Requirements [page 83]. The text of the second edition (in the first paragraph of this topic heading) states that North Carolina law did not then permit state and local government law enforcement officers to use devices to intercept wire, oral, or electronic communications without consent of one of the parties to the communication. The North Carolina General Assembly enacted legislation in 1995 to permit officers to do so with a state court order, but under limited circumstances.[4] Only the Attorney General of North Carolina (or his or her designee) may apply for an order authorizing a state or local law enforcement agency to engage in electronic surveillance (however, state and local law enforcement agencies may ask the attorney general to apply for an order).[5] The attorney general (or his or her designee) must apply for an order from a judicial review panel composed of judges appointed by the Chief Justice of the North Carolina Supreme Court (or an Associate Justice designated by the Chief Justice). This panel is the only judicial body that may issue an order authorizing electronic surveillance—individual judges may not do so. The legislation contains detailed provisions about the issuance and implementation of electronic surveillance orders and the disclosure and use of intercepted communications. It also provides for criminal and civil penalties for unlawful interception of wire, oral, or electronic communications.

The text of the second edition (in the second paragraph of this topic heading) states that federal law does not prohibit the interception of the radio portion of a cordless telephone communication that is transmitted between the cordless telephone

---

cocaine); *In re* Whitley, 122 N.C. App. 290, 468 S.E.2d 610, *review denied*, 344 N.C. 437, 476 S.E.2d 132 (1996) (incriminating character of the seized object was immediately apparent to officer when during frisk it fell from the suspect's buttocks into his pants; seizure of cocaine was proper); State v. Wilson, 112 N.C. App. 777, 437 S.E.2d 387 (1993) (officer during frisk felt lump in the left breast pocket of defendant's jacket and immediately believed that it was crack cocaine; seizure of cocaine was proper).

3. *See* Terry v. Ohio, 392 U.S. 1, 88 S. Ct. 1868, 20 L. Ed. 2d 889 (1968).
4. *See* N.C. GEN. STAT. §§ 15A-286 through -298.
5. *See id.* § 15A-292.

handset and its base unit. However, federal legislation enacted in 1994 prohibits the nonconsensual interception of such a communication without a proper federal court order.[6] State legislation also prohibits such a nonconsensual interception without a proper state court order.[7]

Pen Registers and Trap-and-Trace Devices [page 84]. The text of the second edition states that a court order for a pen register or a trap-and-trace device must be supported by, among other things, reasonable suspicion that a person committed a crime punishable by more than one year. Under the Structured Sentencing Act, which became effective in 1994, no misdemeanor offense is punishable by more than one year's imprisonment. Hence a court order could be issued only for a felony offense. However, the North Carolina General Assembly in 1997 enacted legislation, effective for offenses committed on or after December 1, 1997, to also allow a court order to be issued for a Class A1 or Class 1 misdemeanor.[8]

The second edition also states that a person who willfully and knowingly violates the law by using one of these devices is guilty of a misdemeanor punishable by a fine, or imprisonment up to one year, or both. Under the Structured Sentencing Act, the punishment was changed to a Class 1 misdemeanor.[9]

Bank and Telephone Records

Telephone Records [page 86]

The text of the second edition states that North Carolina law does not authorize a law enforcement officer to issue an administrative subpoena. However, the North Carolina General Assembly enacted legislation in 1995 to authorize agents of the State Bureau of Investigation (SBI) to issue an administrative subpoena to telephone companies, other communications common carriers, and electronic communications services to compel production of their business records, if the records (1) disclose information concerning local or long distance toll records or subscriber information and (2) are material to an active criminal investigation being conducted by the SBI.[10]

The text of the second edition states that a law enforcement officer who obtains a customer's telephone information in violation of federal law is subject to civil damages to the customer. However, a federal appellate court has ruled that civil liability applies only to the telephone company for illegally providing the information, not to the law enforcement officer who obtained the information or to his or her agency—at least in the absence of evidence that the officer or agency aided and abetted or conspired with the telephone company to violate the law.[11]

---

6. Pub. L. No. 103-414, § 202(a), 108 Stat. 4290 (1994). The legislation deleted the exclusion of cordless telephone communications from the definitions of "wire communication" and "electronic communication" in 18 U.S.C. § 2510(1) and (12).

7. *See* G.S. 15A-286(21) as amended by N.C. Sess. Laws 1997-435.

8. N.C. Sess. Laws 1997-80.

9. Although the punishment was inadvertently not modified when the Structured Sentencing Act was enacted, the stated punishment automatically became a Class 1 misdemeanor by the provisions of G.S. 14-3(a)(1).

10. *See* N.C. GEN. STAT. § 15A-298. The terms "communications common carrier" and "electronic communications service" are defined in N.C. GEN. STAT. § 15A-286(6) and (9), respectively.

11. Tucker v. Waddell, 83 F.3d 688 (4th Cir. 1996). The court noted but did not decide whether a law enforcement officer or agency could be civilly liable based on theories of aiding and abetting or conspiracy, because the plaintiff did not allege these potential theories of liability.

Search and Seizure by Valid Consent
Content of a Valid Consent

Warning before Asking Consent [page 90]

The United States Supreme Court in *Ohio v. Robinette*[12] reaffirmed its prior rulings that an officer is not required to give any specific warning to a person before asking consent to search. In *Robinette*, an officer stopped the defendant for speeding. The defendant gave his driver's license to the officer, who ran a computer check that revealed that the defendant had no prior violations. The officer then asked the defendant to step out of his car, issued a verbal warning to the defendant, and returned his license. The officer then asked the defendant if he had any illegal contraband in his car. The defendant said no. The officer then asked the defendant if he could search his car, and the defendant consented. The Court rejected a lower court ruling that an officer must advise a lawfully seized defendant that the defendant is free to go before a consent to search will be recognized as voluntary. The Court noted that the Fourth Amendment requires that a consent to search must be voluntary, and voluntariness is a question of fact that must be determined from all the circumstances. An officer's warning before obtaining consent to search is not required by the Fourth Amendment for a consent to search to be valid.

Invasion of Privacy by a Search or Seizure with Sufficient Reason
Search and Seizure to Protect Officers, Other People, or Property

Search Incident to Arrest

Need for a Valid Custodial Arrest [page 103]. The text of the second edition states that even if an arrest is supported by probable cause, a search incident to arrest may be illegal if officers arrest the person—rather than issuing a citation—only as a pretext to search the person incident to arrest. In 1996 the United States Supreme Court in *Whren v. United States*[13] ruled that stopping a vehicle for a traffic violation, when there is probable cause to believe the traffic violation was committed, does not violate the Fourth Amendment regardless of the officer's motivation for doing so. As a result of this ruling, it is highly unlikely that the Court would recognize as unconstitutional a pretextual search incident to arrest when an officer had probable cause to arrest.[14]

Frisk of a Person for Weapons

Discovering Evidence during a Frisk [page 105]. The text of the second edition states that some courts have upheld an officer's seizure of an item (for example, crack cocaine) if the officer's training and experience provided that officer with probable cause to believe that the item the officer was feeling was evidence of a crime, although it clearly did not feel like a weapon. For a discussion of *Minnesota v. Dickerson* and this issue, see page 15 of this chapter.

---

12. 519 U.S. ___, 117 S. Ct. 417, 136 L. Ed. 2d 347 (1996).
13. 517 U.S. 806, 116 S. Ct. 1769, 135 L. Ed. 2d 89 (1996).
14. *See, e.g.,* United States v. Hudson, 100 F.3d 1409 (9th Cir. 1996) (when probable cause supported arrest under arrest warrant, officer's motive in making arrest was irrelevant under *Whren v. United States*).

Changes to Chapter 3 Notes

Note: Both note and page numbers from the second edition are provided for reference.

109. [page 118] In State v. Worsley, 336 N.C. 268, 443 S.E.2d 68 (1994), the court, over-ruling State v. Hall, 264 N.C. 559, 142 S.E.2d 177 (1965), and other cases, ruled that a wife may consent to a search of the premises she shares with her husband.

170. [page 122] In Pennsylvania v. Labron, 518 U.S. ___, 116 S. Ct. 2485, 135 L. Ed. 2d 1031 (1996), the United States Supreme Court reaffirmed its prior case law that if a car is readily mobile and there is probable cause to believe it contains contraband, officers may search the car without a search warrant and without evidence of exigent circumstances.

198. [page 123] In United States v. James Daniel Good Real Property, 510 U.S. 43, 114 S. Ct. 492, 126 L. Ed. 2d 490 (1993), the Court ruled that the Due Process Clause requires that, absent exigent circumstances, the government first must give the owner of real property a hearing before seizing the real property for forfeiture. However, this ruling does not apply to the seizure of personal property for forfeiture.

Supplement to

4   Search Warrants, Administrative Inspection Warrants, and Nontestimonial Identification Orders

4 Search Warrants, Administrative Inspection Warrants, and Nontestimonial Identification Orders

Note: Headings and page numbers from the second edition are provided for reference.

Part I. Search Warrants

Statement of Facts Showing Probable Cause to Search
Future Events: Anticipatory Search Warrants [page 153]

The North Carolina Court of Appeals in *State v. Smith*[1] set out the state constitutional requirements for the issuance of an anticipatory search warrant. (1) An anticipatory search warrant must set out explicit, clear, and narrowly drawn triggering events that must occur before execution of the warrant may take place. (2) These triggering events, from which probable cause arises, must be (i) ascertainable and (ii) preordained (meaning the property is on a sure and irreversible course to its destination, such as when an undercover officer will deliver the cocaine to the house to be searched). (3) A search may not occur unless and until the property does, in fact, arrive at that destination. The court stated that these three conditions ensure that the required nexus among the criminal act, the evidence to be seized, and the identity of the place to be searched is achieved.

An example of what might be contained in an affidavit for an anticipatory search warrant to search premises, in addition to the statement establishing probable cause, is as follows:

> *I request that a search warrant for the premises described above be issued with its execution contingent on the following procedures having occurred: On August 14, 1996, an officer with the Smithville Police Department will pose as a Super Express employee and will deliver the package described above to the premises described above. The package–which is addressed to the premises described above–will contain a powdery substance containing a small amount of cocaine, with most of the cocaine having been removed when the package was previously intercepted as described in this affidavit. After the package is delivered to the above-described premises and is taken inside, this search warrant will be executed.*

Federal court decisions have ruled that anticipatory search warrants are sufficient when the affidavit instead of the warrant itself contains the contingency language.[2] It is unclear whether North Carolina appellate courts would approve such a procedure. The more cautious approach would be to include the contingency language in the affidavit and add a statement on the face of the warrant, such as "This warrant may be executed only if the contingencies set out in the affidavit to this warrant are satisfied."

---

1. 124 N.C. App. 565, 478 S.E.2d 237 (1996). The court ruled that the search warrant in the case before it was not a valid anticipatory search warrant, based on the requirements for such a warrant. The court noted that the search warrant's most glaring deficiency was the absence of any language denoting it as anticipatory.

2. *See, e.g.,* United States v. Moetamedi, 46 F.3d 225 (2d Cir. 1995).

Part III. Nontestimonial Identification Orders

Application for the Order and Issuance of the Order [page 187]

The text of the second edition (in the second paragraph of this topic heading) states that an application for a nontestimonial identification order must establish, among other things, that an offense punishable by imprisonment for more than one year has been committed. Before the enactment of the Structured Sentencing Act in 1994, there were several misdemeanor offenses punishable by more than one year's imprisonment. However, there are no misdemeanors punishable by more than one year's imprisonment under the Structured Sentencing Act. Hence a nontestimonial identification order could be issued only for a felony offense. However, the North Carolina General Assembly in 1997 enacted legislation, effective for offenses committed on or after December 1, 1997, to also allow an order to be issued for a Class A1 or Class 1 misdemeanor.[3]

Defendant's Request for a Nontestimonial Identification Order [page 189]

The text of the second edition states that a person arrested for or charged with an offense punishable by imprisonment for more than one year may request an order so that nontestimonial identification procedures may be conducted on him or her. For the reasons discussed above, this provision under the Structured Sentencing Act applied only to a felony offense until the North Carolina General Assembly in 1997 enacted legislation, effective for offenses committed on or after December 1, 1997, to also allow an order to be issued for a Class A1 or Class 1 misdemeanor.

Juveniles and Nontestimonial Identification Procedures [page 190]

The text of the second edition states that when officers arrest (take into custody) a juvenile, North Carolina law prohibits officers from conducting any nontestimonial identification procedure, including fingerprinting and photographing, unless a superior or district court judge issues a nontestimonial identification order. The statute setting out the grounds for such an order requires, among other things, that the charged offense must be punishable by imprisonment for more than two years.[4] This provision was not changed with the enactment of the Structured Sentencing Act in 1994. As a result, a nontestimonial identification order for a juvenile (for purposes of this law, a person under sixteen) could be issued for Class A through H felonies only.[5] However, the North Carolina General Assembly in 1997 enacted legislation, effective for offenses committed on or after December 1, 1997, to allow an order to be issued for any felony, thus including Class I felonies.[6]

A recent appellate court case made clear that an officer may not conduct a nontestimonial identification procedure on a juvenile (for example, photographing the juvenile) even with the juvenile's consent.[7] The officer must obtain a nontestimonial identification order.

---

3. N.C. Sess. Laws 1997-80.

4. *See* N.C. Gen. Stat. § 7A-598(1). The requirement that an offense be punishable by more than two years' imprisonment also applies when a juvenile requests that a nontestimonial identification order be conducted on himself or herself; *see* N.C. Gen. Stat. § 7A-600.

5. It could not be issued for a Class I felony, whose maximum punishment is only fifteen months, or for any misdemeanor. *See* N.C. Gen. Stat. § 15A-1340.7(c) and (d).

6. N.C. Sess. Laws 1997-80. This legislation also amended G.S. 7A-600, discussed in note 4, *supra*, to make that statute apply to any felony.

7. State v. Green, 124 N.C. App. 269, 477 S.E.2d 182 (1996).

In 1996 the North Carolina General Assembly enacted legislation to require that a juvenile must be fingerprinted and photographed if adjudicated delinquent of an offense that would be a Class A through E felony if committed by an adult, if the juvenile was ten years old or older at the time the offense was committed.[8] The fingerprints and photographs may be retained and used for future investigative or comparison purposes.

Juvenile's Age [page 190]

The text of the second edition states that although it is unclear what age person constitutes a juvenile for nontestimonial identification procedure, the more persuasive view is that a juvenile is a person under sixteen years old, although another view is that a juvenile is a person under eighteen years old. A 1996 legislative amendment to G.S. 15A-502 (which specifies the circumstances when an adult may be photographed and fingerprinted) lends support to the statement that a juvenile is a person under sixteen years old. The legislative amendment specifically states that G.S. 15A-502 does not authorize the taking of photographs or fingerprints of a juvenile *alleged to be delinquent* (the emphasized words were added by the legislative amendment).[9] Only a juvenile under sixteen years old may be alleged to be delinquent.[10]

Changes to Chapter 4 Notes

Note: Both note and page numbers from the second edition are provided for reference.

105. [page 196] In State v. Witherspoon, 110 N.C. App. 413, 429 S.E.2d 783 (1993), the court ruled that a search warrant for the defendant's home was based on probable cause. The search warrant included the following information. A concerned citizen told officers that he had been in defendant's home within the past thirty days and had seen about one hundred marijuana plants in the home's crawl space that were growing with the use of a lighting system and automatic timers. The concerned citizen had spoken with the defendant often about the defendant's growing these plants, and the concerned citizen had used marijuana and had previously seen it growing. Officers corroborated the concerned citizen's description of the defendant's car and stated that it was parked in the defendant's driveway. Officers also checked the power company's records, which showed that the defendant paid the power bill for the house in the past six months. The court, relying on several cases, including State v. Beam, 325 N.C. 217, 381 S.E.2d 327 (1989), rejected the defendant's argument that the information from the concerned citizen was stale because it described events up to thirty days old. The court noted that, based on the facts set out in the affidavit, the magistrate who issued the search warrant could reasonably infer that the marijuana would likely remain in the defendant's home for thirty days.

137. [page 198] In State v. Lyons, 340 N.C. 646, 459 S.E.2d 770 (1995), the court ruled that entry by force to execute a search warrant for drugs was proper under G.S. 15A-251(2), based on the facts in this case (the defendant was uncooperative and the officers believed that there was a firearm in the defendant's apartment). The court also ruled that merely because the officers announced their identity and purpose did not mean that their entry by force could not be justified under G.S. 15A-251(2).

In Richards v. Wisconsin, 520 U.S. ___, 117 S. Ct. 1416, 137 L. Ed. 2d 615 (1997), officers obtained a search warrant to search a hotel room for drugs. Several officers went to the hotel room to execute the warrant. One officer, dressed as a maintenance man, was the lead officer. Among the other officers was at least one uniformed officer. The lead officer knocked on the hotel room door and, responding to a query from inside the room, stated that he was a maintenance man. The defendant cracked open the door with the chain still on it. The defendant saw a uniformed officer among the officers outside the door. The defendant quickly slammed the door shut. After waiting two or three seconds, the officers began kicking and ramming the door to gain entry. The officers identified themselves as officers while they were kicking the door in. The

---

8. 1996 N.C. Sess. Laws (Second Extra Session) ch. 18. This legislation was codified in G.S. 7A-603.

9. 1996 N.C. Sess. Laws (Second Extra Session) ch. 18.

10. See the definition of "delinquent juvenile" in G.S. 7A-517(12).

Court rejected a lower court ruling in this case that officers executing a search warrant involving felony drug crimes are never required to comply with the knock-and-announce rule under the Fourth Amendment. The Court stated that Wilson v. Arkansas, 514 U.S. 927, 115 S. Ct. 1914, 131 L. Ed. 2d 976 (1995) did not support the lower court's ruling. However, the Court ruled that officers are not required to knock and announce their presence before entering a home if they have *reasonable suspicion* that doing so would be dangerous or futile, or that it would inhibit the effective investigation of crime by, for example, allowing the destruction of evidence. The Court stated that this standard—as opposed to the *probable cause* requirement—strikes the appropriate balance between legitimate law enforcement concerns in executing a search warrant and the individual privacy interests affected by no-knock entries. The Court also ruled that, based on the facts in this case (the defendant's apparent recognition of the officers and the easily disposable nature of drugs), the officers were justified in entering the hotel room without first announcing their presence and authority.

Note that G.S. 15A-251 requires an officer, before executing a search warrant and entering premises without giving notice, to have *probable cause* to believe that giving notice would *endanger the life or safety of any person*. Thus this statute imposes a more stringent standard on officers than the Fourth Amendment. *See also* G.S. 15A-401(e)c, which requires an officer, before entering premises to make an arrest without giving notice of the officer's authority and purpose, to have *reasonable cause* to believe that the giving of such notice would present a *clear danger to human life*.

141. [page 198] In State v. Knight, 340 N.C. 531, 459 S.E.2d 481 (1995), the court ruled that entry by force to execute arrest and search warrants was proper after waiting thirty to sixty seconds and hearing no response from inside the residence, based on the facts in this case (the officers knew that the defendant was dangerous, and they were concerned about the safety of a woman and her children inside the residence).

142. [page 198] In State v. Knight, 340 N.C. 531, 459 S.E.2d 481 (1995), officers entered the defendant's residence to execute arrest and search warrants for murder, conducted a quick sweep for weapons, and arrested the defendant for murder. The search warrant was read to the defendant about ten minutes after the entry into and the initial sweep of the residence but before any search was undertaken. The court ruled that the execution of the search warrant complied with the provisions of Chapter 15A of the General Statutes.

185. [page 200] The ruling in State v. Nobles, 107 N.C. App. 627, 422 S.E.2d 78 (1992), cited in this note, was affirmed by the North Carolina Supreme Court, 333 N.C. 787, 429 S.E.2d 716, *cert. denied*, 510 U.S. 946 (1993).

Supplement to

5   Interrogation and Confessions, Lineups And Other Identification Procedures, And Undercover Officers and Informants

Supplement to

5 Interrogation and Confessions, Lineups And Other Identification Procedures, And Undercover Officers and Informants

Note: Headings and page numbers from the second edition are provided for reference.

Part I: Interrogation and Confessions

The *Miranda* Rule and Additional Statutory Rights
When the *Miranda* Rule Applies: Custody and Interrogation

The Meaning of "Custody"

The Focus of the Investigation [page 213]. The text of the second edition states that just because officers focused their investigation on a person does not mean that the person is in custody under the *Miranda* rule. The United States Supreme Court in *Stansbury v. California*[1] strongly reaffirmed its case law reflecting that view. The Court noted that the determination of custody depends on the objective circumstances of the interview, not the subjective views of the interrogating officers or the person being questioned. An officer's views concerning the nature of an interrogation or beliefs concerning the potential culpability of the person being questioned may be one of many factors in determining the custody issue, but only if the officer's views or beliefs are somehow manifested to the person and would have affected how a reasonable person in that position would perceive his or her custodial status.

The Defendant's Assertion of the Right to Remain Silent and the Right to Counsel

Asserting the Right to Remain Silent [page 215]

The text of the second edition states that if a defendant merely expresses uncertainty about talking, an officer may ask questions that clarify the uncertainty. As a result of the United States Supreme Court's ruling in *Davis v. United States*,[2] which ruled that an officer is not required to stop an interrogation unless the defendant makes an unequivocal (clear) request for counsel, it is highly likely the Court would also rule that an officer is not required to stop an interrogation unless a defendant makes an unequivocal request to remain silent.[3] Thus an officer does not have a duty to clarify a defendant's *equivocal* (uncertain) request to remain silent. However, a prudent officer who is unsure whether a defendant's request is equivocal should seek to clarify whether the defendant wants to remain silent.

---

1. 511 U.S. 318, 114 S. Ct. 1526, 128 L. Ed. 2d 293 (1994).
2. 512 U.S. 452, 114 S. Ct. 2350, 129 L. Ed. 2d 362 (1994).
3. Lower courts have already so ruled. *See* United States v. Mikell, 102 F.3d 470 (11th Cir. 1996); United States v. Banks, 78 F.3d 1190 (7th Cir.), *vacated on other grounds*, 117 S. Ct. 478 (1996); Medina v. Singletary, 59 F.3d 1095 (11th Cir. 1995), *cert. denied*, 116 S. Ct. 2505 (1996); Coleman v. Singletary, 30 F.3d 1420 (11th Cir. 1994), *cert. denied*, 115 S. Ct. 1801 (1995).

Asserting the Right to Counsel [page 215]

The text of the second edition (in the first paragraph under this topic heading) states that the North Carolina Supreme Court has ruled that an in-custody defendant may properly assert the right to counsel before impending custodial interrogation. A different issue arises when a defendant asserts the right to counsel before being taken into custody. The North Carolina appellate courts have ruled that a defendant's request for counsel *before* the defendant is in custody is not a proper request for counsel under *Miranda*.[4] Such a request does not bar an officer from interrogating the defendant. Of course, if the defendant requests counsel again after being taken into custody, the officer is barred from conducting interrogation. A prudent officer who is unsure whether the defendant was in custody when the defendant requested counsel may decide not to attempt to interrogate the defendant or may seek clarification of the defendant's custodial status before attempting to interrogate the defendant.

The text of the second edition (in the second paragraph under this topic heading) states that courts permit officers to clarify a defendant's *equivocal* (uncertain) assertion of the right to counsel. However, the United States Supreme Court ruled in *Davis v. United States*[5] that if a defendant makes an equivocal reference to an attorney, an officer is not required to stop the interrogation if a reasonable officer under the circumstances would have understood only that the defendant *might* be invoking the right to counsel. An officer must stop an interrogation only when the defendant makes an unequivocal assertion of the right to counsel.

The investigators in the *Davis* case gave the in-custody defendant *Miranda* warnings and received a proper waiver of his rights. About an hour and a half into the interrogation, the defendant said, "Maybe I should talk to a lawyer." The investigators told the defendant that they did not want to violate his rights. If he wanted a lawyer then they would stop questioning him, and they would not pursue the matter unless it was clarified whether he was asking for a lawyer or was just making a comment about a lawyer. The defendant said, "No, I'm not asking for a lawyer." He then said, "No, I don't want a lawyer." After a short break, the investigators reminded the defendant of his rights to remain silent and to counsel. The defendant then made incriminating statements that he later sought to suppress at trial, arguing that the investigators violated their duty to stop the interrogation once the defendant had asserted the right to counsel.

Based on these facts, the Court ruled that the defendant did not make an unequivocal request for counsel. Therefore the investigators did not violate the defendant's constitutional rights.[6] The Court noted that when a defendant makes an ambiguous or equivocal request for counsel, it often will be good law enforcement practice for officers to clarify whether or not the defendant wants a lawyer. Clarifying questions protect the rights of the defendant by ensuring that the defendant gets a lawyer if he or she wants one and will minimize the risk of a confession being suppressed by later judicial second-guessing of the meaning of the defendant's statement about counsel. But the Court reiterated that if the defendant's statement is not an unequivocal request for counsel, officers are not obligated to stop questioning the defendant.

---

4. State v. Daughtry, 340 N.C. 488, 459 S.E.2d 747 (1995), *cert. denied*, 116 S. Ct. 789 (1996); State v. Medlin, 333 N.C. 280, 426 S.E.2d 402 (1993); State v. Willis, 109 N.C. App. 184, 426 S.E.2d 471, *review denied*, 333 N.C. 795, 431 S.E.2d 29 (1993).

5. 512 U.S. 452, 114 S. Ct. 2350, 129 L. Ed. 2d 362 (1994).

6. The Court's ruling in *Davis* now casts doubt on the validity of a ruling in State v. Torres, 330 N.C. 517, 412 S.E.2d 20 (1992), that the defendant unequivocally invoked her right to counsel when she asked law enforcement officers whether she needed a lawyer.

It is unclear whether the Court's ruling in *Davis* applies beyond the situation when a defendant makes an equivocal request for counsel *after* proper *Miranda* warnings have been given and a waiver of rights has been obtained. If a defendant makes an equivocal request for counsel *during* the officer's giving of the *Miranda* warnings or obtaining a waiver of rights, the officer should clarify whether or not the defendant wants a lawyer, because the state has the burden of proving that the defendant waived his or her rights, including the right to counsel.

Changes to Chapter 5 Notes

Note: Both note and page numbers from the second edition are provided for reference.

8. [page 230] In State v. Chapman, 343 N.C. 495, 471 S.E.2d 354 (1996), the court ruled that a delay of eleven-and-one-half hours in taking the defendant to a magistrate was not unlawful because the officers were interrogating the defendant about several crimes.

15. [page 230] In State v. Sturgill, 121 N.C. App. 629, 469 S.E.2d 557 (1996), the defendant asked "what would be in it" for him if he provided information about certain break-ins. The detective told him he would not seek to indict him for habitual felon status. The defendant then confessed. Based on these and other facts, the court ruled that the defendant's confession was inadmissible.

22. [page 231] In State v. Chapman, 343 N.C. 495, 471 S.E.2d 354 (1996), a detective falsely implied to the defendant during interrogation that a note found next to the murder victim's body had been the subject of handwriting analysis that showed that it was the defendant's handwriting and that the defendant's fingerprints were on the note. The defendant confessed to the murder. The court, in reviewing these and other facts surrounding the defendant's confession, ruled that the confession was voluntary.

32. [page 231] In State v. Benjamin, 124 N.C. App. 734, 478 S.E.2d 651 (1996), an officer conducted a frisk of the defendant after an investigative stop for a traffic violation. As the officer was patting the defendant, he felt two hard plastic containers in a breast pocket of the defendant's winter jacket. The officer's narcotics training made it immediately apparent that these containers were vials of the type that is customarily used to hold illegal drugs. When the officer felt the container through the jacket, he asked the defendant, "What is that?" The defendant responded that it was "crack." The officer removed two vials from the coat pocket and found cocaine.

The court ruled that the defendant was not in "custody" to require *Miranda* warnings when the officer asked the question while conducting the frisk. The court noted that the fact that a defendant is not free to leave does not necessarily constitute custody under *Miranda*. Instead, the inquiry is whether a reasonable person in the defendant's position would believe that he or she was under arrest or the functional equivalent of arrest; the court cited and discussed Stansbury v. California, 511 U.S. 318, 114 S. Ct. 1526, 128 L. Ed. 2d 293 (1994), and Berkemer v. McCarty, 468 U.S. 420, 104 S. Ct. 3138, 82 L. Ed. 2d 317 (1984). The court concluded that a reasonable person would not have believed he was in custody, based on these facts.

35. [page 232] See the discussion of *State v. Benjamin* in note 32, above.

51. [page 232] In State v. Morrell, 108 N.C. App. 465, 424 S.E.2d 147, *appeal dismissed, review denied, and cert. denied*, 333 N.C. 465, 427 S.E.2d 626 (1993), the defendant was arrested for a federal charge of child abduction and was committed to the county jail. A social worker in the county child protective services unit identified herself to the defendant and told the defendant that she was conducting an investigation of alleged sexual abuse and neglect of a boy with whom the defendant had had a relationship. The defendant confessed to the social worker. Two days later, a detective talked with the defendant in the jail after giving her *Miranda* warnings and obtaining a proper waiver. The defendant again confessed. Based on evidence that the social worker was working with the sheriff's department on the case before interviewing the defendant in jail, the court ruled that the social worker was an agent of the state and thus was required to give *Miranda* warnings before her interview with the defendant.

Note, however, that the court did not discuss Illinois v. Perkins, 496 U.S. 292, 110 S. Ct. 2394, 110 L. Ed. 2d 243 (1990), which ruled that when a person does not know that he or she is talking to a law enforcement officer (or agent of a law enforcement officer), there is no reason to assume the possibility of coercion, which is the underlying principle of the *Miranda* decision. Thus *Miranda* warnings are not required. If the defendant did not know that the social worker was a law enforcement officer (or an agent of a law enforcement officer), then the ruling in *Illinois v. Perkins* did not require the social worker to give *Miranda* warnings. [The court upheld the admissibility of the confession to the detective under the rulings in Oregon v. Elstad, 470 U.S. 298, 105 S. Ct. 1285, 84 L. Ed. 2d 222 (1985), and State v. Barlow, 330 N.C. 133, 409 S.E.2d 906 (1991).]

61. [page 233] The discussion in this note has been superseded by the ruling in Davis v. United States, 511 U.S. 452, 114 S. Ct. 1526, 128 L. Ed. 2d 293 (1994), which is discussed earlier in this supplement to the text of Chapter 5.

68. [page 234] The North Carolina Supreme Court clearly recognized in State v. Murphy, 342 N.C. 813, 467 S.E.2d 428 (1996), that the standard for reinterrogation after a defendant asserts the right to remain silent differs from when a defendant asserts the right to counsel. Thus the court implicitly disavowed contrary statements in State v. Bragg, 67 N.C. App. 759, 314 S.E.2d 1 (1984), and State v. Crawford, 83 N.C. App. 135, 349 S.E.2d 301 (1986), *cert. denied*, 319 N.C. 106, 353 S.E.2d 115 (1987), which are discussed in the first paragraph of this note in the second edition.

71. [page 235] The North Carolina Supreme Court in State v. Murphy, 342 N.C. 813, 467 S.E.2d 428 (1996), clearly rejected a rule that would always require an officer to give new *Miranda* warnings as a prerequisite to reinterrogation after a defendant had asserted the right to remain silent. The court stated that whether or not the defendant had been given new *Miranda* warnings was but one factor in considering if the defendant's rights had been scrupulously honored under the ruling in Michigan v. Mosley, 423 U.S. 96, 96 S. Ct. 321, 46 L. Ed. 2d 313 (1975).

86. [page 236] In State v. Adams, 345 N.C. 745, 483 S.E.2d 156 (1997), the court ruled that defendant did not have a Sixth Amendment right to counsel when the state brought a civil petition for child abuse and neglect against her; the Sixth Amendment right to counsel applies only to criminal charges. In Chewning v. Rogerson, 29 F.3d 418 (8th Cir. 1994), the court ruled that a defendant's request for counsel to represent him at an extradition hearing was not an invocation of the defendant's Sixth Amendment right to counsel for the murder charge for which he was being extradited.

104. [page 237] In State v. Palmer, 334 N.C. 104, 431 S.E.2d 172 (1993), the court ruled that an officer who gave *Miranda* warnings sufficiently established the defendant's waiver of his Sixth Amendment and state constitutional right to counsel. To constitute a valid waiver, the officer was not required to explain specifically to the defendant that he was waiving his right to counsel under these constitutional provisions.

Supplement to

6 **Rules of Evidence in Criminal Cases**

Note: Headings and page numbers from the second edition are provided for reference.

Witnesses
Cross-Examination of Witnesses

Impeaching a Witness with a Prior Conviction [page 245]

The text of the second edition states that any witness, including a defendant, may be impeached by being asked about a prior conviction of a crime punishable by more than sixty days' imprisonment. Under the Structured Sentencing Act, impeachment by a prior conviction would be limited to felonies and Class A1 and Class 1 misdemeanors, because only these misdemeanors are punishable by more than sixty days' imprisonment.[1]

Hearsay
Special Statutory Exceptions

Chemical Analyst's Affidavits [page 252]

In 1997 the North Carolina General Assembly enacted legislation, effective for offenses committed on or after December 1, 1997, that allows a chemical analyst's affidavit to include information about the presence or absence of an impairing substance in addition to a defendant's alcohol concentration.[2]

Drug Laboratory Reports [page 252]

In 1997 the North Carolina General Assembly enacted legislation, effective for offenses committed on or after December 1, 1997, to provide that a report of an analysis to determine whether a substance is a controlled substance is admissible in superior court and in a district court juvenile delinquency adjudicatory hearing under certain condi-

---

1. Rule 609(a) provides that a witness—including a defendant—may be impeached by a conviction of "a crime punishable by more than 60 days confinement." All Class 2 misdemeanors (maximum imprisonment is sixty days) and Class 3 misdemeanors (maximum imprisonment is twenty days) are therefore ineligible for impeachment under Rule 609(a). It would appear that all misdemeanors in Class A1 (maximum imprisonment is 150 days) and Class 1 (maximum imprisonment is 120 days)—regardless of the actual prior conviction level and sentence imposed—are eligible for impeachment under Rule 609(a) if our appellate courts follow, by analogy, the ruling in State v. Stanton, 101 N.C. App. 710 (1991), *cert. denied*, 330 N.C. 853, 413 S.E.2d 556 (1992). The court ruled in *Stanton* that a conviction of impaired driving was for an offense "punishable by more than 60 days confinement" [G.S. 15A-1340.4(a)(1)o] and therefore was a statutory aggravating factor under the Fair Sentencing Act. The court rejected the defendant's argument that since he had received Level Five punishment (maximum imprisonment is sixty days), his conviction was not a statutory aggravating factor. The court stated that the "plain language of the Fair Sentencing Act speaks in terms of potential, not actual, punishment." Thus, because a defendant convicted of a Class A1 or Class 1 misdemeanor potentially could receive a sentence of more than sixty days' confinement, all Class A1 and Class 1 misdemeanors are eligible for impeachment under Rule 609(a).
2. N.C. Sess. Laws 1997-379.

tions. Those conditions include the state's giving the defendant advance notice of its intention to introduce the report into evidence and the defendant's opportunity to timely object to the introduction of the report.[3]

Miscellaneous Evidentiary Issues [page 253]
Authentication of Physical Evidence or Documents: Chain of Custody [page 253]

In 1997 the North Carolina General Assembly enacted legislation, effective for offenses committed on or after December 1, 1997, to allow the state to prove—without calling witnesses to do so—a chain of custody of evidence that consists of or contains a substance tested or analyzed to determine whether it was a controlled substance.[4] The legislation specifies the type of written statement that must be prepared by each person in the chain of custody, requires the state to give the defendant advance notice of its intention to introduce the report into evidence, and allows the defendant to timely object to proof of chain of custody by this method.

Admissibility of a Defendant's Written Confession [new section]

A law enforcement officer may orally testify to what the defendant told the officer during a confession, including a confession that was later reduced to writing. However, before the state may introduce into evidence a written document containing a defendant's confession,[5] the state must show that it was (1) read to or by the defendant and signed or otherwise acknowledged to be correct, or (2) a verbatim record of the questions asked by the officer and answers given by the defendant.[6]

Changes to Chapter 6 Notes
Note: Both note and page numbers from the second edition are provided for reference.

101. [page 258] An additional case for this note is Kyles v. Whitley, 514 U.S. 419, 115 S. Ct. 1555, 131 L. Ed. 2d 490 (1995).
102. [page 258] An additional case for this note is Kyles v. Whitley, 514 U.S. 419, 115 S. Ct. 1555, 131 L. Ed. 2d 490 (1995).
104. [page 258] An additional case for this note is State v. Graham, 118 N.C. App. 231, 454 S.E.2d 878, *cert. denied*, 340 N.C. 262, 456 S.E.2d 834 (1995) (police department's inadvertent destruction of rape kit and victim's clothing did not violate the defendant's due process rights).
113. [page 259] An additional case for this note is State v. Frye, 341 N.C. 470, 461 S.E.2d 664 (1995), *cert. denied*, 116 S. Ct. 1359 (1996) (state's failure to offer evidence concerning which of two people drew blood from the murder victim at the autopsy did not constitute insufficient evidence of chain of custody, based on the facts in this case; any weakness in the chain of custody affected the weight, not the admissibility, of evidence concerning the blood sample).

---

3. N.C. Sess. Laws 1997-304.
4. N.C. Sess. Laws 1997-304.
5. The rules govern a defendant's statement as well as a confession, but the text uses "confession" for ease of reading.
6. State v. Wagner, 343 N.C. 250, 470 S.E.2d 33 (1996) (written confession was admissible because it was an exact word-for-word rendition of the officer's interview of the defendant); State v. Bartlett, 121 N.C. App. 521, 466 S.E.2d 302 (1996) (written confession was inadmissible because it did not comply with rules of admissibility).

Supplement to

Case Summaries:
Arrest, Search, and Investigation

The page numbers in brackets show where these cases should be added to the second edition.

Part I.   Arrest and Investigative Stops

*The following summaries of appellate cases provide the page numbers of the
case summaries section in the second edition where these cases should be added.*

The Authority to Make an Investigative Stop: Reasonable Suspicion

Determination of Reasonable Suspicion

Generally [page 277]

State v. Lovin
339 N.C. 695, 454 S.E.2d 229 (1995)

The murder victim's body was discovered in the afternoon, and the victim's Porsche was reported missing. At 4:00 P.M. a woman saw a Porsche that matched the description of the victim's car, and it was being driven by a male with a lot of hair, a gold watch, and large frame glasses. She followed it until it turned toward the airport. She reported this information to a law enforcement agency. Officers went to the airport and found the hood of the Porsche was still warm. A ticket agent reported that the defendant—whom she described as having long brown hair and wearing a gold watch—was acting suspiciously at the ticket counter. The court ruled this and other information in the officers' possession provided reasonable suspicion to make an investigative stop of the defendant to investigate the murder.

State v. Odum
343 N.C. 116, 468 S.E.2d 245 (1996)

The court, per curiam and without an opinion, reversed the decision of the court of appeals, 119 N.C. App. 676, 459 S.E.2d 826 (1995), that affirmed the defendant's conviction. The court stated that the decision was reversed for the reasons stated in the dissenting opinion in the court of appeals.

Officers were working drug interdiction at the Raleigh train station. They had received information from a ticket agent that the defendant had purchased a train ticket with cash, using small bills; had departed Raleigh for New York City on April 27; and was to return on the afternoon of April 29. The officers also learned that the defendant had previously been arrested for attempted robbery in New Jersey, although the charge had been dismissed. When the train arrived in Raleigh on April 29, the defendant left the train carrying a red nylon gym bag and appeared headed toward a parked car in which a female was sitting. The officers approached the defendant, showed him their badges, and asked him to answer a few questions. The defendant agreed to talk to them, and they moved over to the sidewalk. When asked to produce his train ticket, the defendant showed them his ticket stub bearing the name "D. Odum" (his name was David Odum). The defendant became visibly nervous when he could not find his identification after officers asked for it. When he looked into his gym bag for identification, one of the officers saw that the defendant was apparently trying to conceal the contents of the bag. The defendant finally told the officers that he could not find any identification. Although the defendant objected, the officers then seized his gym bag (to await a drug detection dog to sniff it). They told him that he was free to leave and that if he left an address they would have the bag delivered to him. During this conversation, the defendant informed the officers that the woman sitting in the car was his ride. One officer testified at the suppression hearing that the woman neither spoke nor made eye contact with the defendant during the entire questioning.

The dissenting opinion of the court of appeals concluded that reasonable suspicion did not exist to support the seizure of the gym bag. The evidence as a whole could easily be associated with many travelers. Many travelers daily embark on trips similar to the defendant's, and the fact that the defendant paid for his ticket in cash was not remarkable, considering the price was $107. The opinion noted that one officer testified that there was no evidence that the defendant had any prior involvement with drugs, and the prior robbery charge that was later dismissed was not a sufficient reflection of a person's propensity to be involved in drug trafficking.

The court also noted that one of the officers testified that the defendant did not give him any false information during the interaction at the train station. The officers never inquired about the nature of the defendant's trip, nor was there evidence of any questions that might have bolstered their suspicions. Although the defendant became visibly nervous when he could not find his identification, the opinion noted that it is not uncommon for a person to appear nervous when approached by a law enforcement officer. Also, the actions of the woman in the car and the defendant's reluctance to let the officers see what was in his bag did not provide reasonable suspicion.

State v. Willis
125 N.C. App. 537, 481 S.E.2d 407 (1997)

Officers were conducting surveillance of a residence while a search warrant was being sought to search it for drugs. The defendant, whom the officers did not recognize, left the residence on foot. Concerned that he might be involved in drug activity occurring in the residence, they decided to follow him. When the defendant realized that he was being followed, he took evasive action by cutting through a parking lot. A detective then asked a uniformed officer to stop the defendant and ask him for identification. That officer approached the defendant on foot, told him he was conducting an investigative stop, and asked him for identification and for consent to a pat down for drugs and weapons. The defendant consented to the pat down. The officer began to pat down the exterior and then interior of the defendant's leather jacket. Just as the officer began to check the jacket's interior pocket, the defendant lunged into the jacket with his hand. The officer, believing that the defendant might be reaching for a weapon and fearing for his safety, immediately locked his hands around the defendant's jacket, effectively locking the defendant's hand inside the pocket. Another officer arrived and assisted the officer. When the two officers managed to get the defendant's hand out of his pocket, they put the defendant's hands behind him and reached into the defendant's interior jacket pocket and emptied it, revealing several baggies of crack cocaine.

Relying on State v. Butler, 331 N.C. 227, 415 S.E.2d 719 (1992), the court in State v. Willis ruled that the officer's investigative stop was supported by reasonable suspicion. The court noted that the defendant left a suspected drug house just before the search warrant was to be executed. He took evasive action when he knew that he was being followed, and he exhibited nervous behavior.

State v. Watson
122 N.C. App. 596, 472 S.E.2d 28 (1996)

At about 2:30 A.M., an officer saw a vehicle driving on the dividing line of a two-lane highway near a nightclub. After turning to follow the vehicle, the officer watched the vehicle weave back and forth in its lane for about fifteen seconds. The officer then stopped the vehicle. The court ruled that this was sufficient evidence, based on the totality of the circumstances, to support an investigative stop of the vehicle for impaired driving.

State v. Holmes
109 N.C. App. 615, 428 S.E.2d 277, *review denied*, 334 N.C. 166, 432 S.E.2d 367 (1993)

The court ruled that reasonable suspicion existed to stop a vehicle based on the following facts: A trained drug officer saw the defendant driving slowly into a neighborhood known for violence and illegal drugs. The defendant then engaged two different groups of people in conversation from a car and went inside a house personally known to the officer because he had made drug arrests there. The defendant then returned to the car after a few minutes and lit a cigarette, which he shared with two passengers until the cigarette was gone and the car was filled with smoke. Based on his training, the officer believed the cigarette was a marijuana cigarette. The defendant then placed a plastic bag in the trunk of the car and returned to the house alone for about thirty seconds. When the defendant came back to the car, he carefully concealed an object underneath the driver's seat.

State v. Pittman
111 N.C. App. 808, 433 S.E.2d 822 (1993)

Two officers were on patrol at a train station at 1:30 A.M. They saw the female defendant and a man speaking; the pair parted company when they saw the officers. Officer Gunn approached the defendant and Officer Ferrell approached the man. The defendant showed Gunn a train ticket and stated she was traveling alone and did not know the man with whom she had been seen. Gunn noticed that the defendant was constantly looking over at the man, who was twenty feet away. The defendant consented to a search of her bag; nothing was found. Meanwhile, Ferrell spoke with the man, who said he was traveling alone and did not know the defendant. The man consented to a search of his bag; nothing was found. Later a vehicle pulled up to the train station, and the man put his bag in the trunk. The man then motioned to the defendant to approach the car, he placed her bag in the trunk, and the two of them got in the car and left. The officers compared information they had learned from their encounters with the man and the defendant and had the car stopped by a uniformed officer. The defendant was taken to the police station and searched. (1) The court ruled that Officer Gunn did not seize the defendant at the train station. He merely approached her and asked a few questions, and she voluntarily gave him her train ticket and consented to a search of her bag. The court relied on Florida v. Bostick, 501 U.S. 429, 111 S. Ct. 2382, 115 L. Ed. 2d 389 (1991). (2) The court ruled that the officers had reasonable suspicion to stop the vehicle in which the defendant was a passenger, based on the facts discussed above. (3) The court ruled that the officers did not have probable cause to search the defendant after the vehicle stop, based on the facts discussed above.

State v. Wilson
112 N.C. App. 777, 437 S.E.2d 387 (1993)

A police department received an anonymous phone call that several people were selling drugs in the breezeway of Building 1304 in the Hunter Oaks Apartments. The caller did not provide any names or descriptions of the alleged drug dealers. Two officers familiar with the area knew that if a police car entered the parking lot at one end of the breezeway, the suspects would run out of the other end. They devised a plan in which a police car would enter the parking lot and officers would position themselves so they could stop anyone who ran out of the back of the breezeway. An officer stopped the defendant as he ran out of the back of the breezeway. During the subsequent frisk, the officer felt a lump in the left breast pocket of the defendant's jacket and immediately believed that it was crack cocaine. The officer then asked the defendant if his coat had an inside pocket. The defendant did not respond verbally but instead opened his jacket so the inside pocket was visible. The officer saw and removed a small plastic bag that contained crack cocaine. (1) Distinguishing State v. Fleming, 106 N.C. App. 165, 415 S.E.2d 782 (1992), the court ruled that the officer had authority to stop and frisk the defendant, based on the anonymous phone call, the flight of the defendant and others when the police car pulled into the parking lot, and the officer's experience that weapons were frequently involved in drug transactions. (2) Distinguishing Minnesota v. Dickerson, 508 U.S. 366, 113 S. Ct. 2130, 124 L. Ed. 2d 334 (1993), the court noted that the officer in this case–unlike the officer in Dickerson–did not need to manipulate the item in the defendant's pocket to determine that it was cocaine; he immediately believed it was crack cocaine. The court ruled that the requirement in Dickerson that it must be "immediately apparent" to the officer that the item is illegal means that the officer must have *probable cause* to believe that the item is illegal. (See the discussion in the second edition on page 112 at note 31.) The court also ruled that the officer's tactile senses, based on his experience and the facts in this case, gave him probable cause to believe that the item was crack cocaine. Thus the officer did not exceed the scope of a frisk under the Dickerson ruling.

State v. Watkins
337 N.C. 437, 446 S.E.2d 67 (1994)

An officer received a transmission on an official radio frequency stating that there was a "10-50" (suspicious vehicle) behind a well-drilling company. When the officer arrived there, he saw a car with its lights off moving out of the company parking lot. It was 3:00 A.M., the area was generally rural, and the location was a business that the officer knew was normally closed at that hour. The officer followed the car and stopped it on the highway. The court ruled, based on these facts and the comparable cases of State v. Fox, 58 N.C. App. 692, 294 S.E.2d 410 (1982), aff'd per curiam, 307 N.C. 460, 298 S.E.2d 388 (1983), and State v. Tillett, 50 N.C. App. 520, 274 S.E.2d 361, appeal dismissed, 302 N.C. 633, 280 S.E.2d 448 (1981), that the officer had a reasonable suspicion to stop the car. The court noted, citing Alabama v. White, 496 U.S. 325, 110 S. Ct. 2412, 110 L. Ed. 2d 301 (1990), that an anonymous tip may provide reasonable suspicion when corroborated by independent law enforcement work.

State v. Watkins
120 N.C. App. 804, 463 S.E.2d 802 (1995)

An officer stopped a motorist for impaired driving. A prior appeal of this case determined that anonymous information and the officer's observations provided reasonable suspicion for the stop; see State v. Watkins, 337 N.C. 437, 446 S.E.2d 67 (1994). The defendant then filed a supplemental suppression motion based on newly discovered evidence that the anonymous information had been supplied to the stopping officer by another officer and that this other officer had fabricated the information (there was no evidence that the stopping officer knew that the information was fabricated). The court ruled that reasonable suspicion that is based on information fabricated by a law enforcement officer and supplied to another law enforcement officer may not serve as a basis for the stop by the officer who received the fabricated information, even though that officer did not know the information was fabricated.

State v. Rogers
124 N.C. App. 367, 477 S.E.2d 221 (1996)

An officer was directing traffic with hand signals when the defendant's vehicle approached the intersection where the officer was located. Instead of turning left as the officer directed, the defendant stopped his vehicle in the intersection. The officer approached the vehicle and noticed a strong odor of alcohol on the defendant's breath. The officer directed the defendant to drive to the shoulder of the road, and the defendant complied with that directive. The officer then administered an Alco-Sensor test, which revealed a reading of 0.13, and the officer arrested the defendant for impaired driving. The court upheld the trial judge's ruling that the officer had reasonable suspicion, based on the strong odor of alcohol on the defendant's breath, to stop the defendant's vehicle.

State v. Watson

119 N.C. App. 395, 458 S.E.2d 519 (1995)

Three officers approached a convenience store at night. Officer A had made fifty or more arrests for possessing cocaine in this area. Officer A knew the defendant had previously been arrested for drug charges. The defendant, on seeing the officers, put items in his mouth and started to go back into the store. Officer A grabbed the defendant's jacket, and the defendant then attempted to drink a soft drink. The officer took the drink away, ordered the defendant to spit the objects out of his mouth, and applied pressure to the defendant's throat so he would spit out the items. The defendant spit out three baggies containing crack cocaine. Based on this and other evidence (for example, officers testified at the suppression hearing that drug dealers will attempt to conceal or to swallow drugs when they see officers), the court ruled that the officers had reasonable suspicion to stop the defendant; the court cited State v. Butler, 331 N.C. 227, 415 S.E.2d 719 (1992). The court also ruled that exigent circumstances supported the reasonableness of the officer's actions in applying pressure to the defendant's throat so he would not swallow the drugs he had placed in his mouth (the court considered the officers' training and experience, their familiarity with the area and the defendant, and the practice of drug dealers to hide drugs in their mouths to elude detection).

State v. Clyburn

120 N.C. App. 377, 462 S.E.2d 538 (1995)

Officers were conducting surveillance at night at a place that had a reputation for drug activity and where they had previously made drug arrests. The officers saw three males in front of a vacant duplex. Individuals would approach one of the males, who would disappear behind the duplex with each individual. The other two males remained in front of the duplex as if acting as lookouts. Each time the defendant reappeared, the other two males conferred with him. Based on their training and experience with similar activity, the officers believed that drug transactions were being conducted. After one such activity, one of the males and a female got into a car and drove away. The officers stopped the car and frisked the male (the defendant) and female. An officer searched the passenger area of the car and found a .357 Magnum in the glove compartment. The male was arrested for carrying a concealed weapon. Following the arrest, the car was searched and crack cocaine was found in an ashtray. The court ruled: (1) the officers had reasonable suspicion to stop the car to investigate drug activity; (2) the search of the car for weapons was proper under Michigan v. Long, 463 U.S. 1032, 103 S. Ct. 3469, 77 L. Ed. 2d 1201 (1983),

because after the defendant had been frisked, he had become belligerent, and the officers could reasonably believe that the defendant was potentially dangerous and might be armed because of his involvement in drug trafficking [the court also cited State v. Butler, 331 N.C. 227, 415 S.E.2d 719 (1992)]; and (3) the search of the ashtray was permissible as a search incident to the arrest of a vehicle occupant under New York v. Belton, 453 U.S. 454, 101 S. Ct. 2860, 69 L. Ed. 2d 768 (1981).

State v. Jordan

120 N.C. App. 364, 462 S.E.2d 234, *appeal dismissed and review denied*, 342 N.C. 416, 465 S.E.2d 546 (1995)

An officer received a call that two black males, one wearing dark clothing and the other wearing a green jacket, had just left a Pick-N-Pay shoe store after committing an armed robbery. The officer, less than a mile away from the shopping center when he received the call, went there and saw a small blue car come from behind Revco Drugs in the shopping center as he drove toward the shoe store. The area from which the car came was not used for public parking. The blue car contained three black males. The officer saw no other black people in the area. The officer followed the car and noticed that the backseat passenger kept looking back at his police vehicle. When he saw an arm reach out of the passenger window and drop two small, cardlike objects, he stopped the car. The court ruled that the officer had reasonable suspicion to stop the car to investigate the armed robbery.

State v. Taylor

117 N.C. App. 644, 453 S.E.2d 225 (1995)

Officer A knew that the defendant had been previously arrested for drugs and had a reputation in the community as a drug dealer. Officer A and other officers saw the defendant with others in an area known for drug trafficking. As the officers approached the area in their marked car, the defendant left. The officers saw him at a nearby intersection. The defendant stopped as the police car approached him. As Officer A got out of the car, the defendant walked toward him and dropped something on the ground. The officer approached the defendant and brought him over to the police car. He determined that the dropped item was marijuana and arrested the defendant. He then noticed that the defendant was talking "funny" and ordered him to spit out whatever was in his mouth. The defendant spit out individually wrapped pieces of crack cocaine. The court ruled: (1) the defendant was not seized until after he dropped the item to the ground because he had not yielded to a show of authority before then; *see* California v. Hodari D., 499 U.S. 621, 111 S. Ct. 1547, 113 L. Ed. 2d 690 (1991); (2) after the defendant dropped the item, Officer A had reasonable suspicion to detain the defendant, considering everything the officer knew; (3) Officer A had probable cause to arrest the defendant when he determined the item was marijuana; and (4) even if the defendant did not voluntarily spit out the cocaine, the cocaine was admissible as the result of a search incident to arrest.

United States v. Roberson
90 F.3d 75 (3d Cir. 1996)

A police department operator received an anonymous call stating that a heavyset black male wearing dark green pants, a white hooded sweatshirt, and a brown leather jacket was selling drugs on the 2100 block of a specifically named street. Two officers went to this location in a marked patrol car and saw a man meeting the anonymous caller's description. The defendant, after making eye contact with the officers, walked over to a car and leaned in as if to speak with the car's occupants. The court ruled, distinguishing Alabama v. White, 496 U.S. 325, 110 S. Ct. 2412, 110 L. Ed. 2d 301 (1990), United States v. Clipper, 973 F.2d 944 (1992), cert. denied, 506 U.S. 1070 (1993), and United States v. DeBerry, 76 F.3d 884 (7th Cir. 1996), that this information was insufficient to establish reasonable suspicion to stop the defendant. See also United States v. Packer, 15 F.3d 654 (7th Cir. 1994) (anonymous tip reporting suspicious vehicle, with four black men inside, parked late at night along street for more than one hour was insufficient to support reasonable suspicion for investigative stop).

United States v. DeBerry
76 F.3d 884 (7th Cir. 1996)

An officer received anonymous information that at the corner of two specifically named streets there was a black man wearing a tan shirt and tan shorts who had a gun in his waistband. The officer went to the street corner and saw a black man wearing a tan shirt and tan shorts. The gun was not visible. The officer told him he wanted to talk to him. The man, the defendant, took several steps backward, turned slightly to the side, and moved his hands as if he might be about to draw a gun. The court ruled that (1) the officer's approach and statement to the defendant was not a seizure and (2) the anonymous information and the defendant's reaction to the officer as he approached the defendant supplied reasonable suspicion to stop and frisk him.

United States v. Elkins
70 F.3d 81 (10th Cir. 1995)

An area of a city was known as the "war zone" because gang warfare and shootings occurred there. A car had been identified previously as one involved in a drive-by shooting and had been seen at a known gang member's address on several occasions. The police department received anonymous reports of shots being fired in that area and saw the car leave from that address. While following the car, an officer saw a lot of activity in the rear seat and saw the right rear door open several inches. After the officer turned on his flasher lights, the car stopped but only after going three blocks. The court ruled that this information established reasonable suspicion to stop the car. See also United States v. Mikell, 102 F.3d 470 (11th Cir. 1996) (anonymous information plus officer surveillance supported reasonable suspicion to stop car for drug investigation); United States v. Lee, 68 F.3d 1267 (11th Cir. 1995), cert. denied, 116 S. Ct. 971 (1996) (anonymous information plus officer corroboration supported reasonable suspicion to stop car for drug investigation); United States v. Johnson, 64 F.3d 1120 (8th Cir. 1995) (similar ruling; court stated that Alabama v. White did not create a rule requiring that an anonymous tip predict future action); United States v. Gibson, 64 F.3d 617 (11th Cir. 1995), cert. denied, 116 S. Ct. 1580 (1996) (reasonable suspicion based on anonymous tip about two armed men in a bar and officer's corroboration); United States v. Perrin, 45 F.3d 869, cert. denied, 115 S. Ct. 2287 (4th Cir. 1995) (reasonable suspicion based on two anonymous tips about man selling drugs and officer's corroboration); United States v. Bold, 19 F.3d 99 (2d Cir. 1994), cert. denied, 116 S. Ct. 2511 (1996) (reasonable suspicion based on anonymous tip about four men—one of whom was armed—in car in parking lot, and officer's corroboration); United States v. Clipper, 973 F.2d 944 (D.C. Cir. 1992), cert. denied, 506 U.S. 1070 (1993) (reasonable suspicion based on anonymous tip about armed person on street and officer's corroboration); United States v. Walker, 7 F.3d 26 (2d Cir. 1993) (reasonable suspicion based on anonymous tip about man on trail with automatic weapons when police verified nearly every aspect of tip).

United States v. Lender
985 F.2d 151 (4th Cir. 1993)

At approximately 12:50 A.M., officers were patrolling an area where they knew heavy drug trafficking occurred. They saw a group of four or five men, including the defendant, huddled on a street corner. The defendant had his hand stuck out with his palm up, and the other men were looking down toward his palm. Suspecting a drug transaction, the officers approached the group. The group began to disperse, and the defendant walked away from the officers with his back to them. One officer called for the defendant to stop, but the defendant refused, telling the officer, "You don't want me; you don't want me."

As the defendant continued to walk away, he brought his hands to the front of his waist as though reaching for or fumbling with something there. The officer again called for the defendant to stop. The defendant stopped briefly, and a loaded semiautomatic pistol fell from his waist to the ground. The court ruled that the officers had reasonable suspicion to stop the defendant for drugs.

Airport Investigative Stops [page 281]

State v. Pope
120 N.C. App. 462, 462 S.E.2d 693 (1995)
An officer approached the defendant in an airport and identified himself. After the defendant agreed to talk with the officer, the defendant produced his airline ticket and identification on the officer's request. The officer returned the ticket and identification to the defendant and asked the defendant to accompany him to a more private area. The defendant agreed and accompanied the officer to a private room. There the defendant consented to a search of his bag and person. The court ruled, relying on Florida v. Royer, 460 U.S. 491, 103 S. Ct. 1319, 75 L. Ed. 2d 229 (1983), State v. Casey, 59 N.C. App. 99, 296 S.E.2d 473 (1982), and State v. Grimmett, 54 N.C. App. 494, 284 S.E.2d 144 (1981), review denied and appeal dismissed, 305 N.C. 304, 290 S.E.2d 706 (1982), that the entire encounter between the officer and defendant was consensual and therefore the defendant's Fourth Amendment rights were not violated.

Special Aspects of Stopping Authority

Scope of an Investigative Stop [page 284]

Ohio v. Robinette
519 U.S. ___, 117 S. Ct. 417, 136 L. Ed. 2d 347 (1996)
An officer stopped the defendant for speeding. The defendant gave his driver's license to the officer, who ran a computer check that revealed that the defendant had no prior violations. The officer then asked the defendant to step out of his car, issued a verbal warning to the defendant, and returned his license. The officer then asked the defendant if he had any illegal contraband in his car. The defendant said no. The officer then asked the defendant if he could search his car, and the defendant consented. The Court rejected a lower court ruling that an officer must advise a lawfully seized defendant that the defendant is free to go before a consent to search will be recognized as voluntary. The Court noted that the Fourth Amendment requires that a consent to search must be voluntary, and voluntariness is a question of fact that must be determined from all the circumstances. An officer's warning before obtaining consent to search is not required by the Fourth Amendment for a consent to search to be valid. [Note that the Court did not decide the legality of the scope of the investigative stop in this case.]

Burton v. City of Durham
118 N.C. App. 676, 457 S.E.2d 329, cert. denied, 341 N.C. 419, 461 S.E.2d 756 (1995)
The court ruled that an officer may conduct a registration check when the officer has properly stopped a defendant for committing an infraction (in this case, exceeding a safe speed).

United States v. Shabazz
993 F.2d 431 (5th Cir. 1993)
An officer may, during a valid traffic stop, request a driver's license, insurance papers, and vehicle registration, and may run a computer check of these matters. Questioning about matters unrelated to the traffic stop while officers were waiting for the computer check of the driver's license did not violate the Fourth Amendment by exceeding the scope of the initial purpose of the stop. The questioning did not extend the scope of the initial valid seizure. In this case, the computer check consumed only four minutes.

United States v. Jeffus
22 F.3d 554 (4th Cir. 1994)
A total of fifteen minutes to issue an improper equipment notice and to run a computer check on the defendant's license was not unreasonable under the Fourth Amendment.

United States v. McFarley
991 F.2d 1188 (4th Cir.), cert. denied, 114 S. Ct. 393 (1993)
Based on the facts in this case, a detention of luggage for thirty-eight minutes to subject it to a dog sniff did not elevate an investigatory stop to an arrest requiring probable cause. See also United States v. Daniel, 982 F.2d 146 (5th Cir. 1993) (detention of shipped package for about an hour for drug dog sniff was reasonable).

United States v. White
81 F.3d 775 (8th Cir.), cert. denied, 117 S. Ct. 518 (1996)
After stopping the defendant's car for speeding and erratic driving, an officer decided to issue the defendant a written warning for the traffic violations he observed. The officer, after running a "wants and warrants" computer check on the defendant, returned the defendant's license and registration to him and explained the warning ticket. Then the officer asked the defendant for his consent to search his car. The court ruled that the defendant was no longer seized under the Fourth Amendment after the of-

ficer issued the warning ticket. Therefore the officer's request to search occurred during a consensual encounter and was permissible without reasonable suspicion. The court noted that the facts in this case were similar to those in United States v. White, 42 F.3d 457 (8th Cir. 1994) (similar ruling). The court distinguished United States v. Ramos, 42 F.3d 1160 (8th Cir. 1994), *cert. denied*, 115 S. Ct. 2015 (1995) (additional questioning and delay before asking consent to search constituted an investigative stop unsupported by reasonable suspicion).

United States v. Finke
85 F.3d 1275 (7th Cir. 1996)
After a traffic stop had been completed, a five-minute delay to await the result of a criminal history check did not make the traffic stop unreasonable under the Fourth Amendment, based on the facts of this case. The officer who stopped the vehicle had reason to believe that the behavior of the driver and passengers was consistent with drug trafficking.

United States v. Lattimore
87 F.3d 647 (4th Cir. 1996)
An officer stopped the defendant's car for speeding. After issuing citations and returning the driver's license to the defendant, the officer asked him if there were any drugs or contraband in his car. After further conversation, the defendant consented to a search of his car. The court rejected the defendant's argument that the officer's questioning of the defendant about the drugs in the car without reasonable suspicion that the defendant was involved in criminal activity exceeded the scope of the traffic stop and thereby converted the encounter into an illegal detention that tainted the later consent search. The court noted that the officer did not question the defendant about drugs or request consent to search until after issuing the citations and returning the driver's license, indicating that all business with the defendant was completed and that he was free to leave. The totality of circumstances indicates that the encounter thereafter was consensual and the defendant was not being illegally detained. The court cited Florida v. Bostick, 501 U.S. 429, 111 S. Ct. 2382, 115 L. Ed. 2d 389 (1991).

United States v. Carrazco
91 F.3d 65 (8th Cir. 1996)
The defendant was not being detained illegally when an officer asked the defendant, three seconds after handing him a warning ticket for speeding, to consent for a drug dog to sniff the exterior of the defendant's truck. The three-second delay was a normal pause in a single conversation between the officer and the defendant.

United States v. Dumas
94 F.3d 286 (7th Cir. 1996)
After an officer gave the defendant her traffic ticket and told her she was free to go, the officer asked her if she would answer a few more questions. The court ruled that based on the facts in this case the defendant consented to remain and answer the questions. *See also* United States v. Hernandez, 93 F.3d 1493 (10th Cir. 1996) (similar ruling; asking questions that may elicit incriminating answers is irrelevant in determining whether encounter was consensual, although accusatory, persistent, and intrusive questioning may convert an otherwise voluntary encounter into a coercive one if it conveys the message that compliance is required).

United States v. Torres-Sanchez
83 F.3d 1123 (9th Cir. 1996)
The court noted that there is not a per se rule that a defendant's detention in a patrol car constitutes an arrest. The court discussed the facts in this case and determined that the defendant's twenty-minute detention in a patrol car (particularly when the defendant initially agreed to go there because it was cold) while an officer sought to confirm or dispel his suspicion about the ownership of a truck did not exceed the scope of the investigative stop and become an arrest. *See also* United States v. Bradshaw, 102 F.3d 204 (6th Cir. 1996) (similar ruling).

United States v. Sandoval
29 F.3d 537 (10th Cir. 1994)
An officer wrote a speeding warning citation, ran computer checks on the defendant and his truck, and returned the defendant's license and registration to him. The defendant asked, "That's it?" and the officer responded, "No, wait a minute." The court ruled that the detention exceeded the scope of the traffic stop, and there was no reasonable suspicion to continue the detention.

United States v. Edwards
103 F.3d 90 (11th Cir. 1996)
A drug stop based on reasonable suspicion exceeded the scope of an investigative stop after thirty minutes of detention, because the defendant had fully cooperated with the officers and searches of his car and himself did not reveal any evidence of illegal activity or danger to the officers.

Ordering a Person out of a Vehicle [page 285]

Maryland v. Wilson
519 U.S. ___, 117 S. Ct. 882, 137 L. Ed. 2d 41 (1997)
The Court ruled that an officer who has lawfully stopped a vehicle may order the passengers out of the vehicle without showing any reason to do so under the Fourth

Amendment. [Note: The court previously had ruled in Pennsylvania v. Mimms, 434 U.S. 106, 98 S. Ct. 330, 54 L. Ed. 2d 331 (1977), that an officer could automatically order the driver out of a vehicle.]

Using Weapons or Handcuffs [page 286]

Burton v. City of Durham
118 N.C. App. 676, 457 S.E.2d 329, *cert. denied*, 341 N.C. 419, 461 S.E.2d 756 (1995)

The court ruled that the officers' use of handcuffs to subdue the arrestee after he resisted arrest was reasonable, based on the facts in this case.

When an Officer's Interaction with a Person Is a Seizure under the Fourth Amendment [page 286]

State v. Farmer
333 N.C. 172, 424 S.E.2d 120 (1993)

Based on the facts in this case, the court ruled that the officers' encounter and conversation with the defendant on the roadside was not a seizure under the Fourth Amendment or the North Carolina Constitution. The defendant had no objective reason to believe that he was not free to end his encounter with the officers and to proceed on his way.

State v. Brooks
337 N.C. 132, 446 S.E.2d 579 (1994)

An SBI agent accompanied other law enforcement officers in executing a search warrant for a nightclub to search for illegal drugs. On arriving at the nightclub, the agent saw a vehicle parked in the parking lot with the defendant sitting in the driver's seat. The agent walked over to the driver's side of the vehicle and shone his flashlight into the car's interior. He saw on the passenger side of the bucket seats an empty unsnapped holster within the defendant's reach. The agent asked the defendant, "Where is your gun?" The defendant replied, "I'm sitting on it." The agent was unable to see the gun although he shone his light all about the vehicle. He asked the defendant to get out of the vehicle; the defendant reached under his right thigh and handed the gun to the agent. The agent did not place the defendant under arrest for carrying a concealed weapon, but he eventually obtained permission to search the vehicle and found cocaine in a nylon pouch there. The court ruled, relying on Florida v. Bostick, 501 U.S. 429, 111 S. Ct. 2382, 115 L. Ed. 2d 389 (1991), that the agent's initial encounter with the defendant was not a seizure under the Fourth Amendment and therefore did not require justification, such as reasonable suspicion. There was no evidence tending to show that the agent made a

physical application of force or that the defendant submitted to any show of force. Further, there was no indication that a reasonable person in the defendant's position would have believed he or she was not free to leave or otherwise terminate the encounter.

State v. Pittman
111 N.C. App. 808, 433 S.E.2d 822 (1993)

Two officers were on patrol at a train station at 1:30 A.M. They saw the female defendant and a man speaking, and the pair parted company when they saw the officers. Officer Gunn approached the defendant and Officer Ferrell approached the man. The defendant showed Gunn a train ticket and stated she was traveling alone and did not know the man with whom she had been seen. Gunn noticed that the defendant was constantly looking over at the man, who was twenty feet away. The defendant consented to a search of her bag; nothing was found. Meanwhile, Ferrell spoke with the man, who said he was traveling alone and did not know the defendant. The man consented to a search of his bag; nothing was found.

Later a vehicle pulled up to the train station, and the man put his bag in the trunk. The man then motioned to the defendant to approach the car, he placed her bag in the trunk, and the two of them got in the car and left. The officers compared information they had learned from their encounters with the man and the defendant and had the car stopped by a uniformed officer. The defendant was taken to the police station and searched. (1) The court ruled that Officer Gunn did not seize the defendant at the train station. He merely approached her and asked a few questions, and she voluntarily gave him her train ticket and consented to a search of her bag. The court relied on Florida v. Bostick, 501 U.S. 429, 111 S. Ct. 2382, 115 L. Ed. 2d 389 (1991). (2) The court ruled that the officers had reasonable suspicion to stop the vehicle in which the defendant was a passenger, based on the facts discussed above. (3) The court ruled that the officers did not have probable cause to search the defendant after the vehicle stop, based on the facts discussed above.

State v. Johnston
115 N.C. App. 711, 446 S.E.2d 135 (1994)

An officer was conducting a license check at an intersection. He saw the defendant turn off into an apartment complex parking lot about 200 yards before the intersection, and the defendant remained seated there about five minutes. The officer drove over to the defendant's car. As the officer got out of his car, the defendant got out of his car. The officer noticed that the defendant was unsteady on his feet. The officer walked over to the defendant and asked him why he turned off the road before the license check. The defendant responded that he lived there. The officer noticed a strong odor of alcohol about the defendant's breath; he asked him for his driver's license. The defendant was unable to produce a license. The officer then asked him to step back to his vehicle; he eventually arrested him for impaired driving. The court ruled that the officer did not seize the defendant when he approached him and asked him for his driver's license, citing Florida v. Bostick, 501 U.S. 429, 111 S. Ct. 2382, 115 L. Ed. 2d 389 (1991), that a seizure does not occur simply when an officer approaches a person and asks a few questions. Once the defendant admitted that he did not have a license, the officer had probable cause to arrest him. While the officer could have arrested him, he chose to ask the defendant to step back to his vehicle so he could investigate further. He then arrested the defendant after he failed field sobriety tests. The court concluded that the officer's actions were consistent with the Fourth Amendment.

State v. Cuevas
121 N.C. App. 553, 468 S.E.2d 425, *review denied*, 343 N.C. 307, 471 S.E.2d 77 (1996)
Officers who were conducting drug surveillance followed the defendant and an acquaintance as they took a cab from a bus station. The cab eventually stopped at a restaurant. The officers drove up in their car. An officer approached the cab, opened its rear passenger door, identified himself as a police officer, and asked the defendant and the acquaintance for consent to search them and their luggage. Drugs were discovered and the defendant was arrested. The defendant argued that he had been illegally seized without reasonable suspicion before he consented to the search. The court ruled, relying on State v. West, 119 N.C. App. 562, 459 S.E.2d 55, *appeal dismissed and review denied*, 341 N.C. 656, 462 S.E.2d 524 (1995), that the defendant had not been seized before the consent search. The court noted that law enforcement conduct does not constitute a seizure unless "a reasonable person would not feel free to decline the officer's request or otherwise terminate the encounter." *See* Florida v. Bostick, 501 U.S. 429, 111 S. Ct. 2382, 115 L. Ed. 2d 389 (1991). In other words, the court said, a seizure does not occur until there is a physical application of force or submission to a show of authority. *See* California v. Hodari D., 499 U.S. 621, 111 S. Ct. 1547, 113 L. Ed. 2d 690 (1991). The court stated that the officer did not order the cab to stop, turn on the law enforcement car's siren, or order the defendant to stay in place. Rather, the officer opened the cab's rear door and asked the defendant and

his acquaintance for consent to search them and their luggage. Nothing during this encounter suggested that the defendant was not free to leave.

State v. West
119 N.C. App. 562, 459 S.E.2d 55, *appeal dismissed and review denied*, 341 N.C. 656, 462 S.E.2d 524 (1995)
Two officers, dressed in civilian clothes, were at an airport with a drug interdiction unit. They noticed two suspicious males at the terminal and followed them to the parking lot. They approached the defendant and his acquaintance as they stood on each side of a parked car. Officer Black presented his credentials, identified himself as a police officer, and asked to speak to the defendant. At the officer's request, the defendant provided his airline ticket and identification. The defendant was extremely nervous and his hands were shaking. Black told the defendant that he was investigating drugs and asked the defendant for his consent to search his luggage. The defendant agreed and handed it to Black. As the defendant gave his luggage to Black, Black noticed the defendant's hands trembling and jerking back briefly. This jerking motion startled Black. Concerned for his own safety, Black asked the defendant for permission to frisk him before checking his luggage. Without responding to Black, the defendant ran. (The defendant later threw down a bag containing crack cocaine.) The court ruled that, based on this evidence, the defendant was not seized under the Fourth Amendment. Applying the principles of California v. Hodari D., 499 U.S. 621, 111 S. Ct. 1547, 113 L. Ed. 2d 690 (1991), that a seizure does not occur until there is a physical application of force or the submission to a show of authority, the court ruled that neither had occurred at the time the defendant ran from the officers. The court noted that while there was testimony that Black may have reached for the defendant, there was no evidence indicating that Black physically applied force or that the defendant submitted to any show of force. When Black asked for permission to frisk the defendant, the encounter was consensual and did not require reasonable suspicion. The court also rejected the defendant's argument that the ruling in *Hodari D.* should not be accepted in interpreting provisions of the North Carolina Constitution.

State v. James
118 N.C. App. 221, 454 S.E.2d 858 (1995)
An officer saw the defendant nervously pacing, then reboarding a bus. The defendant moved toward the rear of the bus and picked up a duffel-type bag from a seat and put it in the overhead luggage bin. Officers went through the typical bus boarding procedures designed to find illegal drugs. The defendant agreed to allow an officer to

look in his bag. The officer removed a portable radio from the bag and noticed that screws on the radio had been unscrewed several times. The officer asked the defendant if he would get off the bus so they could talk privately. The defendant did not respond verbally but left the bus with the officer. They went to a private area of the bus terminal, where the officer again obtained a consent to search. The officer discovered cocaine in the radio. (1) Relying on State v. McDowell, 329 N.C. 363, 407 S.E.2d 200 (1991), and other cases, the court reviewed the facts of the bus boarding and ruled that the defendant's consent to search was voluntarily given, although he had an IQ of 70. (2) Relying on State v. Christie, 96 N.C. App. 178, 385 S.E.2d 181 (1989), and State v. Bromfield, 332 N.C. 24, 418 S.E.2d 491 (1992), the court ruled that the defendant was not seized when he was on the bus or when he left the bus with the officers.

State v. Taylor
117 N.C. App. 644, 453 S.E.2d 225 (1995)

Officer A knew that the defendant had been previously arrested for drugs and had a reputation in the community as a drug dealer. Officer A and other officers saw the defendant with others in an area known for drug trafficking. As the officers approached the area in their marked car, the defendant left. The officers saw him at a nearby intersection. The defendant stopped as the police car approached him. As Officer A got out of the car, the defendant walked toward him and dropped something on the ground. The officer approached the defendant and brought him over to the police car. He determined that the dropped item was marijuana and arrested the defendant. He then noticed that the defendant was talking "funny" and ordered him to spit out whatever was in his mouth. The defendant spit out individually wrapped pieces of crack cocaine. The court ruled: (1) the defendant was not seized until after he dropped the item to the ground, because he had not yielded to a show of authority before then; see California v. Hodari D., 499 U.S. 621, 111 S. Ct. 1547, 113 L. Ed. 2d 690 (1991); (2) after the defendant dropped the item, Officer A had reasonable suspicion to detain the defendant, considering everything the officer knew; (3) Officer A had probable cause to arrest the defendant when he determined the item was marijuana; and (4) even if the defendant did not voluntarily spit out the cocaine, the cocaine was admissible as the result of a search incident to arrest.

United States v. $32,400 in U.S. Currency
82 F.3d 135 (7th Cir. 1996)

Officers in two patrol cars surrounded defendant in her car. An officer got out of one of the patrol cars, held up his police badge, and yelled, "Police, stop." The defendant backed her car into one of the patrol cars, striking its fender, and sped away. The court ruled, relying on California v. Hodari D., 499 U.S. 621, 111 S. Ct. 1547, 113 L. Ed. 2d 690 (1991), that the defendant was not seized under the Fourth Amendment. The court stated that if physical force does not accompany an officer's show of authority and a person chooses to ignore or reject that show of authority, that person is not seized until the officer applies physical force and the person submits to the officer's show of authority. In this case the officers' blocking a path of egress was not an intentional application of physical force, and, in any event, the defendant did not submit to any asserted show of authority.

United States v. Alarcon-Gonzalez
73 F.3d 289 (10th Cir. 1996)

A defendant was seized under the Fourth Amendment when an immigration officer (accompanied by as many as seven other armed immigration officers) yelled "freeze" at a co-worker, who was only five feet from the defendant, and the co-worker and the defendant complied with the command.

United States v. Segars
31 F.3d 655 (8th Cir. 1994), cert. denied, 513 U.S. 1099 (1995)

Officers ordered the defendant and others to get on the ground. The defendant dropped a package and attempted to flee. The officers chased and apprehended the defendant. The court ruled that the defendant was not seized under the Fourth Amendment when he dropped the package because he had not submitted to the officers' show of authority. Therefore the defendant abandoned the package under the Fourth Amendment.

United States v. Hernandez
27 F.3d 1403 (9th Cir. 1994), cert. denied, 115 S. Ct. 1147 (1996)

An officer told the defendant to stop because he needed to talk to him. The defendant hesitated a moment, made direct eye contact with the officer, and ran. The court ruled that the defendant's actions were not sufficient to constitute a submission to authority to constitute a seizure under the Fourth Amendment.

United States v. Washington
12 F.3d 1128 (D.C. Cir.), cert. denied, 513 U.S. 828 (1994)

The defendant was not seized under the Fourth Amendment when a law enforcement officer activated his siren and ordered the defendant's vehicle to stop. The vehicle stopped. However, as the officer approached the car on foot, the car sped away. The court ruled that the defendant was not seized under the Fourth Amendment because the defendant did not submit to the officer's order. *See also* United States v. Lender, 985 F.2d 151 (4th Cir. 1993) (similar ruling; defendant did not stop pursuant to officer's command to stop).

United States v. Laboy
979 F.2d 795 (10th Cir. 1992)

An officer's mere motioning to a person to approach the officer, unaccompanied by any verbal communication or show of force, is not inherently coercive. A seizure does not occur simply because an officer waves at a person, signaling the person to come over, and then asks a few questions. The test of whether a seizure has occurred is an objective one: whether a reasonable innocent person (as opposed to a person knowingly carrying contraband) would have felt free to leave. The court ruled, based on the facts of this case, that the defendant was not seized under the Fourth Amendment.

The Officer's Personal Knowledge of Facts Constituting "Reasonable Suspicion" [page 288]

State v. Battle
109 N.C. App. 367, 427 S.E.2d 156 (1993)

Officer Harmon responded to a disturbance call at a washerette and saw the defendant seated behind the steering wheel of a red Pontiac. The officer noticed the odor of alcohol on the defendant's breath (the defendant also performed physical tests poorly). The officer told the defendant not to drive the vehicle because he believed the defendant was impaired by alcohol. The officer left the washerette and radioed Officer Beekin to be on the lookout for this Pontiac and gave Beekin the vehicle's license plate number. Officer Beekin later saw the Pontiac leave the washerette, followed it for four blocks (and did not see anything unusual about its operation), and then stopped it. The court ruled that Officer Harmon, before he communicated his request to be on the lookout for the Pontiac, had reasonable suspicion that the defendant, impaired by alcohol, would leave the parking lot operating the vehicle. Although Officer Beekin did not personally have the information to establish reasonable suspicion and had not been told that information by Officer Harmon, Officer Beekin validly stopped the Pontiac based on Harmon's request, which was based on reasonable suspicion.

The Authority to Make an Investigative Stop or Take Other Action without Reasonable Suspicion

Conducting Impaired-Driving Highway Checkpoints [page 289]

State v. Barnes
123 N.C. App. 144, 472 S.E.2d 784 (1996)

A Highway Patrol sergeant, who was acting shift supervisor, decided to organize a roadblock to check licenses and vehicle registrations. He considered the likelihood of detecting people who were violating motor vehicle laws, the traffic conditions, the traffic volume that would pass through the roadblock, and the convenience of the public. Patrol officers intended to stop all vehicles that approached the roadblock from either direction to detect driver's license and registration violations as well as other motor vehicle violations, including impaired driving. A roadblock was established on a road at about 12:45 A.M., taking into account that there is a higher incidence of impaired driving on weekend early-morning hours. The sergeant's unmarked patrol car was parked in the paved median dividing the lanes of the road, and another unmarked patrol car was parked on the road's shoulder. At least one of the patrol cars had its blue lights on. The defendant's car was stopped, and the defendant was asked to show his license and registration; his conduct led to his arrest and conviction for impaired driving. The court noted the provisions of G.S. 20-16.3A (impaired driving roadblocks) and State Highway Patrol Directive No. 63. The directive requires that "[a]ll roadblocks shall be marked by signs, activated emergency lights, marked Patrol vehicles parked in conspicuous locations, or other ways to assure motorists are aware that an authorized roadblock is being conducted. A blue light on at least one Patrol vehicle shall be operated at all times." Reviewing the facts set out above, the court ruled the roadblock substantially complied with G.S. 20-16.3A and Directive 63 [the court noted its ruling in State v. Sanders, 112 N.C. App. 477, 435 S.E.2d 842 (1993)], and the stopping of the defendant's car did not violate the Fourth Amendment.

Conducting Driver's License Checkpoint [new section]

State v. Barnes
123 N.C. App. 144, 472 S.E.2d 784 (1996)

A Highway Patrol sergeant, who was acting shift supervisor, decided to organize a roadblock to check licenses and vehicle registrations. He considered the likelihood of detecting people who were violating motor vehicle laws, the traffic conditions, the traffic volume that would pass through the roadblock, and the convenience of the public. Patrol officers intended to stop all vehicles that approached the roadblock from either direction to detect driver's license and registration violations as well as other motor vehicle violations, including impaired driving. A roadblock was established on a road at about 12:45 A.M., taking into account that there is a higher incidence of impaired driving on weekend early-morning hours. The sergeant's unmarked patrol car was parked in the paved median dividing the lanes of the road, and another unmarked patrol car was parked on the road's shoulder. At least one of the patrol cars had its blue lights on. The defendant's car was stopped and the defendant was asked to show his license and registration; his conduct led to his arrest and conviction for impaired driving. The court noted the provisions of G.S. 20-16.3A (impaired driving roadblocks) and State Highway Patrol Directive No. 63. The directive requires that "[a]ll roadblocks shall be marked by signs, activated emergency lights, marked Patrol vehicles parked in conspicuous locations, or other ways to assure motorists are aware that an authorized roadblock is being conducted. A blue light on at least one Patrol vehicle shall be operated at all times." Reviewing the facts set out above, the court ruled the roadblock substantially complied with G.S. 20-16.3A and Directive 63 [the court noted its ruling in State v. Sanders, 112 N.C. App. 477, 435 S.E.2d 842 (1993)], and the stopping of the defendant's car did not violate the Fourth Amendment.

State v. Sanders
112 N.C. App. 477, 435 S.E.2d 842 (1993)
Two State Highway Patrol officers set up a driver's license check at a ramp off a highway. They did not post signs warning the public that a license check was being conducted. The officers checked every car that approached the checkpoint unless they were busy writing citations. The defendant entered the ramp and, as he approached the checkpoint, he stopped his car 150 feet from one of the troopers. The defendant then drove up to the checkpoint, stopped the car, and rolled down his window. In response to the trooper's request for driver's license and registration, the defendant said that he did not have the registration or any identification and that he was not the owner of the car. The passenger in the car also failed to produce any identification. The trooper asked the defendant to get out of the car. As the defendant stepped out of the car, the trooper saw a bulge about the size of two fists in the right pocket of the defendant's jacket. The trooper then told the defendant to face the car and place his hands on the car so he could pat him down for weapons. As the defendant was doing so, the trooper saw plastic protruding from the right pocket.

While frisking the defendant, the trooper touched the bulge and noted that it felt like "hard flour dough." The trooper removed the plastic bag from the defendant's pocket. It contained three smaller bags with cocaine inside. Distinguishing Delaware v. Prouse, 440 U.S. 648, 99 S. Ct. 1391, 59 L. Ed. 2d 660 (1979), the court ruled that the stop of the defendant's vehicle for the license check was constitutional. The court noted that the troopers followed guidelines of their agency in selecting the location and time for the license check and detained every car that passed through (except for those that came through while they were issuing citations). *See also* State v. Grooms, 126 N.C. App. 88, 483 S.E.2d 445 (1997) (court upheld license check roadblock by deputy sheriffs approved in advance by sheriff).

Merrett v. Moore
58 F.3d 1547 (11th Cir. 1995), *cert. denied*, 117 S. Ct. 58 (1996)
Officers set up a driver's license and vehicle registration checkpoint, although its primary purpose was to intercept illegal drugs. While checking a person's driver's license and vehicle registration, officers walked a drug detection dog around the person's vehicle. The use of the drug detection dog did not prolong the time to check the driver's license and vehicle registration. The court ruled that this checkpoint did not violate the Fourth Amendment. The court noted that when the state has one lawful purpose to justify a checkpoint, the checkpoint is not unconstitutional because the state also uses it to intercept illegal drugs (the court noted that it was not required in this case to decide the constitutionality of a checkpoint used solely to intercept illegal drugs). The court also noted that walking a drug detection dog around a person's vehicle is not a search under the Fourth Amendment.

Pretextual Stop or Arrest [page 289]

Whren v. United States
517 U.S. 806, 116 S. Ct. 1769, 135 L. Ed. 2d 89 (1996)
Drug officers stopped a vehicle for traffic violations. The Court ruled that stopping a vehicle for a traffic violation, when there is probable cause to believe the traffic violation was committed, does not violate the Fourth Amendment regardless of the officer's motivation for doing so. The Court also stated that stopping a vehicle for an improper racial purpose must be considered under the Equal Protection Clause of the Fourteenth Amendment, not the Fourth Amendment.

[Notes: (1) This decision effectively overruled State v. Morocco, 99 N.C. App. 421, 393 S.E.2d 545 (1990), which had ruled that the test for determining whether a stop is pretextual is what a reasonable officer *would* do rather than what an officer legally *could* do. The North Carolina Court of Appeals, in State v. Hamilton, 125 N.C. App. 396, 481 S.E.2d 98 (1997), recognized the *Whren* ruling effectively overruled *Morocco*. (2) The Court did not discuss whether its ruling would also apply when an officer has only reasonable suspicion to stop a vehicle for a traffic violation (although it likely would so rule). Of course, the Court's ruling in no way changes Fourth Amendment law that an officer may make an investigative stop of a vehicle based on reasonable suspicion; *see, e.g.,* Alabama v. White, 496 U.S. 325, 110 S. Ct. 2412, 110 L. Ed. 2d 301 (1990); United States v. Brignoni-Ponce, 422 U.S. 873, 95 S. Ct. 2574, 45 L. Ed. 2d 607 (1975).]

See also Holland v. City of Portland, 102 F.3d 6 (1st Cir. 1996) (officers' subjective motives in arresting defendant did not affect validity of arrest under Fourth Amendment based on probable cause); United States v. Hudson, 100 F.3d 1409 (9th Cir. 1996) (when probable cause supported arrest under arrest warrant, officer's motive in making arrest was irrelevant under *Whren v. United States*); United States v. Bullock, 94 F.3d 896 (4th Cir. 1996) (judge at suppression hearing properly prohibited defendant from introducing evidence of the officer's prior traffic stops because the officer's subjective motives are irrelevant, citing *Whren v. United States*); United States v. Stribling, 94 F.3d 321 (7th Cir. 1996) (when initial traffic stop for traffic violations was supported by probable cause, the fact that the stopping officer was assigned to drug enforcement duties was irrelevant, citing *Whren v. United States*); United States v. Dumas, 94 F.3d 286 (7th Cir. 1996) (court noted that any argument that investigative stop was invalid as mere pretext to search for drugs was foreclosed by *Whren v. United States*); United States v. Bell, 86 F.3d 820 (8th Cir.), *cert. denied,* 117 S. Ct. 372 (1996) (person asserting unequal enforcement of facially neutral statute must show both that the enforcement had a discriminatory effect and that it was motivated by a discriminatory purpose).

State v. Hamilton
125 N.C. App. 396, 481 S.E.2d 98 (1997)
An officer involved in drug surveillance stopped a vehicle because the driver and front-seat passenger were not wearing seat belts as required by law. The court ruled, based on Whren v. United States, 517 U.S. 806, 116 S. Ct. 1769, 135 L. Ed. 2d 89 (1996), that because the officer had probable cause to believe that the seat belt law had been violated, the stop was consistent with the Fourth Amendment even though a reasonable officer may not have made the stop. The court recognized that the *Whren* de-

cision effectively overruled State v. Morocco, 99 N.C. App. 421, 393 S.E.2d 545 (1990), which had ruled that the test for determining whether a stop is pretextual is what a reasonable officer *would* do rather than what an officer legally *could* do.

The Authority to Arrest: Probable Cause

Determination of Probable Cause [page 289]
State v. Medlin
333 N.C. 280, 426 S.E.2d 402 (1993)
Atlantic Beach officers arrested the defendant in a breezeway outside a motel room in Atlantic Beach for a murder and robbery committed in Wake County, based on the mistaken belief that an arrest warrant had been issued in Wake County for these offenses. The court determined, however, that the Atlantic Beach officers had sufficient information to establish probable cause to arrest, based on the facts in this case. Therefore the warrantless arrest was proper.

Best v. Duke University
337 N.C. 742, 448 S.E.2d 506 (1994)
An officer saw the plaintiff's vehicle enter the Duke Faculty Club driveway at 5:00 A.M., turn its lights off, and continue down the driveway. Ten or fifteen minutes later, the officer saw the plaintiff's vehicle exit the driveway and go toward the rear of the Washington-Duke Hotel. The officer knew that the hotel was having problems with thefts. He decided to stop the vehicle by blocking it. However, the plaintiff drove his vehicle around the officer and sped away. The plaintiff did not stop even when the officer pulled beside him, rolled down his window, and flashed his badge. Eventually, the plaintiff's vehicle stopped. The officer saw wrought-iron furniture inside. The plaintiff said to another officer there (Russell) that he was taking the furniture to a friend's house. A check of the Faculty Club then indicated that there was no missing furniture. The plaintiff was allowed to leave. The next day Russell learned that furniture similar in description to the plaintiff's furniture had in fact been stolen from the Faculty Club that night. Arrest warrants for larceny and trespass were obtained and the plaintiff was arrested. At the criminal trial, the state at the close of the state's evidence took a voluntary dismissal of the trespass charge without an explanation, and the judge found the defendant not guilty of the larceny charge.

The plaintiff sued the defendant, Duke University, for malicious prosecution (and other torts) based on his arrest and prosecution for trespass and larceny. (1) The court examined the evidence and ruled that probable cause existed as a matter of law for the plaintiff's arrest for trespass and larceny and for his later prosecution for larceny; thus the university's motion for a directed verdict on the malicious prosecution claim should have been granted at trial. (2) The court rejected the plaintiff's argument that the state's voluntary dismissal of a criminal charge without an explanation is a prima facie showing of absence of probable cause in a malicious prosecution claim. The court distinguished its ruling in Pitts v. Village Inn Pizza, Inc., 296 N.C. 81, 249 S.E.2d 375 (1978) (disputed issue of whether probable cause existed in malicious prosecution claim when evidence showed prosecutor had voluntarily dismissed criminal charge before trial), because in Pitts the only evidence presented was the issuance of an arrest warrant charging a criminal offense and the prosecutor's dismissal of that charge. In this case, uncontroverted evidence established probable cause as a matter of law; thus the prosecutor's voluntary dismissal was not sufficient evidence of a lack of probable cause to establish a question of fact for the jury. The court stated that it disapproves Pitts to the extent that Pitts may be read to suggest otherwise. The court also noted that, unlike in Pitts, the prosecutor in this case had prosecuted the plaintiff on a second charge—the larceny charge.

State v. Crawford
125 N.C. App. 279, 480 S.E.2d 422 (1997)

Responding to a call from a department dispatcher about a suspicious vehicle on the side of a road in a rural area, a deputy sheriff investigated and saw a car parked there with its engine off. The driver's door was open and the defendant was sitting in the driver's seat with one leg hanging out of the car. The defendant was in a semiconscious state. His knee and shirt were wet with drool, and his pants were undone. The deputy asked the defendant if he was okay. The defendant was initially unresponsive and appeared to have trouble speaking. As the deputy looked for a medical alert bracelet, he detected a strong odor of alcohol on the defendant's breath. He then felt the hood of the car and, although the outdoor temperature was twenty-six degrees, the hood was warm. When the defendant finally spoke, he had a slight slur in his speech. The deputy asked him if he had been drinking, to which the defendant responded, "Yes." When asked how much he had to drink, the defendant replied, "Some." The deputy then asked the defendant several times to step out of the car. The defendant failed to respond to the deputy's first request to get out of the car and answered "no" to the second request. After the third re-

quest, the defendant replied, "I'm not going anywhere with you." The defendant then started to put a key into the ignition. The deputy removed the defendant from the car and arrested him for impaired driving. The court noted that the degree of certainty necessary for probable cause is a "fair probability," and ruled that this evidence supplied probable cause to arrest the defendant for impaired driving.

The court also ruled, relying on In re Pinyatello, 36 N.C. App. 542, 245 S.E.2d 185 (1978), that this evidence supported, under G.S. 15A-401(b)(2), the officer's warrantless arrest for the misdemeanor of impaired driving committed outside the officer's presence, because the defendant presented a danger to himself and others if not immediately arrested. [Note: Although not applicable to the date on which the offense in this case occurred, G.S. 15A-401(b)(2)(c) now authorizes an officer to make a warrantless impaired-driving arrest without any additional justification (such as danger to the defendant or others), even if the offense was committed outside the officer's presence.]

State v. Rogers
124 N.C. App. 367, 477 S.E.2d 221 (1996)

An officer was directing traffic with hand signals when the defendant's vehicle approached the intersection where the officer was located. Instead of turning left as the officer directed, the defendant stopped his vehicle in the intersection. The officer approached the vehicle and noticed a strong odor of alcohol on the defendant's breath. The officer directed the defendant to drive to the shoulder of the road, and the defendant complied with that directive. The officer then administered an Alco-Sensor test, which revealed a reading of 0.13, and the officer arrested the defendant for impaired driving. (1) The court upheld the trial judge's ruling that the officer had reasonable suspicion, based on the strong odor of alcohol on the defendant's breath, to stop the defendant's vehicle. (2) The trial judge also ruled that the strong odor of alcohol was sufficient to establish probable cause to arrest the defendant for impaired driving. The judge declined to base a finding of probable cause on the Alco-Sensor test reading because the officer failed to give a second test in what the judge stated was a violation of G.S. 20-16.3(b). The court upheld the trial judge's ruling that there was probable cause to arrest the defendant for DWI. The court noted the evidence of the strong odor of alcohol on the defendant's breath, but stated that the evidence of the Alco-Sensor reading could also be considered in establishing probable cause, even though the failure to give a second test violated G.S. 20-16.3(b). The court stated, "There is no prohibition against the results of this test being used by the officer to form probable cause, although this evidence may not have been admissible at trial."

[Note: The Alco-Sensor is an approved screening test. G.S. 20-16.3(c) provides that "[n]o screening test for alcohol concentration is a valid one . . . unless . . . the screening test is conducted in accordance with the applicable regulations . . . as to the manner of its use." Rule 19B.0502(b)(2) provides that "[u]nless the driver volunteers the information that he has consumed an alcoholic beverage within the previous 15 minutes, the officer shall administer a screening test as soon as feasible. If a test made without observing a waiting period results in an alcohol concentration reading of 0.08 or more, the officer shall wait five minutes and administer an additional test. If the results of the additional test show an alcohol concentration reading more than 0.02 under the first reading, the officer shall disregard the first reading."

Note also that G.S. 20-16.3(d) provides that the results of an alcohol-screening test or a driver's refusal to submit to the test may be used by a law enforcement officer in determining if there are reasonable grounds for believing that the driver committed an implied-consent offense. With a limited exception not applicable to this case, the results of an alcohol-screening test may not be admitted in evidence in court.]

State v. Trapp
110 N.C. App. 584, 430 S.E.2d 484 (1993)
On January 3, 1991, a confidential informant advised Detective Hines that Steven James would be driving from Jacksonville to Maysville that night to make a cocaine purchase and that James would return to Jacksonville and go to 106 Circle Drive and then to the Triangle Motel. Another confidential informant advised Detective Selogy that drugs were being sold at 106 Circle Drive and that James and his girlfriend, defendant Trapp, lived at that address. The informant also said that defendant Trapp hid the drugs in her vagina while they were being transported. (It did not appear from the court's opinion that either informant told the detectives their basis of knowledge about James's and defendant Trapp's activities.) That night the detectives saw people matching one of the informant's descriptions leave a car and enter 106 Circle Drive and later leave that address in the same car and arrive at the Triangle Motel. When they left the motel, Detective Selogy followed the car and activated his blue lights. He saw the female passenger, later identified as defendant Trapp, move closer to the driver, later identified as James, and then saw the male driver put his hand over the female's lap as he was looking in the rearview mirror. After the car was stopped, defendant Trapp was taken to the police station. The court ruled that, based on the informants' information and the officers' corroboration of that information, the detectives had probable cause to arrest the defendant when they stopped the car. The court relied on several cases, including Draper v. United States, 358 U.S. 307, 79 S. Ct. 329, 3 L. Ed. 2d 327 (1959), and Illinois v. Gates, 462 U.S. 213, 103 S. Ct. 2317, 76 L. Ed. 2d 527 (1983).

Davis v. Town of Southern Pines
116 N.C. App. 663, 449 S.E.2d 240 (1994), *review denied*, 339 N.C. 737, 454 S.E.2d 648 (1995)
Civil pzlaintiff sued law enforcement officers and town for violating her Fourth Amendment rights by taking her to jail for allegedly being intoxicated in public. The evidence, taken in the light most favorable to the plaintiff on the defendant's motion for summary judgment, showed that the plaintiff was publicly intoxicated at 1:30 A.M. and that she tripped and fell while walking to a phone booth to call a cab. The plaintiff told the law enforcement officers that she was not bothering anybody and that she was going to call a cab to take her home. The plaintiff's sister offered to call a cab for the plaintiff and take care of her. The officers then took the plaintiff to jail against her will, which the court ruled constituted an arrest under the Fourth Amendment. The court also ruled, based on these proffered facts, the officers did not have probable cause to believe the plaintiff was in need of assistance under G.S. 122C-303 (which authorizes officers to take a publicly intoxicated person to jail if the person is apparently in need of and apparently unable to provide for oneself food, clothing, or shelter, but is not apparently in need of immediate medical care and if no other facility is readily available to receive the person).

Moore v. Hodges
116 N.C. App. 727, 449 S.E.2d 218 (1994)
A trooper arrived at the scene of a one-car accident and saw Moore's vehicle in the ditch on the side of the road. Moore was lying down in the back of a rescue squad vehicle while being treated for injuries. She told the trooper at the hospital that she was driving the vehicle and it went off the road. She admitted that she had some liquor earlier in the day. The trooper noticed her mumbled speech and detected a faint odor of alcohol about her. He administered an alcohol-screening test [authorized for probable cause determinations under G.S. 20-16.3(d)] with an Alco-Sensor [approved under N.C. Administrative Code Title 15A, rule 19B.0503(a)]. The test registered a result higher than 0.10. The court ruled that, based on these facts, the trooper had probable cause to believe that Moore had committed impaired driving.

State v. Taylor
117 N.C. App. 644, 453 S.E.2d 225 (1995)

Officer A knew that the defendant had been previously arrested for drugs and had a reputation in the community as a drug dealer. Officer A and other officers saw the defendant with others in an area known for drug trafficking. As the officers approached the area in their marked car, the defendant left. The officers saw him at a nearby intersection. The defendant stopped as the police car approached him. As Officer A got out of the car, the defendant walked toward him and dropped something on the ground. The officer approached the defendant and brought him over to the police car. He determined that the dropped item was marijuana and arrested the defendant. He then noticed that the defendant was talking "funny" and ordered him to spit out whatever was in his mouth. The defendant spit out individually wrapped pieces of crack cocaine. The court ruled: (1) the defendant was not seized until after he dropped the item to the ground, because he had not yielded to a show of authority before then; see California v. Hodari D., 499 U.S. 621, 111 S. Ct. 1547, 113 L. Ed. 2d 690 (1991); (2) after the defendant dropped the item, Officer A had reasonable suspicion to detain the defendant, considering everything the officer knew; (3) Officer A had probable cause to arrest the defendant when he determined the item was marijuana; and (4) even if the defendant did not voluntarily spit out the cocaine, the cocaine was admissible as the result of a search incident to arrest.

United States v. Marshall
79 F.3d 68 (7th Cir.), cert. denied, 117 S. Ct. 155 (1996)

When officers mistake a person for someone else they seek to validly arrest, the arrest is constitutionally reasonable under the Fourth Amendment if the arresting officers have probable cause to arrest the person sought and reasonably believe that the person arrested is the person sought. See Hill v. California, 401 U.S. 797, 91 S. Ct. 1106, 28 L. Ed. 2d 484 (1971). Based on the facts in this case, the court ruled that the officers were reasonable in mistakenly believing that the arrestee was a fugitive named in the arrest warrant so that a gun seized from the defendant incident to his arrest was admissible.

Collective Knowledge of All Officers [page 292]

State v. Watkins
120 N.C. App. 804, 463 S.E.2d 802 (1995)

An officer stopped a motorist for impaired driving. A prior appeal of this case determined that anonymous information and the officer's observations provided reasonable suspicion for the stop; see State v. Watkins, 337 N.C.

437, 446 S.E.2d 67 (1994). The defendant then filed a supplemental suppression motion based on newly discovered evidence that the anonymous information had been supplied to the stopping officer by another officer and that this other officer had fabricated the information (there was no evidence that the stopping officer knew that the information was fabricated). The court ruled that reasonable suspicion that is based on information fabricated by a law enforcement officer and supplied to another law enforcement officer may not serve as a basis for the stop by the officer who received the fabricated information, even though that officer did not know the information was fabricated.

The Arrest Procedure

Notice of Authority

Before Entering a Dwelling [page 296]
Wilson v. Arkansas
514 U.S. 927, 115 S. Ct. 1914, 131 L. Ed. 2d 976 (1995)

Officers made an unannounced entry into a home to execute a search warrant. The Arkansas Supreme Court ruled that the Fourth Amendment does not require officers to knock and announce before entering a home. The Court, rejecting the state court's ruling, ruled that an officer's unannounced entry into a home must be reasonable under the Fourth Amendment. Whether an officer announced his or her presence and authority before entering a home is among the factors (along with the threat of physical harm to the officer, pursuit of a recently escaped arrestee, and the likely destruction of evidence if advance notice was given) to be considered in determining whether the entry was reasonable. The Court specifically stated that it will leave to lower courts the task of determining whether an unannounced entry was reasonable and remanded this case to the Arkansas Supreme Court for that purpose.

[Note: G.S. 15A-249 sets standards in entering private premises to execute a search warrant, and G.S. 15A-401(e) sets standards in entering private premises to arrest.]

Lee v. Greene
114 N.C. App. 580, 442 S.E.2d 547 (1994)

An officer arrested the suspect's husband in the driveway of the home of the suspect and her husband. Because the suspect blocked the front door of the officer's car in which the husband was sitting, the officers (another officer had arrived by then) decided to arrest her for obstructing and delaying the arrest of her husband. When the suspect began moving toward her house, they ran after her. As she entered her house and was closing the door, the officers grabbed the door and entered the house. The court ruled that the officers, under these circumstances, were not required to give notice of their authority and purpose under G.S. 15A-401(e). The suspect knew the officers' identities and their reason for being at her house. Moreover, the officers were about to arrest the suspect as she entered her house and attempted to close the door. Under these circumstances, compliance with G.S. 15A-401(e) was not required.

Entrance onto Premises to Arrest

Generally [page 296]

State v. Workman
344 N.C. 482, 476 S.E.2d 301 (1996)

The court ruled that officers had probable cause to believe that the defendant was inside his home when they entered his home late at night to execute an arrest warrant for two murders, based on the following facts. His accomplice in the murders pointed out the trailer as the defendant's home. Officers maintained surveillance on the trailer while another officer obtained an arrest warrant. They did not see anyone leave the trailer. As the officers approached the trailer, they saw lights on and heard noises inside.

United States v. Risse
83 F.3d 212 (8th Cir. 1996)

Officers had a reasonable belief that the female person (Rhoads) for whom they had an arrest warrant resided with a male person (Risse) at his home, and therefore an arrest warrant was sufficient to enter Risse's home to arrest her. Rhoads had previously told the officers that she was "staying with" Risse and that the officers could contact her there. In addition, a confidential reliable informant had told an officer that Rhoads was living with Risse. While officers twice successfully contacted her at Risse's residence, they were unable to contact her at her permanent residence elsewhere. The court rejected the defendant's argument that a person can have only one residence for Fourth Amendment purposes.

United States v. May
68 F.3d 515 (D.C. Cir. 1995)

Officers had a reasonable belief that the person (Thomas) named in an arrest warrant for murder was in the dwelling that they entered to execute the arrest warrant. Police records disclosed that Thomas lived there. Two witnesses

placed Thomas at that dwelling after the murder. The murder occurred on a Saturday afternoon, the arrest warrant was issued on Monday, and the officers entered the dwelling on Tuesday morning.

United States v. Gooch
6 F.3d 673 (9th Cir. 1993)

The defendant had a reasonable expectation of privacy in his tent located on a public campground, and the officers' warrantless entry into the tent to arrest him—without a warrant, exigent circumstances, or consent—violated the Fourth Amendment.

Exigent Circumstances [page 296]

State v. Worsley
336 N.C. 268, 443 S.E.2d 68 (1994)

Officers arrived at the murder scene and discovered the victim's body, the subject of a brutal stabbing, lying in a common area of an apartment complex. An eyewitness to the murder identified the defendant as the killer. Another witness informed the officers that he had seen the defendant running toward the defendant's apartment shortly after the murder. The officers went to the defendant's nearby apartment and discovered fresh blood on the doorknob of the back door. The officers knocked loudly on the defendant's door and identified themselves as officers but received no response. They then entered the apartment. The court ruled that the officers had exigent circumstances to enter the defendant's home—without consent or an arrest warrant—to arrest the defendant.

Completion of Custody: Taking the Arrestee to a Magistrate without Unnecessary Delay [page 298]

State v. Chapman
343 N.C. 495, 471 S.E.2d 354 (1996)

On August 23, 1993, about 9:30 A.M., the defendant was arrested at a bank for attempting to cash a forged check. He waived his *Miranda* rights and admitted that he had attempted to cash a check that he had forged after taking it in a robbery. Officers took the defendant to a school to search for a purse that had been taken in the robbery. They then returned the defendant to the police station, where he confessed to forgery and uttering charges. A detective procured arrest warrants for these charges at 12:15 P.M. and served them on the defendant. The defendant then was questioned by another detective who was investigating the robbery in which the checks were taken, and the defendant confessed to the robbery at 1:27 P.M. Officers prepared an arrest warrant to charge the robbery, but it was not presented to the magistrate then. The defendant then was interviewed by another detective about a robbery and murder (not related to the crimes discussed previously). The detective put nine photos of the murder victim on the walls of the interrogation room and one photo of the victim on the floor directly in front of the chair in which the defendant sat during the interrogation. Thus the defendant saw a photo of the victim in every direction he turned. During the interview, the detective falsely implied to the defendant that a note found next to the victim's body had been the subject of handwriting analysis that showed it was the defendant's handwriting, and the defendant's fingerprints were on the note. The defendant confessed to the murder at about 7:05 P.M. and was taken to the magistrate at about 8:00 P.M.

(1) The court ruled that there was no unreasonable delay in a magistrate's determination of whether there was probable cause to issue an arrest warrant. Distinguishing County of Riverside v. McLaughlin, 500 U.S. 44, 111 S. Ct. 1661, 114 L. Ed. 2d 49 (1991), and Gerstein v. Pugh, 420 U.S. 103, 95 S. Ct. 854, 43 L. Ed. 2d 54 (1975), the court noted that the defendant was arrested at 9:30 A.M. without a warrant, and a magistrate issued an arrest warrant based on probable cause at 12:30 P.M. This procedure satisfied the rulings in these cases that a magistrate promptly determine probable cause. The court noted that the defendant was then in lawful custody and could be interrogated about other crimes. (2) The court ruled that the defendant's statutory right, under G.S. 15A-501(2), to be taken to a magistrate without unnecessary delay was not violated. The court noted that much of the time from the defendant's arrest at 9:30 A.M. until he was taken before a magistrate at 8:00 P.M. was spent interrogating the

defendant about several crimes. The court stated that the officers had the right to conduct these interrogations and that they did not cause an unnecessary delay by doing so. (3) In violation of G.S. 15A-501(5), the officers failed to advise the defendant of his right to communicate with friends. The court ruled that, based on State v. Curmon, 295 N.C. 453, 245 S.E.2d 503 (1978), the defendant was not prejudiced by this violation, based on the facts in this case.

State v. Littlejohn
340 N.C. 750, 459 S.E.2d 629 (1995)

The defendant was arrested for murder and other offenses; interrogated for ten hours, during which time he confessed; and then taken to the magistrate. The total period of time between the arrest and appearance before the magistrate was thirteen hours. The court ruled, based on these and other facts (for example, the officers advised him of his constitutional rights before they began interrogation), the delay did not violate G.S. 15A-501(2) (duty to take arrestee before magistrate without unnecessary delay).

State v. Daniels
337 N.C. 243, 446 S.E.2d 298 (1994), *cert. denied*, 115 S. Ct. 953 (1995)

An officer's one-hour delay from arresting the defendant to informing him of his rights under G.S. 15A-501(5) was not an unnecessary delay because during that time period the officer was involved with interactions with the defendant, which included taking him to a house at the defendant's request.

Part II.   Search and Seizure

The following summaries of appellate cases provide the page numbers of the case summaries section in the second edition where these cases should be added.

What Is a Search and Seizure and What Evidence May Be Searched for and Seized

Definition of a Search [page 299]

State v. Church
110 N.C. App. 569, 430 S.E.2d 462 (1993)
Based on a first-time informant's information that marijuana was being grown near a white frame house located behind an oil company, officers went there to investigate. They saw a white frame house and a second house with wood siding, which was about 150 feet west of the white frame house. The officers walked to the front porch of the white house, knocked on the door, and received no answer. From the front porch, they saw two marijuana plants growing along a fence that went from the white house to another residence east of the white house and a third marijuana plant growing directly behind the second house. After seeing these marijuana plants, the officers walked to the second house to determine who lived in the houses. One officer knocked on the front and side doors and then saw the defendant walk from the garage that was next to the second house. The defendant informed the officers that he owned both houses but lived in the second house. The officers asked the defendant if they could search the houses and garage, but he refused. After arresting the defendant, the officers asked him for a garage door key, which he produced. An officer inserted the key in the lock, found that it fit, and withdrew the key without opening the door.

The officers learned that the defendant was on probation, contacted his probation officer, and were informed by her that as a condition of probation, the defendant was obligated to submit to warrantless searches by his probation officer. An officer informed the probation officer of the discovery of marijuana and asked her if she would be interested in conducting a warrantless search under the probation condition. She told the officer that she would be willing to conduct a warrantless search if she saw marijuana growing outside the defendant's house and determined that the plants more than likely belonged to him. She went to the house, saw the plants, determined that the plants probably belonged to the defendant, and authorized a warrantless search of the defendant's premises. She and nine law enforcement officers conducted the search.

The court ruled that the officers' entry onto the defendant's property (that is, walking to the front and side doors to look for the resident) was permissible, based on State v. Prevette, 43 N.C. App. 450 (1979), *review denied*, 299 N.C. 124, 261 S.E.2d 925, *cert. denied*, 447 U.S. 906 (1980). The court also noted that the *inadvertence* component of the plain-view doctrine was deleted in Horton v. California, 496 U.S. 128, 110 S. Ct. 2301, 110 L. Ed. 2d 112 (1990), and ruled that the plain-view doctrine was satisfied in this case. (Note, however, that the plain-view doctrine must be satisfied only when there is a seizure of property, not when only a search takes place. See page 112 of the second edition at note 31. The officers' initial observation of the marijuana, before any seizure took place, did not need to satisfy the plain-view doctrine.) The court also ruled that insertion of the key in the lock was not an unlawful search. [Other courts have disagreed about whether inserting a key in a lock is a search. *Compare* United States v. Lyon, 898 F.2d 210 (1st Cir.), *cert. denied*, 498 U.S. 920 (1990) (inserting key is not a search), *with* United States v. Concepcion, 942 F.2d 1170 (7th Cir. 1991) (inserting key is a search, but only reasonable suspicion is required to do so).]

United States v. Gault
92 F.3d 990 (10th Cir. 1996)
An officer noticed a nylon gym bag in front of a train seat, but the bag protruded five inches into the aisle. An officer kicked and lifted the bag to determine its weight. He then knelt down and sniffed the seam of the bag to determine if an odor of marijuana was coming from it. The court ruled that the officer did not conduct a search under the Fourth Amendment. The bag, protruding into the aisle, could have been kicked or lifted by another passenger or railroad employee who encountered it. There is no reasonable expectation of privacy in the air surrounding one's possessions, and therefore the officer's sniff of the bag was not a search under the Fourth Amendment.

United States v. Guzman
75 F.3d 1090 (6th Cir.), *cert. denied*, 117 S. Ct. 266 (1996)
An officer's touching of a cloth bag on a luggage rack inside of a bus and asking to whom it belonged was not a search under the Fourth Amendment. *See also* United States v. McDonald, 100 F.3d 1320 (7th Cir. 1996) (similar ruling).

United States v. Ryles
988 F.2d 13 (5th Cir.), *cert. denied*, 510 U.S. 858 (1993)
An officer conducted a search under the Fourth Amendment when he placed his head and torso into the defendant's van, although his action was reasonable based on the facts in this case.

Definition of a Seizure [page 299]

United States v. Letsinger
93 F.3d 140 (4th Cir. 1996)
Drug task force officers were standing outside the defendant's train compartment. The defendant was standing in the doorway, and his bag was behind him inside the compartment. During a conversation between the officers and the defendant, an officer told the defendant that they were going to detain his bag. However, the officers made no effort then to take possession of the bag, and the defendant did not give the bag to them or otherwise assent to their taking it. Relying on California v. Hodari D., 499 U.S. 621, 111 S. Ct. 1547, 113 L. Ed. 2d 690 (1991), the court ruled that, based on these facts, the bag was not seized under the Fourth Amendment. The defendant did not acquiesce to the officer's statement that they were going to detain his bag.

Observations and Actions That May Not Implicate Fourth Amendment Rights

Private Search or Seizure [page 300]

United States v. Leffall
82 F.3d 343 (10th Cir. 1996)
The court stated that the test to determine when a search by a private person becomes government action under the Fourth Amendment is a two-part inquiry: (1) whether the government knew of and acquiesced in the intrusive conduct and (2) whether the party performing the search intended to assist law enforcement efforts or to further the party's own ends. In this case, the court ruled that an airline employee who independently decided to open a package because he believed it contained contraband conducted a private search even though he asked a law enforcement officer to witness his opening of the package. The officer neither participated in the search nor encouraged the airline employee to search the package.

United States v. Cleaveland
38 F.3d 1092 (9th Cir. 1994)
A public power company received an anonymous tip that there was an illegal power diversion and possible marijuana manufacturing at the defendant's residence. Power company employees planned to visit the residence to investigate the power diversion and asked police to be present in case danger arose. While the employees investigated the power meter, an officer waited a block away. Based on the information learned by the employees, the officer obtained a search warrant to search the residence for marijuana. The court ruled that the search by the power company employees was a private search because they initiated the plan to inspect the meter. Even though they may have had dual motives to conduct the inspection—to recover money for the company's loss of power and to assist the police in capturing the power thief and uncovering the marijuana manufacturing—the motive to recover for the loss of power was independent of the other motive.

Abandoned Property and Garbage [page 302]

State v. Hauser
342 N.C. 382, 464 S.E.2d 443 (1995)
A detective made arrangements with the city sanitation department to collect trash at the defendant's residence and give it to two detectives. A sanitation worker collected the garbage left at the back of the residence for pickup. The collection was routine except that the sanitation worker prevented the garbage from commingling with other garbage by depositing the defendant's garbage into his own container in the back of the garbage truck instead of into the truck's collection bin.

    The sanitation worker gave the defendant's garbage to the detectives, who found cocaine residue in it. One of the detectives then obtained a search warrant based on the cocaine found in the garbage and on information received from four informants. One of the informants stated that the defendant had sold him cocaine at the defendant's residence. In addition, the officers provided facts showing the reliability of the informants' information. The officers executed the search warrant and found more than a pound of cocaine in the defendant's residence.

    The court, disavowing a contrary conclusion in the court of appeals opinion in this case, 115 N.C. App. 431,

445 S.E.2d 73 (1994), ruled that the search of the defendant's garbage did not violate the Fourth Amendment, based on the ruling in California v. Greenwood, 486 U.S. 35, 108 S. Ct. 1625, 100 L. Ed. 2d 30 (1988) (no reasonable expectation of privacy under the Fourth Amendment in garbage left for collection). The defendant sought to distinguish the *Greenwood* ruling by noting that the garbage was left at the curb in *Greenwood* while the garbage in this case was left for collection within the curtilage of the home, the defendant's backyard.

The court rejected the defendant's argument, relying on United States v. Hedrick, 922 F.2d 396 (7th Cir.), *cert. denied*, 502 U.S. 847 (1991) (no Fourth Amendment violation when officers seized garbage placed for collection eighteen to twenty feet within home's curtilage; garbage was placed in view of public passing by on the sidewalk, distance between garbage and sidewalk was short, and there was no fence or other barrier preventing public access to garbage). The North Carolina Supreme Court stated that the location of the defendant's garbage within the home's curtilage did not automatically establish that he possessed a reasonable expectation of privacy in the garbage. Relying on the ruling in United States v. Biondich, 652 F.2d 743 (8th Cir.), *cert. denied*, 454 U.S. 975 (1981) (no Fourth Amendment violation when officer arranged with regular trash collection service to deliver defendant's garbage to officer, even though there may be an expectation of privacy in garbage while it remains within the curtilage), and distinguishing United States v. Certain Real Property Located at 987 Fisher Road, 719 F. Supp. 1396 (E.D. Mich. 1989) (Fourth Amendment was violated when police went onto defendant's property and seized garbage bags placed against back wall of house), the court ruled that the defendant did not retain a reasonable expectation of privacy in his garbage once it left his yard in the usual manner, based on the facts in this case. The court also ruled that, even assuming that the search of the defendant's garbage violated the Fourth Amendment, the information supplied by the informants provided a substantial basis for probable cause to support the search warrant for the defendant's house.

United States v. Shanks
97 F.3d 977 (7th Cir. 1996)

After receiving an anonymous tip that someone was selling drugs from a residence on the upper floor of two-story duplex condominium, officers attempted to corroborate the tip by looking for evidence of drug activity in garbage containers located next to a garage that was approximately twenty feet away from the residence. The garbage containers were located on a narrow strip of land occupying the space between the garage and the alley. The officers confiscated the containers in the early hours of the morning and replaced them with identical containers so no one would notice. They found drug items in opaque bags located in the containers and obtained a search warrant of the defendant's residence based on this information. The court ruled that the containers were not within the curtilage of the residence because they were located adjacent to the alley. The court also ruled that, even assuming the containers were within the curtilage, the defendant did not have a reasonable expectation of privacy in them. The containers were readily accessible to and visible from a public thoroughfare (the alley), and scavengers commonly snoop through garbage containers found in such alleys. The court also ruled that the defendant did not have a reasonable expectation of privacy merely because officers, rather than the regular garbage service, rummaged through his garbage or because his garbage was hidden in opaque bags.

United States v. Leshuk
65 F.3d 1105 (4th Cir. 1995)

The defendant's disclaimer of ownership of a garbage bag and backpacks located near him was a voluntary abandonment of the property. Thus he was precluded from seeking to suppress evidence found in them.

United States v. Boone
62 F.3d 323 (10th Cir.), *cert. denied*, 116 S. Ct. 576 (1995)

After officers conducted an illegal search of the defendant's vehicle and discovered marijuana, the defendant got in his vehicle and a high-speed chase occurred. During the chase, the defendant threw illegal drugs from the vehicle. The court ruled that the defendant abandoned the drugs. Although abandonment did not occur as a direct result of the officers' illegal conduct, the defendant's independent and voluntary decision to throw the illegal drugs from the vehicle during the high-speed chase was sufficient intervening conduct to remove the taint from the prior illegal search of the vehicle.

United States v. Washington
12 F.3d 1128 (D.C. Cir.), *cert. denied*, 513 U.S. 828 (1994)

Officers in a patrol car were in a high-speed chase of a car in which the defendant and others were passengers. The car crashed, and the defendant and the other passengers fled from the car. The court ruled that the car was abandoned under the Fourth Amendment.

Areas Outside the Home:
Curtilage and Open Fields [page 303]

State v. Hauser
342 N.C. 382, 464 S.E.2d 443 (1995)

A detective made arrangements with the city sanitation department to collect trash at the defendant's residence and give it to two detectives. A sanitation worker collected the garbage left at the back of the residence for pickup. The collection was routine except that the sanitation worker prevented the garbage from commingling with other garbage by depositing the defendant's garbage into his own container in the back of the garbage truck instead of into the truck's collection bin.

The sanitation worker gave the defendant's garbage to the detectives, who found cocaine residue in it. One of the detectives then obtained a search warrant based on the cocaine found in the garbage and information received from four informants. One of the informants stated that the defendant had sold him cocaine at the defendant's residence. In addition, the officers provided facts showing the reliability of the informants' information. The officers executed the search warrant and found more than a pound of cocaine in the defendant's residence.

The court, disavowing a contrary conclusion in the court of appeals opinion in this case, 115 N.C. App. 431, 445 S.E.2d 73 (1994), ruled that the search of the defendant's garbage did not violate the Fourth Amendment, based on the ruling in California v. Greenwood, 486 U.S. 35, 108 S. Ct. 1625, 100 L. Ed. 2d 30 (1988) (no reasonable expectation of privacy under the Fourth Amendment in garbage left for collection). The defendant sought to distinguish the *Greenwood* ruling by noting that the garbage was left at the curb in *Greenwood* while the garbage in this case was left for collection within the curtilage of the home, the defendant's backyard. The court rejected the defendant's argument, relying on United States v. Hedrick, 922 F.2d 396 (7th Cir.), *cert. denied*, 502 U.S. 847 (1991) (no Fourth Amendment violation when officers seized garbage placed for collection eighteen to twenty feet within home's curtilage; garbage was placed in view of public passing by on the sidewalk, distance between garbage and sidewalk was short, and there was no fence or other barrier preventing public access to garbage). The North Carolina Supreme Court stated that the location of the defendant's garbage within the home's curtilage did not automatically establish that he possessed a reasonable expectation of privacy in the garbage. Relying on the ruling in United States v. Biondich, 652 F.2d 743 (8th Cir.), *cert. denied*, 454 U.S. 975 (1981) (no Fourth Amendment violation when officer arranged with regular trash collection service to deliver defendant's garbage to

officer, even though there may be an expectation of privacy in garbage while it remains within the curtilage), and distinguishing United States v. Certain Real Property Located at 987 Fisher Road, 719 F. Supp. 1396 (E.D. Mich. 1989) (Fourth Amendment was violated when police went onto defendant's property and seized garbage bags placed against back wall of house), the court ruled that the defendant did not retain a reasonable expectation of privacy in his garbage once it left his yard in the usual manner, based on the facts in this case. The court also ruled that, even assuming that the search of the defendant's garbage violated the Fourth Amendment, the information supplied by the informants provided a substantial basis for probable cause to support the search warrant for the defendant's house. *See also* United States v. Shanks, 97 F.3d 977 (7th Cir. 1996), discussed above on page 63.

State v. Church
110 N.C. App. 569, 430 S.E.2d 462 (1993)

Based on a first-time informant's information that marijuana was being grown near a white frame house located behind an oil company, officers went there to investigate. They saw a white frame house and a second house with wood siding, which was about 150 feet west of the white frame house. The officers walked to the front porch of the white house, knocked on the door, and received no answer. From the front porch, they saw two marijuana plants growing along a fence that went from the white house to another residence east of the white house and a third marijuana plant growing directly behind the second house. After seeing these marijuana plants, the officers walked to the second house to determine who lived in the houses. One officer knocked on the front and side doors and then saw the defendant walk from the garage that was next to the second house. The defendant informed the officers that he owned both houses but lived in the second house. The officers asked the defendant if they could search the houses and garage, but he refused. After arresting the defendant, the officers asked him for a garage door key, which he produced. An officer inserted the key in the lock, found that it fit, and withdrew the key without opening the door.

The officers learned that the defendant was on probation, contacted his probation officer, and were informed by her that as a condition of probation, the defendant was obligated to submit to warrantless searches by his probation officer. An officer informed the probation officer of the discovery of marijuana and asked her if she would be interested in conducting a warrantless search under the probation condition. She told the officer that she would be willing to conduct a warrantless search if she saw marijuana growing outside the defendant's house and determined that the plants more than likely belonged to him. She went to the house, saw the plants, determined that the plants probably belonged to the defendant, and authorized a warrantless search of the defendant's premises. She and nine law enforcement officers conducted the search.

The court ruled that the officers' entry onto the defendant's property (that is, walking to the front and side doors to look for the resident) was permissible, based on State v. Prevette, 43 N.C. App. 450 (1979), *review denied,* 299 N.C. 124, 261 S.E.2d 925, *cert. denied,* 447 U.S. 906 (1980). The court also noted that the *inadvertence* component of the plain-view doctrine was deleted in Horton v. California, 496 U.S. 128, 110 S. Ct. 2301, 110 L. Ed. 2d 112 (1990), and ruled that the plain-view doctrine was satisfied in this case. (Note, however, that the plain-view doctrine must be satisfied only when there is a seizure of property, not when only a search takes place. See page 112 of the second edition at note 31. The officers' initial observation of the marijuana, before any seizure took place, did not need to satisfy the plain-view doctrine.) The court also ruled that the insertion of the key in the lock was not an unlawful search. [Other courts have disagreed about whether inserting a key in a lock is a search. *Compare* United States v. Lyon, 898 F.2d 210 (1st Cir.), *cert. denied,* 498 U.S. 920 (1990) (inserting key is not a search), *with* United States v. Concepcion, 942 F.2d 1170 (7th Cir. 1991) (inserting key is a search, but only reasonable suspicion is required to do so).]

United States v. Reilly
76 F.3d 1271 (2d Cir. 1996)

The court ruled that the curtilage of the defendant's residence included a cottage that was 375 feet from the residence on a 10.71-acre farm. The property was enclosed by a wire fence, hedgerows, and thick woods. There was no interior fencing separating the cottage from the residence. The defendant and his guests used the cottage area for a variety of private activities, including fishing, naked swimming, croquet, cooking, and sexual intercourse. The area's parklike appearance made it readily apparent to observers that the area was private. *See also* United States v. Depew, 8 F.3d 1424 (9th Cir. 1993) (area six feet from the defendant's garage and fifty to sixty feet from the defendant's house was within the curtilage; area was not readily visible from the road).

United States v. Friend
50 F.3d 548 (8th Cir. 1995), *vacated on other grounds,* 116 S. Ct. 1538 (1996)

The defendant's residence was located within a locked gate and fence. An officer entered onto the defendant's property with a drug detection dog, which alerted to the defendant's car. The car was parked outside the locked gate and fence, between the garage and a public alley. The court ruled that the car was not located within the curtilage of the defendant's residence and that therefore the officer's entry onto the defendant's property did not violate the Fourth Amendment.

United States v. Van Damme
48 F.3d 461 (9th Cir. 1995)

The court ruled that the defendant's three greenhouses were not within the curtilage of his home. The greenhouses were more than 200 feet from the home. A wire fence surrounding the home and greenhouses was a perimeter fence enclosing several acres, not a fence surrounding only the home and curtilage. A board fence surrounding one of the greenhouses made it a distinct portion of the property quite separate from the home. The greenhouses lacked any indicia of activities commonly associated with domestic life. The cultivation of crops, such as the marijuana involved in this case, is an activity that occurs in open fields, not an intimate activity of the home. Thus the officers were not within the curtilage when they saw the marijuana through the board fence and the greenhouse doors, and neither were any of the greenhouses. *See also* United States v. Wright, 991 F.2d 1182 (4th Cir. 1993) (barn on path from defendant's house was not within curtilage, based on facts in this case); United States v. Traynor, 990 F.2d 1153 (9th Cir. 1993) (outbuilding about seventy-five feet away from house was not within curtilage, based on facts in this case).

United States v. Hall
47 F.3d 1091 (11th Cir.), *cert. denied,* 116 S. Ct. 71 (1995)

An officer entered a commercial company's property and removed a bag of paper shreddings from a garbage dumpster located near the company's offices in a parking area reserved for company employees. The officer drove forty yards on a private paved road to get to the dumpster. However, there were no signs that indicated that the road was private, and the dumpster was readily accessible to the public. The court noted that the United States Supreme Court has consistently stated that a commercial proprietor has a reasonable expectation of privacy only in those areas where affirmative steps have been taken to exclude the public. The court concluded that the company's subjective expectation of privacy was not one that society was prepared to accept as objectively reasonable. Thus the officer's search of the dumpster did not violate the Fourth Amendment.

Plain View (Sensory Perception) [page 307]

Minnesota v. Dickerson
508 U.S. 366, 113 S. Ct. 2130, 124 L. Ed. 2d 334 (1993)
An officer had reasonable suspicion to stop the defendant and to frisk him for weapons. Based on the record before the Court, during the frisk the officer felt a lump (a small, hard object wrapped in plastic) that he knew was not a weapon in the defendant's jacket pocket. However, after concluding that the lump was not a weapon, the officer determined that the lump was cocaine *only after* "squeezing, sliding and otherwise manipulating the contents of the defendant's pocket." The Court ruled that the "plain-view" doctrine [which provides that if officers are lawfully in a position in which they view an object, if its incriminating character is immediately apparent (i.e., they have probable cause to seize it), and if the officers have a lawful right of access to the object, they may seize it without a warrant] applies by analogy to cases in which an officer discovers contraband through the sense of touch during an otherwise lawful search. However, the Court also ruled that the officer in this case was not justified in seizing the cocaine, because the officer exceeded the search for weapons permitted by Terry v. Ohio, 392 U.S. 1, 88 S. Ct. 1868, 20 L. Ed. 2d 889 (1968). Once the officer determined the lump was not a weapon, his continued exploration of the lump until he developed probable cause to believe it was cocaine was an additional search that was not justified by *Terry v. Ohio.* (Thus the officer's action would have been permissible in this case only if he had developed probable cause to believe the lump was cocaine at the time he determined the lump was not a weapon.) *See also* United States v. Ashley, 37 F.3d 678 (D.C. Cir. 1994) (officer felt hard object during initial patdown; based on facts in this case, it was immediately apparent to officer that object was crack cocaine); United States v. Craft, 30 F.3d 1044 (8th Cir. 1994) (officer at airport felt hard, compact packages attached to defendant's ankles; it was immediately apparent to officer that packages contained controlled substances).

State v. Beveridge
336 N.C. 601, 444 S.E.2d 223 (1994)
The court, per curiam and without an opinion, affirmed the court of appeals opinion, 112 N.C. App. 688, 436 S.E.2d 912 (1993), that is discussed below.

   While Officer Johnson was arresting a driver for impaired driving, Officer Gregory (while securing the car) asked the defendant, a passenger, to get out. Officer Gregory noticed a strong odor of alcohol about the defendant, who also was acting "giddy." The officer believed, based on the facts in this case, that the defendant was under the influence of alcohol and a controlled sub-stance. He told the defendant he was going to pat him down for weapons. During the patdown, the officer noticed that there was a cylindrical-shaped rolled-up plastic bag in the defendant's front pocket. The officer asked him what it was, and the defendant started laughing and pulled out some money. However, the officer could still see the long cylindrical bulge he had in his pocket. He asked the defendant what it was. The defendant then stuck his hand in his pocket and tried to palm what he had. The officer asked him what he was trying to hide, and the defendant rolled open his hand and showed the officer a white plastic bag with a white powdery substance in it. The officer believed that the substance was cocaine and then arrested the defendant for possession of cocaine. The court ruled that Officer Gregory was justified in conducting a limited patdown of the defendant to determine whether the defendant was armed, but once he concluded that there was no weapon, he could not continue to search or question the defendant to determine whether the bag contained illegal drugs. (The court's specific ruling that the officer could not continue to question the defendant does not appear consistent with prevailing federal constitutional law.) The court ruled that the search exceeded the scope of the frisk under Minnesota v. Dickerson, 508 U.S. 366, 113 S. Ct. 2130, 124 L. Ed. 2d 334 (1993), because it was not immediately apparent that the item in the defendant's pocket was an illegal substance. *See also* United States v. Schiavo, 29 F.3d 6 (1st Cir. 1994) (officer's continued manipulation of bulge in defendant's pocket, which was a paper bag with money, was not justified).

State v. Corpening
109 N.C. App. 586, 427 S.E.2d 892 (1993)
A deputy sheriff responded to a report that the defendant's van had caught fire and was off the highway in the lot of an old store. The fire had been extinguished and a wrecker had been called before the deputy arrived. The deputy, who had been an officer for thirteen years and had smelled "white liquor" many times, detected the odor of that substance coming from the van. The court ruled: (1) the deputy's detection of the odor was sufficient to establish probable cause to search the van (in addition, the defendant had acted very nervous and had placed cardboard over a burned-out window); and (2) the warrantless search of the van was proper, based on State v. Isleib, 319 N.C. 634, 356 S.E.2d 573 (1987).

State v. Church
110 N.C. App. 569, 430 S.E.2d 462 (1993)
Based on a first-time informant's information that marijuana was being grown near a white frame house located

behind an oil company, officers went there to investigate. They saw a white frame house and a second house with wood siding, which was about 150 feet west of the white frame house. The officers walked to the front porch of the white house, knocked on the door, and received no answer. From the front porch, they saw two marijuana plants growing along a fence that went from the white house to another residence east of the white house and a third marijuana plant growing directly behind the second house. After seeing these marijuana plants, the officers walked to the second house to determine who lived in the houses. One officer knocked on the front and side doors and then saw the defendant walk from the garage that was next to the second house. The defendant informed the officers that he owned both houses but lived in the second house. The officers asked the defendant if they could search the houses and garage, but he refused. After arresting the defendant, the officers asked him for a garage door key, which he produced. An officer inserted the key in the lock, found that it fit, and withdrew the key without opening the door.

The officers learned that the defendant was on probation, contacted his probation officer, and were informed by her that as a condition of probation, the defendant was obligated to submit to warrantless searches by his probation officer. An officer informed the probation officer of the discovery of marijuana and asked her if she would be interested in conducting a warrantless search under the probation condition. She told the officer that she would be willing to conduct a warrantless search if she saw marijuana growing outside the defendant's house and determined that the plants more than likely belonged to him. She went to the house, saw the plants, determined that the plants probably belonged to the defendant, and authorized a warrantless search of the defendant's premises. She and nine law enforcement officers conducted the search.

The court ruled that the officers' entry onto the defendant's property (that is, walking to the front and side doors to look for the resident) was permissible, based on State v. Prevette, 43 N.C. App. 450 (1979), *review denied*, 299 N.C. 124, 261 S.E.2d 925, *cert. denied*, 447 U.S. 906 (1980). The court also noted that the *inadvertence* component of the plain-view doctrine was deleted in Horton v. California, 496 U.S. 128, 110 S. Ct. 2301, 110 L. Ed. 2d 112 (1990), and ruled that the plain-view doctrine was satisfied in this case. [Note, however, that the plain-view doctrine must be satisfied only when there is a seizure of property, not when only a search takes place. See page 112 of the second edition at note 31. The officers' initial observation of the marijuana, before any seizure took place, did not need to satisfy the plain-view doctrine.] The

court also ruled that the insertion of the key in the lock was not an unlawful search. [Other courts have disagreed about whether inserting a key in a lock is a search. *Compare* United States v. Lyon, 898 F.2d 210 (1st Cir.), *cert. denied*, 498 U.S. 920 (1990) (inserting key is not a search), *with* United States v. Concepcion, 942 F.2d 1170 (7th Cir. 1991) (inserting key is a search, but only reasonable suspicion is required to do so).]

State v. Wilson
112 N.C. App. 777, 437 S.E.2d 387 (1993)

A police department received an anonymous phone call that several people were selling drugs in the breezeway of Building 1304 in the Hunter Oaks Apartments. The caller did not provide any names or descriptions of the alleged drug dealers. Two officers familiar with the area knew that if a police car entered the parking lot at one end of the breezeway, the suspects would run out of the other end. They devised a plan in which a police car would enter the parking lot and officers would position themselves so they could stop anyone who ran out of the back of the breezeway. An officer stopped the defendant as he ran out of the back of the breezeway. During the subsequent frisk, the officer felt a lump in the left breast pocket of the defendant's jacket and immediately believed that it was crack cocaine. The officer then asked the defendant if his coat had an inside pocket. The defendant did not respond verbally but instead opened his jacket so the inside pocket was visible. The officer saw and removed a small plastic bag that contained crack cocaine. (1) Distinguishing State v. Fleming, 106 N.C. App. 165, 415 S.E.2d 782 (1992), the court ruled that the officer had authority to stop and frisk the defendant, based on the anonymous phone call, the flight of the defendant and others when the police car pulled into the parking lot, and the officer's experience that weapons were frequently involved in drug transactions. (2) Distinguishing Minnesota v. Dickerson, 508 U.S. 366, 113 S. Ct. 2130, 124 L. Ed. 2d 334 (1993), the court noted that the officer in this case—unlike the officer in *Dickerson*—did not need to manipulate the item in the defendant's pocket to determine that it was cocaine; he immediately believed it was crack cocaine. The court ruled that the requirement in *Dickerson* that it must be "immediately apparent" to the officer that the item is illegal means that the officer must have *probable cause* to believe that the item is illegal. (See the discussion in the second edition on page 112 at note 31.) The court also ruled that the officer's tactile senses, based on his experience and the facts in this case, gave him probable cause to believe that the item was crack cocaine. Thus the officer did not exceed the scope of a frisk under the *Dickerson* ruling.

State v. Whitted

112 N.C. App. 640, 436 S.E.2d 275 (1993)

A car parked in front of a residence fled at a high rate of speed after the driver saw a marked patrol car. The area from which the car fled was known for frequent sales of drugs, especially crack cocaine. People commonly pulled over to the curbside, after being flagged down, and purchased drugs. This area had been under surveillance for thirty days, and several arrests had been made based on drug sales at the residence from which the car had fled. After officers stopped the car, they went on each side of the car to investigate. The defendant was sitting in the front passenger seat, and an officer saw that the defendant kept his hand by his front pants pocket and "kept pushing something down." The defendant did not move his hand when the officer asked him to do so, and the officer then frisked the defendant for weapons. During the frisk, the officer felt a "pebble" (i.e., a hard substance) in the defendant's pocket that he believed, based on his experience and knowledge of the circumstances, was crack cocaine. He removed the object and discovered that it was crack cocaine. The court ruled, based on all the circumstances in this case, including the suspicious behavior and flight from the officers, that the officer had probable cause to search the defendant after the officer felt the pebble in the defendant's pocket. [Although the court did not discuss Minnesota v. Dickerson, 508 U.S. 366, 113 S. Ct. 2130, 124 L. Ed. 2d 334 (1993), its ruling is consistent with the *Dickerson* ruling.]

In re Whitley

122 N.C. App. 290, 468 S.E.2d 610, *review denied*, 344 N.C. 437, 476 S.E.2d 132 (1996)

Two officers responded to a call that drug sales were occurring between two black males on a certain street. Officers saw the respondent and another person under a tree. They approached them and told them they were going to search them for weapons. During the search of the respondent, an officer noticed that his lower body and legs were really tight so he asked him to spread his legs. The officer's hands were outside of the respondent's trousers in the bottom crotch area when an item fell from the respondent's buttocks into his pants. (The officer testified at a hearing that, based on his personal experience as a law enforcement officer, he had probable cause to believe that the object was some kind of illegal substance.) When the officer felt the item fall on his hand, he held it in one hand and put his other hand into the pants and retrieved it. It was a plastic bag with a white powdered substance, and the officer placed the respondent under arrest. The court ruled: (1) there was reasonable suspicion that the respondent might be armed, dangerous, and involved in

criminal activity to frisk him; and (2) the incriminating character of the object seized was immediately apparent to the officer, noting State v. Wilson, 112 N.C. App. 777, 437 S.E.2d 387 (1993), and Minnesota v. Dickerson, 508 U.S. 366, 113 S. Ct. 2130, 124 L. Ed. 2d 334 (1993). The court noted that there was no evidence that the officer improperly manipulated the object to determine if it was an illegal substance.

State v. Benjamin

124 N.C. App. 734, 478 S.E.2d 651 (1996)

An officer conducted a frisk of the defendant after an investigative stop for a traffic violation. As the officer was patting the defendant, he felt two hard plastic containers in a breast pocket of the defendant's winter jacket. Based on his narcotics training, it was immediately apparent that these containers were vials of the type that is customarily used to hold illegal drugs. When the officer felt the container through the jacket, he asked the defendant, "What is that?" The defendant responded that it was "crack." The officer removed two vials from the coat pocket and found cocaine. (1) The court ruled that the defendant was not in "custody" to require *Miranda* warnings when the officer asked the question while conducting the frisk. The court noted that the fact that a defendant is not free to leave does not necessarily constitute custody under *Miranda*. Instead, the inquiry is whether a reasonable person in the defendant's position would believe that he or she was under arrest or the functional equivalent of arrest; the court cited and discussed Stansbury v. California, 511 U.S. 318, 114 S. Ct. 1526, 128 L. Ed. 2d 293 (1994), and Berkemer v. McCarty, 468 U.S. 420, 104 S. Ct. 3138, 82 L. Ed. 2d 317 (1984). The court concluded that a reasonable person would not have believed he was in custody, based on these facts. (2) The court ruled that the seizure of the cocaine was proper under the plain-feel theory set out in Minnesota v. Dickerson, 508 U.S. 366, 113 S. Ct. 2130, 124 L. Ed. 2d 334 (1993). The court stated that the officer had probable cause to believe (or to state it a different way, it became immediately apparent to the officer) that the object was contraband based on the officer's experience and narcotics training; on the size, shape, and mass of the objects; and on the defendant's response to the officer's question. The court also ruled that an officer may ask a suspect the nature of an object in the suspect's pocket during a lawful frisk even after the officer has determined that the object is not a weapon.

State v. Brooks

337 N.C. 132, 446 S.E.2d 579 (1994)

The court ruled that the officer's shining his flashlight into a car's interior was not a search, citing Texas v. Brown, 460 U.S. 730, 103 S. Ct. 1535, 75 L. Ed. 2d 502 (1983), and State v. Whitley, 33 N.C. App. 753, 236 S.E.2d 720 (1977).

State v. Wooding

117 N.C. App. 109, 449 S.E.2d 760 (1994)

An officer received a radio communication that a person at the Southern Lights Restaurant had seen a black man of a given description get out of a 1980s gray Monte Carlo car and hide behind a dumpster near the restaurant. The person believed that the man lived in one of the apartments at 109 North Cedar Street. While investigating this communication, the officer received another radio communication that a robbery had occurred at the Equinox Restaurant. The description of the robber matched the description of the suspicious person at the Southern Lights Restaurant. The officer went to 109 North Cedar Street. He saw a gray Monte Carlo car parked in front of the building, which contained four apartments, two at ground level and two upstairs. Before leaving his vehicle, the officer saw—through an open window in the side of one of the downstairs apartments—a black male matching the earlier descriptions. After getting out of his vehicle, the officer saw this same person through the open window walking around the apartment and "heard a lot of noise which appeared to [him] to be coins hitting metal." He believed that the noise was definitely change being counted or sifted through.

The officer went to the back porch of the apartment in which he had seen the black male (there was a partition that separated the porches of the two lower-level apartments). Once on the porch, the officer leaned over a couch next to the window, got close to the window, and looked into the apartment through a three- to four-inch opening in the window curtains. The officer saw two black males sitting on the floor in the hallway counting money. The officer radioed what he had seen to an officer who was in the front of the apartment with the robbery victim (the victim heard the officer's communication). Shortly thereafter, the defendant came out onto the front porch and was arrested for the robbery. Then the other person came out of the apartment and was identified as the robber by the victim. Both men thereafter consented to a search of the apartment, and the officers found a handgun and money in the apartment.

The court, relying on State v. Tarantino, 322 N.C. 386, 368 S.E.2d 588 (1988), *cert. denied*, 489 U.S. 1010

(1989) (looking through cracks in building violated Fourth Amendment), ruled that the officer's looking into the apartment window was an unlawful search under the Fourth Amendment. Also, the court rejected the state's argument that the later consent search of the apartment (when a handgun and money were found) was based on lawful activity independent of the officer's initial unlawful observation into the apartment window. The court ruled that (1) the arrest of the defendant was based entirely on the officer's unlawful search and was therefore itself unlawful; (2) the consent to search, given by the defendant after his arrest, was tainted by the unlawful search; and (3) the victim's identification of the second person in the apartment was made only after the victim learned what the officer had seen, through the back window—two people counting money in the apartment. Thus the identification and the later consent to search were also tainted by the unlawful search.

United States v. Taylor

90 F.3d 903 (4th Cir. 1996)

Two law enforcement officers came to the defendant's home to return a handgun pursuant to a court order. As they approached the front door, they could clearly see into a well-lit dining room through unclosed vertical blinds in a picture window. The court ruled, based on these facts, the defendant did not possess a reasonable expectation of privacy from the officers' observations, and thus their observations were not a search under the Fourth Amendment.

United States v. Williams

41 F.3d 192 (4th Cir. 1994), *cert. denied*, 115 S. Ct. 1442 (1995)

An officer properly conducted a warrantless search of five legally seized packages located in lost luggage at an airport because their contents, cocaine, were clearly indicated (the court stated their contents were a "foregone conclusion") based on the following facts: (1) the manner in which the cocaine was packaged (each apparently weighing about one kilogram, heavily wrapped in cellophane with a brown opaque material inside); (2) the officer's firm belief, based on ten years' experience, that packages appearing in this manner always contain narcotics; (3) an airline baggage agent's belief that the packages contained narcotics; and (4) the fact that the only items found in the suitcase besides the five packages of cocaine were towels, dirty blankets, and a shirt with a cigarette burn.

G & G Jewelry, Inc. v. City of Oakland

989 F.2d 1093 (9th Cir. 1993)

The court ruled that an officer's warrantless seizure of stolen property being held at a pawn shop under a pawn agreement was proper under the plain-view theory, if the seizure was for investigatory purposes—but not if the stolen property was seized simply to return it to the rightful owner.

Beepers

Tracking Beepers [page 310]

United States v. Jones
31 F.3d 1304 (4th Cir. 1994)
A postal inspector's use of an electronic tracking device to monitor the movement of a government mail pouch was not a search under the Fourth Amendment when the defendant stole the mail pouch and hid it in his van.

Dogs [page 311]

United States v. Jeffus
22 F.3d 554 (4th Cir. 1994)
The use of a drug dog to walk around the defendant's car while it was lawfully stopped for a traffic offense was not a search under the Fourth Amendment. When the dog alerted positively for the presence of drugs, officers had probable cause to search the car without a search warrant.

United States v. Ludwig
10 F.3d 1523 (10th Cir. 1993)
The use of a drug dog to randomly sniff vehicles in a motel parking lot open to the public was not a search under the Fourth Amendment. The dog's alerting to the defendant's car in the parking lot gave an officer probable cause to conduct a warrantless search of the car.

Thermal Imagers [new section]

United States v. Robinson
62 F.3d 1325 (11th Cir. 1995), *cert. denied*, 116 S. Ct. 1848 (1996)
The warrantless use of a thermal imager to detect heat emanating from a person's home does not violate a person's reasonable expectation of privacy under the Fourth Amendment. *See also* United States v. Pinson, 24 F.3d 1056 (8th Cir.), *cert. denied*, 513 U.S. 1057 (1994) (similar ruling); United States v. Ford, 34 F.3d 992 (11th Cir. 1194) (similar ruling); United States v. Myers, 46 F.3d 668 (7th Cir.), *cert. denied*, 116 S. Ct. 684 (1995) (similar ruling); United States v. Ishmael, 48 F.3d 850 (5th Cir.), *cert. denied*, 116 S. Ct. 74 (1995).

Search and Seizure by Valid Consent

Voluntariness

Generally [page 312]

Ohio v. Robinette
519 U.S. ___, 117 S. Ct. 417, 136 L. Ed. 2d 347 (1996)
An officer stopped the defendant for speeding. The defendant gave his driver's license to the officer, who ran a computer check that revealed that the defendant had no prior violations. The officer then asked the defendant to step out of his car, issued a verbal warning to the defendant, and returned his license. The officer then asked the defendant if he had any illegal contraband in his car. The defendant said no. The officer then asked the defendant if he could search his car, and the defendant consented. The Court rejected a lower court ruling that an officer must advise a lawfully seized defendant that the defendant is free to go before a consent to search will be recognized as voluntary. The Court noted that the Fourth Amendment requires that a consent to search must be voluntary, and voluntariness is a question of fact that must be determined from all the circumstances. An officer's warning before obtaining consent to search is not required by the Fourth Amendment for a consent to search to be valid.

State v. Wooding
117 N.C. App. 109, 449 S.E.2d 760 (1994)
An officer received a radio communication that a person at the Southern Lights Restaurant had seen a black man of a given description get out of a 1980s gray Monte Carlo car and hide behind a dumpster near the restaurant. The person believed that the man lived in one of the apartments at 109 North Cedar Street. While investigating this communication, the officer received another radio communication that a robbery had occurred at the Equinox Restaurant. The description of the robber matched the description of the suspicious person at the Southern Lights Restaurant. The officer went to 109 North Cedar Street. He saw a gray Monte Carlo car parked in front of the building, which contained four apartments, two at ground level and two upstairs. Before leaving his vehicle, the officer saw—through an open window in the side of one of the downstairs apartments—a black male matching the earlier descriptions. After getting out of his vehicle, the officer saw this same person through the open window walking around the apartment and "heard a lot of noise which appeared to [him] to be coins hitting metal." He believed that the noise was definitely change being counted or sifted through. The officer went to the back

porch of the apartment in which he had seen the black male (there was a partition that separated the porches of the two lower-level apartments). Once on the porch, the officer leaned over a couch next to the window, got close to the window, and looked into the apartment through a three- to four-inch opening in the window curtains. The officer saw two black males sitting on the floor in the hallway counting money. The officer radioed what he had seen to an officer who was in the front of the apartment with the robbery victim (the victim heard the officer's communication). Shortly thereafter, the defendant came out onto the front porch and was arrested for the robbery. Then the other person came out of the apartment and was identified as the robber by the victim. Both men thereafter consented to a search of the apartment, and the officers found a handgun and money in the apartment.

The court, relying on State v. Tarantino, 322 N.C. 386, 368 S.E.2d 588 (1988), *cert. denied*, 489 U.S. 1010 (1989) (looking through cracks in building violated Fourth Amendment), ruled that the officer's looking into the apartment window was an unlawful search under the Fourth Amendment. Also, the court rejected the state's argument that the later consent search of the apartment (when a handgun and money were found) was based on lawful activity independent of the officer's initial unlawful observation into the apartment window. The court ruled that (1) the arrest of the defendant was based entirely on the officer's unlawful search and was therefore itself unlawful; (2) the consent to search, given by the defendant after his arrest, was tainted by the unlawful search; and (3) the victim's identification of the second person in the apartment was made only after the victim learned what the officer had seen, through the back window—two people counting money in the apartment. Thus the identification and the later consent to search were also tainted by the unlawful search.

State v. Wise
117 N.C. 105, 449 S.E.2d 774 (1994)

[Note: Although there was a dissenting opinion, the state did not seek further review.] A State Highway Patrol trooper stopped a vehicle for speeding. He saw the defendant, a passenger, grab his midsection between his stomach and his belt line with both hands. The trooper patted down the defendant, reaching from the driver's side of the car, and felt a "round cylinder object" in the area where the defendant had grabbed, but he determined that it was not a weapon. The trooper asked the defendant what he had grabbed, which prompted the defendant to reach inside his jacket and hand the trooper a white, nontransparent Bayer aspirin bottle.

The trooper shook the bottle and it "rattled lightly," sounding as if it had "BBs in it." He was suspicious because such a bottle normally has cotton in it, so the rattle would not sound the same. The trooper then opened the bottle, shone his flashlight in it, looked inside, and saw what he determined was rock cocaine. The court ruled that the officer unconstitutionally opened the bottle: (1) there was no evidence that the defendant consented to a search of the bottle and (2) there was not probable cause to believe, based on these facts, that the bottle contained illegal drugs.

State v. James
118 N.C. App. 221, 454 S.E.2d 858 (1995)

An officer saw the defendant nervously pacing, then reboarding a bus. The defendant moved toward the rear of the bus and picked up a duffel-type bag from a seat and put it in the overhead luggage bin. Officers went through the typical bus boarding procedures designed to find illegal drugs. The defendant agreed to allow an officer to look in his bag. The officer removed a portable radio from the bag and noticed that screws on the radio had been unscrewed several times. The officer asked the defendant if he would get off the bus so they could talk privately. The defendant did not respond verbally but left the bus with the officer. They went to a private area of the bus terminal, where the officer again obtained a consent to search. The officer discovered cocaine in the radio. (1) Relying on State v. McDowell, 329 N.C. 363, 407 S.E.2d 200 (1991), and other cases, the court reviewed the facts of the bus boarding and ruled that the defendant's consent to search was voluntarily given, although he had an IQ of 70. (2) Relying on State v. Christie, 96 N.C. App. 178, 385 S.E.2d 181 (1989), and State v. Bromfield, 332 N.C. 24, 418 S.E.2d 491 (1992), the court ruled that the defendant was not seized when he was on the bus or when he left the bus with the officers.

Scope of the Search [page 315]

United States v. McSween
53 F.3d 684 (5th Cir.), *cert. denied*, 116 S. Ct. 199 (1995)

The defendant's consent to search his car included a search under the car's hood. In this case, the officer made a general request for a search without identifying his objective, and the defendant did not attempt to limit the scope of the search. *See also* United States v. Snow, 44 F.3d 133 (2d Cir. 1995) (similar ruling; scope of consent included containers within vehicle); United States v. Crain, 33 F.3d 480 (5th Cir. 1994), *cert. denied*, 115 S. Ct. 1142 (1995) (similar ruling); United States v. Rich, 992 F.2d 502 (5th Cir.), *cert. denied*, 510 U.S. 933 (1993) (officer's request to "look in your truck" included suitcase behind passenger seat).

Undercover Officers and Informants [page 317]

United States v. Akinsanya
53 F.3d 852 (7th Cir. 1995)

An undercover informant agreed to arrange a purchase of heroin from the defendant. The informant went to the defendant's apartment to consummate the purchase. He saw the heroin there and called an officer (pretending the officer was the buyer) to tell him. The informant then left the apartment, pretending to get the money to buy the heroin. Officers then entered the apartment without a warrant and seized the heroin. The court ruled that the doctrine of "consent once removed" justified the entry and seizure. The doctrine applies when an undercover officer or informant (1) enters a place with the express invitation of someone with the authority to consent; (2) establishes then the existence of probable cause to arrest or to search; and (3) immediately summons help from other officers. The court ruled that all three criteria were met and that the officers' actions did not violate the Fourth Amendment.

Special Relationships

Spouses and Other Shared Relationships [page 318]

State v. Garner
340 N.C. 573, 459 S.E.2d 718 (1995), *cert. denied*, 116 S. Ct. 948 (1996)

A homeowner consented to a search of her residence after officers said that they were looking for a pistol involved in a shooting. An officer saw a pile of men's and women's clothes in a room. He picked them up and squeezed them to see if he could find a weapon. He found a weapon in a man's jacket (the officer did not know to whom the jacket belonged), which later was determined to be the defendant's. The court ruled that the homeowner's consent was valid under United States v. Matlock, 415 U.S. 164, 94 S. Ct. 988, 39 L. Ed. 2d 242 (1974).

State v. Worsley
336 N.C. 268, 443 S.E.2d 68 (1994)

Overruling State v. Hall, 264 N.C. 559, 142 S.E.2d 177 (1965), and other cases, the court ruled that a wife may consent to a search of the premises she shares with her husband.

State v. Weathers
339 N.C. 441, 451 S.E.2d 266 (1994)

The court ruled that the defendant's stepdaughter had the authority to consent to a search of the house and bedroom that she shared with the defendant. (The opinion did not provide the age of the stepdaugther.)

Reasonable Belief That Person Is Entitled to Give Consent [page 320]

United States v. Jenkins
92 F.3d 430 (6th Cir. 1996)

The court ruled that an officer is justified in believing that the driver of a tractor trailer has the authority to consent to a search of the trailer unless the officer knows or is told other information indicating that the officer's assumption is incorrect.

United States v. Dearing
9 F.3d 1428 (9th Cir. 1993)

The court ruled that an officer's belief that a person who lived in a house as a caretaker and occasional housekeeper had use and access to or control over the homeowner's bedroom—to establish apparent authority to consent to a search of the bedroom—was unreasonable under the Fourth Amendment. Even though the officer knew that the caretaker had been in the bedroom on prior occasions, there was nothing to indicate that the prior access was authorized, the bedroom door was closed at the time of the search, and the officer knew that the caretaker's relationship with the homeowner was nearing an end.

United States v. Welch
4 F.3d 761 (9th Cir. 1993)

A male person's (McGee) consent to search a vehicle did not give officers the actual or apparent authority to search the female defendant's purse in the rental car's trunk. When the officers decided to search the purse, they knew that the defendant was McGee's girlfriend, that she had traveled with him in the rental car, and that the purse belonged to a woman. The officers did not have a reasonable belief that McGee shared the use of and had joint access to or control over her purse.

Evidence of Refusal to Consent Is Inadmissible [new section]

State v. Jennings
333 N.C. 579, 430 S.E.2d 188, *cert. denied*, 510 U.S. 1028 (1993)

The court ruled that evidence of the defendant's refusal to give consent to search is not admissible at trial.

Search and Seizure of Evidence with Probable Cause, Reasonable Suspicion, or Other Justification

Vehicles, Including Containers within Vehicles

Generally [page 321]

Pennsylvania v. Labron
518 U.S. ___, 116 S. Ct. 2485, 135 L. Ed. 2d 1031 (1996)
The court, per curiam, reaffirmed its prior rulings [*see, e.g.*, California v. Carney, 471 U.S. 386, 105 S. Ct. 2066, 85 L. Ed. 2d 406 (1985)] that an officer who has probable cause to search a readily mobile vehicle for contraband may conduct a search of the vehicle without a search warrant. A showing of exigent circumstances to conduct such a warrantless vehicle search is unnecessary.

United States v. Gastiaburo
16 F.3d 582 (4th Cir.), *cert. denied*, 115 U.S. 102 (1994)
An officer's warrantless search of a hidden compartment of a car that occurred thirty-eight days after the car had been seized and impounded was reasonable under the Fourth Amendment. The officer conducted the warrantless search on the day he learned that the hidden compartment contained drugs, money, and a handgun. *See also* United States v. Spires, 3 F.3d 1234 (9th Cir. 1993) (warrantless search of truck seven days after it was impounded as a forfeited asset was proper).

United States v. Hatley
15 F.3d 856 (9th Cir. 1994)
The court ruled that the automobile exception to the search warrant requirement applied to a car that appeared to the officer to be mobile, even though it was not actually mobile. An officer is not required to determine the actual functional capacity of a car to satisfy the automobile exception.

Probable Cause to Search a Vehicle [page 324]

State v. Corpening
109 N.C. App. 586, 427 S.E.2d 892 (1993)
A deputy sheriff responded to a report that the defendant's van had caught fire and was off the highway in the lot of an old store. The fire had been extinguished and a wrecker had been called before the deputy arrived. The deputy, who had been an officer for thirteen years and had smelled "white liquor" many times, detected the odor of that substance coming from the van. The court ruled: (1) the deputy's detection of the odor was sufficient to establish probable cause to search the van (in addition, the defendant had acted very nervous and had placed cardboard over a burned-out window) and (2) the warrantless search of the van was proper, based on State v. Isleib, 319 N.C. 634, 356 S.E.2d 573 (1987).

State v. Holmes
109 N.C. App. 615, 428 S.E.2d 277, *review denied*, 334 N.C. 166, 432 S.E.2d 367 (1993)
The court ruled that reasonable suspicion existed to stop a vehicle based on following facts: A trained drug officer saw the defendant driving slowly into a neighborhood known for violence and illegal drugs. The defendant then engaged two different groups of people in conversation from a car and went inside a house personally known to the officer, as he had made drug arrests there. The defendant then returned to the car after a few minutes and lit a cigarette, which he shared with two passengers until the cigarette was gone and the car was filled with smoke. Based on his training, the officer believed the cigarette was a marijuana cigarette. The defendant then placed a plastic bag in the trunk of the car and returned to the house alone for about thirty seconds. When the defendant returned to the car, he carefully concealed an object underneath the driver's seat. After the officer stopped the car, he opened a passenger door to question a passenger and saw two needles and syringes in a small compartment on the car door. The officer then arrested the passenger for possession of drug paraphernalia. The court ruled that the officer then had probable cause to search the rest of the car for more contraband, including the area underneath the driver's seat, based on United States v. Ross, 456 U.S. 798, 102 S. Ct. 2157, 72 L. Ed. 2d 572 (1982), and State v. Martin, 97 N.C. App. 19, 387 S.E.2d 211 (1990).

United States v. Padro
52 F.3d 120 (6th Cir. 1995)
The court ruled that an anonymous informant's detailed information (including license plate number) about a specific vehicle bringing cocaine to a particular city was sufficient evidence to establish probable cause to search the vehicle, when an officer extensively corroborated the information.

Containers (Other Than in Vehicles)

Probable Cause [page 326]

State v. Wise
117 N.C. 105, 449 S.E.2d 774 (1994)
[Note: Although there was a dissenting opinion, the state did not seek further review.] A State Highway Patrol trooper stopped a vehicle for speeding. He saw the defendant, a passenger, grab his midsection between his stomach

and his belt line with both hands. The trooper patted down the defendant, reaching from the driver's side of the car, and felt a "round cylinder object" in the area where the defendant had grabbed, but he determined that it was not a weapon. The trooper asked the defendant what he had grabbed, which prompted the defendant to reach inside his jacket and hand the trooper a white, nontransparent Bayer aspirin bottle. The trooper shook the bottle and it "rattled lightly," sounding as if it had "BBs in it." He was suspicious because such a bottle normally has cotton in it, so the rattle would not sound the same. The trooper then opened the bottle, shone his flashlight in it, looked inside, and saw what he determined was rock cocaine. The court ruled that the officer unconstitutionally opened the bottle: (1) there was no evidence that the defendant consented to a search of the bottle and (2) there was not probable cause to believe, based on these facts, that the bottle contained illegal drugs.

Reasonable Suspicion [page 327]

State v. Odum
343 N.C. 116, 468 S.E.2d 245 (1996)

The court, per curiam and without an opinion, reversed the decision of the court of appeals, 119 N.C. App. 676, 459 S.E.2d 826 (1995), that affirmed the defendant's conviction. The court stated that the decision was reversed for the reasons stated in the dissenting opinion in the court of appeals.

Officers were working drug interdiction at the Raleigh train station. They had received information from a ticket agent that the defendant had purchased a train ticket with cash using small bills, had left Raleigh for New York City on April 27, and was to return on the afternoon of April 29. The officers also learned that the defendant had previously been arrested for attempted robbery in New Jersey, although the charge had been dismissed. When the train arrived in Raleigh on April 29, the defendant left the train carrying a red nylon gym bag and appeared headed toward a parked car in which a female was sitting. The officers approached the defendant, showed him their badges, and asked him to answer a few questions. The defendant agreed to talk to them, and they moved over to the sidewalk. When asked to produce his train ticket, the defendant showed them his ticket stub bearing the name, "D. Odum" (his name was David Odum). The defendant became visibly nervous when he could not find his identification after officers asked for it. When the defendant looked into his gym bag for identification, one of the officers saw that the defendant was apparently trying to conceal the contents of the bag. The defendant finally told the officers that he could not find any identification. Although the defendant objected, the

officers then seized his gym bag (to await a drug detection dog to sniff it). They told him he was free to leave and if he left an address they would have the bag delivered to him. During this conversation, the defendant informed the officers that the woman sitting in the car was his ride. One officer testified at the suppression hearing that the woman neither spoke nor made eye contact with the defendant during the entire questioning.

The dissenting opinion of the court of appeals concluded that reasonable suspicion did not exist to support the seizure of the gym bag. The evidence as a whole could easily be associated with many travelers. Many travelers daily embark on trips similar to the defendant's, and the fact that the defendant paid for his ticket in cash was not remarkable, considering the price was $107. The opinion noted that one officer testified that there was no evidence that the defendant had any prior involvement with drugs, and the prior robbery charge that was later dismissed was not a sufficient reflection of a person's propensity to be involved in drug trafficking. The court also noted that one of the officers testified that the defendant did not give him any false information during the interaction at the train station. The officers never inquired about the nature of the defendant's trip, nor was there evidence of any questions that might have bolstered their suspicions. Although the defendant became visibly nervous when he could not find his identification, the opinion noted that it is not uncommon for a person to appear nervous when approached by a law enforcement officer. Also, the actions of the woman in the car and the defendant's reluctance to let the officers see what was in his bag did not provide reasonable suspicion.

Probable Cause to Search a Person [new section]

State v. Smith
342 N.C. 407, 464 S.E.2d 45 (1995), *cert. denied*, 116 S. Ct. 1676 (1996)

The court, per curiam and without an opinion, reversed the decision of the court of appeals, 118 N.C. App. 106, 454 S.E.2d 680 (1995), that awarded the defendant a new trial. The court stated that the decision was reversed for the reasons stated in the dissenting opinion in the court of appeals. The dissenting opinion concurred (without additional comment) with the majority opinion on issue (1), discussed below, and disagreed with the majority opinion on issue (2), which is set out below as discussed in the dissenting opinion (with some facts excerpted from the majority opinion). (1) An officer knew the defendant for two to three years and had information that he was operating a drug house and selling drugs in a certain area of Fayetteville. The officer received a phone call at 12:15

A.M. on May 12, 1992, from a reliable informant, who told the officer that the defendant would be driving a red Ford Escort with a specific license plate and would be going to an unknown location to purchase cocaine. The defendant then would go to a particular apartment on Johnson Street, where he was to package the cocaine, and then would go to a house on Buffalo Street, where he would sell the cocaine. The informant said that the defendant would have the cocaine concealed in or under his crotch when he left the Johnson Street apartment. The officer and other officers took the informant to Johnson Street, where the informant pointed out the apartment and Ford Escort. At approximately 1:15 A.M. on May 12, 1992, the defendant left the apartment in the Ford Escort. The officers stopped the defendant's car in the middle of Johnson Street where it intersected with Bragg Boulevard. All three judges on the court of appeals hearing this case ruled, based on these facts, that the officers had probable cause to make a warrantless search of the defendant, including his crotch area. (2) After stopping the defendant's vehicle, the officer informed the defendant that he was going to search him completely by using his flashlight and hands. He asked the defendant to step behind the door of the defendant's vehicle, which was open, and the officer stood between him and the car door on the outside. After the defendant opened his trousers, the officer could not see underneath the defendant's scrotum and testicles and therefore asked the defendant to pull down his underwear. Because the defendant resisted, the officer slid the defendant's underwear down and pointed his flashlight there. He saw the corner of a small paper towel underneath the defendant's scrotum. He pulled the underwear further. The defendant resisted. The officer pushed the defendant into the door, reached underneath the defendant's scrotum, and removed the paper towel that contained cocaine. The dissenting opinion in the court of appeals, adopted by the supreme court, noted that this search was conducted in the intersection of two streets in Fayetteville at 1:30 A.M. The state's evidence showed that before the search the officer asked the defendant to step behind the open door of his vehicle and that the officer positioned himself between the defendant and the car door on the outside. The officer testified that he took these steps because he did not want to embarrass the defendant in public. The defendant did not dispute the officer's testimony. The opinion stated that the officer took reasonable precautions to prevent the public exposure of the defendant's private areas and "[w]hile there may have been other less intrusive means of conducting the search . . . the availability of those less intrusive means does not automatically transform an otherwise reasonable search into a Fourth Amendment violation." The opinion

concluded that the search did not violate the Fourth Amendment.

State v. Pittman
111 N.C. App. 808, 433 S.E.2d 822 (1993)

Two officers were on patrol at a train station at 1:30 A.M. They saw the female defendant and a man speaking, and the pair parted company when they saw the officers. Officer Gunn approached the defendant and Officer Ferrell approached the man. The defendant showed Gunn a train ticket and stated she was traveling alone and did not know the man with whom she had been seen. Gunn noticed that the defendant was constantly looking over at the man, who was twenty feet away. The defendant consented to a search of her bag; nothing was found. Meanwhile, Ferrell spoke with the man, who said he was traveling alone and did not know the defendant. The man consented to a search of his bag; nothing was found. Later a vehicle pulled up to the train station, and the man put his bag in the trunk. The man then motioned to the defendant to approach the car, he placed her bag in the trunk, and the two of them got in the car and left. The officers compared information they had learned from their encounters with the man and the defendant and had the car stopped by a uniformed officer. The defendant was taken to the police station and searched. (1) The court ruled that Officer Gunn did not seize the defendant at the train station. He merely approached her and asked a few questions, and she voluntarily gave him her train ticket and consented to a search of her bag. The court relied on Florida v. Bostick, 501 U.S. 429, 111 S. Ct. 2382, 115 L. Ed. 2d 389 (1991). (2) The court ruled that the officers had reasonable suspicion to stop the vehicle in which the defendant was a passenger, based on the facts discussed above. (3) The court ruled that the officers did not have probable cause to search the defendant after the vehicle stop, based on the facts discussed above.

Warrantless Entry with Exigent Circumstances to Search a Place for Evidence or Weapons [page 327]

State v. Wallace
111 N.C. App. 581, 433 S.E.2d 238, *review denied*, 335 N.C. 242, 439 S.E.2d 161 (1993)

Officers received information that marijuana was being grown in the basement of a residence. However, the officers were unable to corroborate the informant's information. Therefore they went to the residence to confirm or refute the information. After the officers knocked on the door, Jolly came out and closed the door behind him. The officers told him why they were there and asked him if there were others in the residence. Jolly told the officers that one of his roommates was asleep inside. The officers then asked for consent to search the residence. Before Jolly could answer, Wallace came out of the residence. The officers then asked for consent to search, which Wallace and Jolly denied. According to the court's opinion, "Jolly then stated that '*there might be some drug paraphernalia and marijuana seeds in the house,*' and that he would not consent to a search until he had time to get rid of the contraband." After the officers were denied consent to search, they heard footsteps in the residence and a door shut on the inside. The officers asked Wallace and Jolly who was in the residence, and they said they did not know because they had just arrived. The officers then went inside to execute a protective sweep before leaving the residence to obtain a search warrant. The officers saw what appeared to be marijuana plants while inside. The defendants were detained in the residence while other officers obtained a search warrant, which included information about their observation of marijuana in the house.

The court ruled: (1) Uncorroborated information initially given to the officers was insufficient to establish probable cause to search the residence. (2) The officers did not violate the defendants' rights by going to the residence to investigate the information they had received. (3) Probable cause existed to search the residence when Jolly made the statement noted in italics in the paragraph above. (4) The officers did not have exigent circumstances to enter the residence without a search warrant. The court stated that the "record is devoid of any evidence that the officers entered the residence with a reasonably objective belief that evidence was about to be removed or destroyed." The court noted that the only purpose of the officers' entry into the residence was to conduct a protective sweep until a search warrant could be obtained, and the officers did not believe they were in danger at any time. (5) The state could not justify the search of the residence under the independent-source exception to the exclusionary rule, Murray v. United States, 487 U.S. 533, 108 S. Ct. 2529, 101 L. Ed. 2d 472 (1988), and Segura v. United States, 468 U.S. 796, 104 S. Ct. 3380, 82 L. Ed. 2d 599 (1984). In this case, the search warrant was prompted by what the officers saw in their unlawful entry, and the information obtained during the illegal entry was presented to the magistrate and affected the decision to issue the search warrant.

United States v. Scroger
98 F.3d 1256 (10th Cir. 1996)

Four plain-clothed officers arrived at a house to conduct a "knock and talk" in response to reports of drug activity. As the officers approached the house, they heard noises coming from inside that sounded like someone was running through the house and heard someone say, "Go out the back." The person (the defendant) who responded to an officer's knock on the front door was holding a hot plate in his hands, his fingertips were stained with a rust-colored residue that the officers knew was associated with methamphetamine manufacturing, and the officers saw inside the house glassware commonly used in the manufacturing of this illegal drug. There also was a strong odor of methamphetamine production coming from the house and from the defendant himself. The officers identified themselves and informed the defendant that they were investigating allegations that someone was manufacturing methamphetamine inside the house. The defendant then attempted to push an officer out of the doorway and shut the door. The officers then entered the house, conducted a protective sweep, and obtained a search warrant to search the house. The court ruled that exigent circumstances supported the officers' warrantless entry into the house. The court noted that the trial judge had found that the officers had not manipulated or abused their authority because the drug information they had before approaching the house was insufficient to obtain a search warrant to search the house.

United States v. Tovar-Rico
61 F.3d 1529 (11th Cir. 1995)

Officers did not have exigent circumstances to enter an apartment to seize illegal drugs when evidence of the only reason supporting exigent circumstances—that the suspects were aware of the officers' presence and might destroy the drugs—was not supported by the evidence presented at the suppression hearing.

Reasonableness of a Strip Search of a Person
[new section]

State v. Smith
342 N.C. 407, 464 S.E.2d 45 (1995), *cert. denied*, 116 S. Ct. 1676 (1996)

The court, per curiam and without an opinion, reversed the decision of the court of appeals, 118 N.C. App. 106, 454 S.E.2d 680 (1995), that awarded the defendant a new trial. The court stated that the decision was reversed for the reasons stated in the dissenting opinion in the court of appeals. The dissenting opinion concurred (without additional comment) with the majority opinion on issue (1), discussed below, and disagreed with the majority opinion on issue (2), which is set out below as discussed in the dissenting opinion (with some facts excerpted from the majority opinion). (1) An officer knew the defendant for two to three years and had information that he was operating a drug house and selling drugs in a certain area of

Fayetteville. The officer received a phone call at 12:15 A.M. on May 12, 1992, from a reliable informant, who told the officer that the defendant would be driving a red Ford Escort with a specific license plate and would be going to an unknown location to purchase cocaine. The defendant then would go to a particular apartment on Johnson Street, where he was to package the cocaine, and then would go to a house on Buffalo Street, where he would sell the cocaine. The informant said that the defendant would have the cocaine concealed in or under his crotch when he left the Johnson Street apartment. The officer and other officers took the informant to Johnson Street, where the informant pointed out the apartment and Ford Escort.

At approximately 1:15 A.M. on May 12, 1992, the defendant left the apartment in the Ford Escort. The officers stopped the defendant's car in the middle of Johnson Street where it intersected with Bragg Boulevard. All three judges on the court of appeals hearing this case ruled, based on these facts, that the officers had probable cause to make a warrantless search of the defendant, including his crotch area. (2) After stopping the defendant's vehicle, the officer informed the defendant that he was going to search him completely by using his flashlight and hands. He asked the defendant to step behind the door of the defendant's vehicle, which was open, and the officer stood between him and the car door on the outside. After the defendant opened his trousers, the officer could not see underneath the defendant's scrotum and testicles and therefore asked the defendant to pull down his underwear. Because the defendant resisted, the officer slid the defendant's underwear down and pointed his flashlight there. He saw the corner of a small paper towel underneath the defendant's scrotum. He pulled the underwear further. The defendant resisted. The officer pushed the defendant into the door, reached underneath the defendant's scrotum, and removed the paper towel that contained cocaine.

The dissenting opinion in the court of appeals, adopted by the supreme court, noted that this search was conducted in the intersection of two streets in Fayetteville at 1:30 A.M. The state's evidence showed that before the search the officer asked the defendant to step behind the open door of his vehicle and that the officer positioned himself between the defendant and the door on the outside. The officer testified that he took these steps because he did not want to embarrass the defendant in public. The defendant did not dispute the officer's testimony. The opinion stated that the officer took reasonable precautions to prevent the public exposure of the defendant's private areas and "[w]hile there may have been other less intrusive means of conducting the search . . . the availability of

those less intrusive means does not automatically transform an otherwise reasonable search into a Fourth Amendment violation." The opinion concluded that the search did not violate the Fourth Amendment.

Search and Seizure of Evidence from a Person's Body [page 329]

Vernonia School District 47J v. Acton
515 U.S. 646, 115 S. Ct. 2386, 132 L. Ed. 2d 564 (1995)
The court ruled that random urinalysis testing of public school students participating in interscholastic athletics was reasonable under the Fourth Amendment, based on the facts in this case, even though the testing was not based on reasonable suspicion.

State v. Watson
119 N.C. App. 395, 458 S.E.2d 519 (1995)
Three officers approached a convenience store at night. Officer A had made fifty or more arrests for possessing cocaine in this area. Officer A knew the defendant had previously been arrested for drug charges. The defendant, on seeing the officers, put items in his mouth and started to go back into the store. Officer A grabbed the defendant's jacket, and the defendant then attempted to drink a soft drink. The officer took the drink away, ordered the defendant to spit the objects out of his mouth, and applied pressure to the defendant's throat so he would spit out the items. The defendant spit out three baggies containing crack cocaine. Based on this and other evidence (for example, officers testified at the suppression hearing that drug dealers will attempt to conceal or to swallow drugs when they see officers), the court ruled that the officers had reasonable suspicion to stop the defendant; the court cited State v. Butler, 331 N.C. 227, 415 S.E.2d 719 (1992). The court also ruled that exigent circumstances supported the reasonableness of the officer's actions in applying pressure to the defendant's throat so he would not swallow the drugs he had placed in his mouth (the court considered the officers' training and experience and their familiarity with the area, the defendant, and the practice of drug dealers to hide drugs in their mouth to elude detection).

Probation or Parole Officer's Search of Home [page 331]

State v. Church
110 N.C. App. 569, 430 S.E.2d 462 (1993)
Based on a first-time informant's information that marijuana was being grown near a white frame house located

behind an oil company, officers went there to investigate. They saw a white frame house and a second house with wood siding, which was about 150 feet west of the white frame house. The officers walked to the front porch of the white house, knocked on the door, and received no answer. From the front porch, they saw two marijuana plants growing along a fence that went from the white house to another residence east of the white house and a third marijuana plant growing directly behind the second house. After seeing these marijuana plants, the officers walked to the second house to determine who lived in the houses. One officer knocked on the front and side doors and then saw the defendant walk from the garage that was next to the second house. The defendant informed the officers that he owned both houses but lived in the second house. The officers asked the defendant if they could search the houses and garage, but he refused. After arresting the defendant, the officers asked him for a garage door key, which he produced. An officer inserted the key in the lock, found that it fit, and withdrew the key without opening the door.

The officers learned that the defendant was on probation, contacted his probation officer, and were informed by her that as a condition of probation, the defendant was obligated to submit to warrantless searches by his probation officer. An officer informed the probation officer of the discovery of marijuana and asked her if she would be interested in conducting a warrantless search under the probation condition. She told the officer that she would be willing to conduct a warrantless search if she saw marijuana growing outside the defendant's house and determined that the plants more than likely belonged to him. She went to the house, saw the plants, determined that the plants probably belonged to the defendant, and authorized a warrantless search of the defendant's premises. She and nine law enforcement officers conducted the search.

The court ruled that the officers' entry onto the defendant's property (that is, walking to the front and side doors to look for the resident) was permissible, based on State v. Prevette, 43 N.C. App. 450 (1979), *review denied*, 299 N.C. 124, 261 S.E.2d 925, *cert. denied*, 447 U.S. 906 (1980). The court also noted that the *inadvertence* component of the plain-view doctrine was deleted in Horton v. California, 496 U.S. 128, 110 S. Ct. 2301, 110 L. Ed. 2d 112 (1990), and ruled that the plain-view doctrine was satisfied in this case. (Note, however, that the plain-view doctrine must be satisfied only when there is a seizure of property, not when only a search takes place. See page 112 of the second edition at note 31. The officers' initial observation of the marijuana, before any seizure took place, did not need to satisfy the plain-view doctrine.) The

court also ruled that the insertion of the key in the lock was not an unlawful search. [Other courts have disagreed about whether inserting a key in a lock is a search. *Compare* United States v. Lyon, 898 F.2d 210 (1st Cir.), *cert. denied*, 498 U.S. 920 (1990) (inserting key is not a search), *with* United States v. Concepcion, 942 F.2d 1170 (7th Cir. 1991) (inserting key is a search, but only reasonable suspicion is required to do so).]

Wiretapping and Eavesdropping [page 331]

United States v. Ortiz
84 F.3d 977 (7th Cir.), *cert. denied*, 117 S. Ct. 250 (1996)

Officers seized an electronic pager incident to the defendant's arrest. They pushed a button on the pager that revealed the numeric messages previously transmitted to the pager. The court ruled, relying on United States v. Meriwether, 917 F.2d 955 (6th Cir. 1990), that the officers' actions were proper as a search incident to arrest.

Brown v. Waddell
50 F.3d 285 (4th Cir. 1995)

Officers used pager clones to receive and record numeric messages being simultaneously received by a person's digital display pager. The court rejected the officers' argument that their use of pager clones was effectively a pen register and that therefore they did not need an appropriate court order under Title III of the Omnibus Crime Control and Safe Roads Act of 1968 and the Electronic Communications Privacy Act of 1986 (ECPA). The court ruled that using pager clones without an appropriate court order was an unauthorized interception of an electronic communication under the ECPA.

Adams v. Sumner
39 F.3d 933 (9th Cir. 1994)

The court ruled that a hotel telephone operator did not violate federal wiretapping law by staying on the line after inadvertently hearing the occupant of the hotel refer to guns; the operator was concerned that there might be a danger to people in the hotel.

Steve Jackson Games, Inc. v. U.S. Secret Service
36 F.3d 457 (5th Cir. 1994)

The court ruled that officers' seizure of a computer used to operate an electronic bulletin board system and containing private electronic mail that had been sent to the bulletin board, but had not been read by the intended recipients, was not an unlawful interception under federal wiretapping and electronic communications privacy laws, because the acquisition of the communications was not contemporaneous with their transmission. [Note, however, that the officers in this case violated 18 U.S.C.A. § 2701 (West Supp. 1997) by accessing stored electronic communications without proper authorization.]

United States v. Clark
22 F.3d 799 (8th Cir. 1994)

Before an officer left his patrol car to conduct a search, he surreptitiously activated a tape recorder while two suspects sat in the patrol car's backseat. Their conversations were recorded, and the officer played them back and heard incriminating remarks by one of the suspects. The court ruled that the suspects did not have a reasonable expectation of privacy in the backseat of the patrol car, and the recording of their conversations did not violate the Fourth Amendment or federal wiretapping law. *See also* United States v. McKinnon, 985 F.2d 525 (11th Cir.), *cert. denied*, 510 U.S. 843 (1993) (similar ruling).

Angel v. Williams
12 F.3d 786 (8th Cir. 1993)

The tape-recording of conversations between law enforcement officers and a prisoner in a jail did not violate federal wiretapping law because the officers and the prisoner did not have a reasonable expectation of privacy that their conversations would not be intercepted.

Protective Searches

Scope of Search Incident to Arrest

Generally [page 332]

State v. Brooks
337 N.C. 132, 446 S.E.2d 579 (1994)

The court upheld a search of a nylon pouch as a proper search incident to the arrest of the defendant for carrying a concealed weapon. The agent had probable cause to arrest the defendant, and the search may be made before the actual arrest and still be justified as a search incident to arrest when, as here, the agent made the search contemporaneously with the arrest; *see* Rawlings v. Kentucky, 448 U.S. 98, 100 S. Ct. 2556, 65 L. Ed. 2d 633 (1980).

State v. Taylor
117 N.C. App. 644, 453 S.E.2d 225 (1995)

Officer A knew that the defendant had been previously arrested for drugs and had a reputation in the community as a drug dealer. Officer A and other officers saw the defendant with others in an area known for drug trafficking. As the officers approached the area in their marked car,

the defendant left. The officers saw him at a nearby intersection. The defendant stopped as the police car approached him. As Officer A got out of the car, the defendant walked toward him and dropped something on the ground. The officer approached the defendant and brought him over to the police car. He determined that the dropped item was marijuana and arrested the defendant. He then noticed that the defendant was talking "funny" and ordered him to spit out whatever was in his mouth. The defendant spit out individually wrapped pieces of crack cocaine. The court ruled: (1) the defendant was not seized until after he dropped the item to the ground, because he had not yielded to a show of authority before then; *see* California v. Hodari D., 499 U.S. 621, 111 S. Ct. 1547, 113 L. Ed. 2d 690 (1991); (2) after the defendant dropped the item, Officer A had reasonable suspicion to detain the defendant, considering everything the officer knew; (3) Officer A had probable cause to arrest the defendant when he determined the item was marijuana; and (4) even if the defendant did not voluntarily spit out the cocaine, the cocaine was admissible as the result of a search incident to arrest.

State v. Clyburn
120 N.C. App. 377, 462 S.E.2d 538 (1995)

Officers were conducting surveillance at night at a place that had a reputation for drug activity and where they had previously made drug arrests. The officers saw three males in front of a vacant duplex. Individuals would approach one of the males, who would disappear behind the duplex with each individual. The other two males remained in front of the duplex as if acting as lookouts. Each time the defendant reappeared, the other two males conferred with him. Based on their training and experience with similar activity, the officers believed that drug transactions were being conducted. After one such activity, one of the males and a female got into a car and drove away. Other officers stopped the car and frisked the male (the defendant) and female. An officer searched the passenger area of the car and found a .357 Magnum in the glove compartment. The male was arrested for carrying a concealed weapon. Following the arrest, the car was searched and crack cocaine was found in an ashtray. The court ruled: (1) the officers had reasonable suspicion to stop the car to investigate drug activity; (2) the search of the car for weapons was proper under Michigan v. Long, 463 U.S. 1032, 103 S. Ct. 3469, 77 L. Ed. 2d 1201 (1983); after the defendant had been frisked, he had become belligerent and the officers could reasonably believe that the defendant was potentially dangerous and possibly armed because of his involvement in drug trafficking; the court also cited State v. Butler, 331 N.C. 227, 415 S.E.2d 719

(1992); and (3) the search of the ashtray was permissible as a search incident to the arrest of a vehicle occupant under New York v. Belton, 453 U.S. 454, 101 S. Ct. 2860, 69 L. Ed. 2d 768 (1981).

United States v. Ortiz
84 F.3d 977 (7th Cir.), *cert. denied*, 117 S. Ct. 250 (1996)
Officers seized an electronic pager incident to the defendant's arrest. They pushed a button on the pager that revealed the numeric messages previously transmitted to the pager. The court ruled, relying on United States v. Meriwether, 917 F.2d 955 (6th Cir. 1990), that the officers' actions were proper as a search incident to arrest.

United States v. Han
74 F.3d 537 (4th Cir.), *cert. denied*, 116 S. Ct. 1890 (1996)
A travel bag was next to the feet of the defendant, who was inside a residence. An officer moved the bag for safety purposes, and a safety sweep of the residence was conducted. The officer interviewed a witness in the back room and then searched the bag. The court ruled that a search of the bag was properly incident to the defendant's arrest although there was a delay of a few minutes between the search and the arrest. A reasonable delay in conducting a search incident to arrest is permitted so any danger to the officers can be eliminated.

United States v. Hudson
100 F.3d 1409 (9th Cir. 1996)
Officers arrested the defendant in a bedroom and removed him for safety reasons to another part of the house. About three minutes later they returned to that bedroom, found a rifle case that had been located at the defendant's feet when he was arrested, and searched it without a warrant. The court ruled that the search was justified as incident to the defendant's arrest. *See also* United States v. Nelson, 102 F.3d 1344 (4th Cir. 1996) (search of shoulder bag incident to arrest of defendant was constitutional although search occurred a few minutes after defendant had been taken to another room in house).

Arrest of an Occupant of a Vehicle [page 335]

United States v. Snook
88 F.3d 605 (8th Cir. 1996)
The defendant stepped out of his car immediately before an officer arrested him. The court ruled that the car was properly searched incident to the arrest of an occupant of the car under New York v. Belton, 453 U.S. 454, 101 S. Ct. 2860, 69 L. Ed. 2d 768 (1981).

United States v. Willis
37 F.3d 313 (7th Cir. 1994)
For the purpose of a search incident to the arrest of an occupant of a vehicle, the defendant was an "occupant" of a car when an officer saw the defendant sitting inside the car and then squatting at the rear of the car. The officer then approached the defendant and arrested him in an area immediately next to the car for possession of a gun. The officer's search of the car was contemporaneous with the defendant's arrest when the officer began the search after he had secured the defendant and well before the defendant had been transported to the police station.

Protective Sweep of Premises [page 336]

United States v. Ford
56 F.3d 265 (D.C. Cir. 1995)
An officer conducting a protective sweep of the premises could not lift a mattress or look behind a window shade when the officer knew that a person could not be found there.

United States v. Henry
48 F.3d 1282 (D.C. Cir. 1995)
The mere fact that an arrest occurs outside a residence does not bar officers from conducting a protective sweep of the residence under Maryland v. Buie, 494 U.S. 325, 110 S. Ct. 1093, 108 L. Ed. 2d 276 (1990), if there is a reasonable belief that a sweep is necessary to protect the safety of the arresting officers.

Frisk [page 336]

State v. Beveridge
336 N.C. 601, 444 S.E.2d 223 (1994)
The court, per curiam and without an opinion, affirmed the court of appeals opinion, 112 N.C. App. 688, 436 S.E.2d 912 (1993), that is discussed below.

While Officer Johnson was arresting a driver for impaired driving, Officer Gregory (while securing the car) asked the defendant, a passenger, to get out. Officer Gregory noticed a strong odor of alcohol about the defendant, who also was acting "giddy." The officer believed, based on the facts in this case, that the defendant was under the influence of alcohol and a controlled substance. He told the defendant he was going to pat him down for weapons. During the patdown, the officer noticed that there was a cylindrical-shaped rolled-up plastic bag in the defendant's front pocket. The officer asked him what it was, and the defendant started laughing and pulled out some money. However, the officer could still see the long cylindrical bulge he had in his pocket. He asked the defendant what it was. The defendant then stuck his hand in his pocket and tried to palm what he had. The officer asked him what he was trying to hide, and the defendant rolled open his hand and showed the officer a white plastic bag with a white powdery substance in it. The officer believed that the substance was cocaine and then arrested him for possession of cocaine. The court ruled that Officer Gregory was justified in conducting a limited patdown of the defendant to determine whether the defendant was armed, but once he concluded that there was no weapon, he could not continue to search "or question" the defendant to determine whether the bag contained illegal drugs. (The court's specific ruling that the officer could not continue to question the defendant does not appear consistent with prevailing federal constitutional law.) The court ruled that the search exceeded the scope of the frisk under Minnesota v. Dickerson, 508 U.S. 366, 113 S. Ct. 2130, 124 L. Ed. 2d 334 (1993), because it was not immediately apparent that the item in the defendant's pocket was an illegal substance.

State v. McGirt
345 N.C. 624, 481 S.E.2d 288 (1997)

The court, per curiam and without an opinion, affirmed the majority opinion of the court of appeals at 122 N.C. App. 237, 468 S.E.2d 833 (1996). An officer stopped a vehicle because the defendant, the driver, was not wearing his seat belt. The officer testified at the suppression hearing that he had been looking for the defendant's vehicle the prior night and was investigating the defendant for cocaine trafficking. The officer knew the defendant had prior felony drug convictions and in his experience knew that cocaine traffickers normally carry weapons. After stopping the vehicle, the defendant complied with the officer's request to exit the vehicle. The officer asked the defendant if he had anything on him. The defendant said, "No," and raised his hands. The officer then frisked the defendant and felt a hard object, which the officer believed was a gun. The officer asked the defendant to identify the object, to which the defendant replied that it was a pistol and handed it to the officer. The majority opinion ruled that the officer, based on this evidence, had reasonable suspicion to frisk the defendant. The majority opinion noted: (1) the defendant was a convicted felon and this was known to the arresting officer; (2) the defendant was under investigation by the officer for cocaine trafficking; and (3) it was the officer's experience that cocaine traffickers normally carry weapons. The majority opinion stated that the totality of circumstances, even in the face of a cooperative defendant who presents no obvious signs of carrying a weapon, supports the legality of the frisk for weapons.

State v. Willis
125 N.C. App. 537, 481 S.E.2d 407 (1997)

Officers were conducting surveillance of a residence while a search warrant was being sought to search it for drugs. The defendant, whom the officers did not recognize, left the residence on foot. Concerned that he might be involved in drug activity occurring in the residence, they decided to follow him. When the defendant realized that he was being followed, he took evasive action by cutting through a parking lot. A detective then asked a uniformed officer to stop the defendant and ask him for identification. That officer approached the defendant on foot, told him he was conducting an investigative stop, and asked the defendant for identification and for consent to a patdown for drugs and weapons. The defendant consented to the patdown. The officer began to pat down the exterior and then interior of the defendant's leather jacket. Just as the officer began to check the jacket's interior pocket, the defendant lunged his hand into the jacket. The officer, believing that the defendant might be reaching for a weapon and fearing for his safety, immediately locked his hands around the defendant's jacket, effectively locking the defendant's hand inside the pocket. Another officer arrived and assisted the officer. When the two officers managed to get the defendant's hand out of his pocket, they put the defendant's hands behind him, and reached into the defendant's interior jacket pocket and emptied it, revealing several baggies of crack cocaine. (1) Relying on State v. Butler, 331 N.C. 227, 415 S.E.2d 719 (1992), the court ruled that the officer's investigative stop was supported by reasonable suspicion. The court noted that the defendant left a suspected drug house just before the search warrant was to be executed. He took evasive action when he knew that he was being followed, and he exhibited nervous behavior. (2) The court also ruled that the frisk and resulting search of the defendant's jacket pocket was proper. The court noted that the officers reasonably feared for their personal safety based on (i) their knowledge that people involved with drugs often carry weapons; (ii) the defendant's exit from the suspected drug house; (iii) the defendant's later furtive, evasive behavior; and (iv) the defendant's sudden lunge of his hand into the interior of his jacket.

State v. Hamilton
125 N.C. App. 396, 481 S.E.2d 98 (1997)

An officer involved in drug surveillance stopped a vehicle because the driver and front-seat passenger were not wearing seat belts as required by law. As the officer approached the front passenger side of the vehicle and informed the defendant (the front seat passenger) that he was a police officer, the defendant's right hand began to reach toward his left side. The officer believed that the defendant was reaching for a weapon. The officer then asked the defendant to step outside the vehicle and told him that he was going to frisk him. The court ruled that, based on this evidence, the officer was justified in conducting the frisk.

State v. Artis
123 N.C. App. 114, 472 S.E.2d 169, *review denied*, 344 N.C. 633, 477 S.E.2d 45 (1996)

An officer was part of a drug interdiction task force at an airport. He saw the defendant operating a video game machine in the airport game room, a location that had a reputation for drug activity. The game room was located so that a person could reach it without first having to go through the airport's metal detectors. The officer approached the defendant, identified himself, and learned that the defendant intended to take a departing flight. The officer saw a large crescent-shaped bulge in the defendant's left front pocket that appeared to be either brass knuckles or a weapon's handgrip. When the officer asked the defendant several times if he was carrying any weapons or drugs, the defendant responded each time by asking, "Why would I carry weapons or drugs?" The officer then told the defendant that he thought the defendant was carrying a weapon in his left front pocket. He informed the defendant that he wanted to pat the area down to satisfy himself that the object was not a weapon. As he made this statement, the officer reached for the pocket. The defendant, however, turned away from the officer and attempted to take a step backwards. As the defendant stepped back, the officer placed his hand on the object from outside the defendant's pants pocket and controlled it with his hand. The officer thought it was brass knuckles. The defendant attempted to reach into the pocket despite the officer's request not to do so. The officer reached into the pocket to get control of the suspected weapon and removed a clear plastic bag that contained crack cocaine. The court ruled that the officer's frisk violated the Fourth Amendment. The court stated that the officer had only a generalized suspicion to conduct the frisk. It was not reasonable to infer that the bulge in the defendant's pants pocket was a weapon simply because the defendant had not yet passed through the airport's metal detectors. Also, the officer had no apparent need to check that the defendant was armed with a weapon that could be used against him or others. When the officer approached the defendant, the defendant was merely operating a video game machine.

State v. Wilson
112 N.C. App. 777, 437 S.E.2d 387 (1993)

A police department received an anonymous phone call that several people were selling drugs in the breezeway of Building 1304 in the Hunter Oaks Apartments. The caller did not provide any names or descriptions of the alleged drug dealers. Two officers familiar with the area knew that if a police car entered the parking lot at one end of the breezeway, the suspects would run out of the other end. They devised a plan in which a police car would enter the parking lot and officers would position themselves so they could stop anyone who ran out of the back of the breezeway. An officer stopped the defendant as he ran out of the back of the breezeway. During the subsequent frisk, the officer felt a lump in the left breast pocket of the defendant's jacket and immediately believed that it was crack cocaine. The officer then asked the defendant if his coat had an inside pocket. The defendant did not respond verbally but instead opened his jacket so the inside pocket was visible. The officer saw and removed a small plastic bag that contained crack cocaine. (1) Distinguishing State v. Fleming, 106 N.C. App. 165, 415 S.E.2d 782 (1992), the court ruled that the officer had authority to stop and frisk the defendant, based on the anonymous phone call, the flight of the defendant and others when the police car pulled into the parking lot, and the officer's experience that weapons were frequently involved in drug transactions. (2) Distinguishing Minnesota v. Dickerson, 508 U.S. 366, 113 S. Ct. 2130, 124 L. Ed. 2d 334 (1993), the court noted that the officer in this case—unlike the officer in *Dickerson*—did not need to manipulate the item in the defendant's pocket to determine that it was cocaine; he immediately believed it was crack cocaine. The court ruled that the requirement in *Dickerson* that it must be "immediately apparent" to the officer that the item is illegal means that the officer must have *probable cause* to believe that the item is illegal. (See the discussion in the second edition on page 112 at note 31.) The court also ruled that the officer's tactile senses, based on his experience and the facts in this case, gave him probable cause to believe that the item was crack cocaine. Thus the officer did not exceed the scope of a frisk under the *Dickerson* ruling.

State v. Sanders
112 N.C. App. 477, 435 S.E.2d 842 (1993)

Two State Highway Patrol officers set up a driver's license check at a ramp off a highway. They did not post signs warning the public that a license check was being conducted. The officers checked every car that approached the checkpoint unless they were busy writing citations. The defendant entered the ramp, and as he approached the checkpoint, he stopped his car 150 feet from one of the troopers. The defendant then drove up to the checkpoint, stopped the car, and rolled down his window. In response to the trooper's request for driver's license and registration, the defendant said that he did not have the registration or any identification and that he was not the owner of the car. The passenger in the car also failed to produce any identification. The trooper asked the defendant to get out of the car. As the defendant stepped out of the car, the trooper saw a bulge about the size of two fists in the right pocket of the defendant's jacket. The trooper then told the defendant to face the car and place his hands on the car so he could pat him down for weapons. As the defendant was doing so, the trooper saw plastic protruding from the right pocket. While frisking the defendant, the trooper touched the bulge and noted that it felt like "hard flour dough." The trooper removed the plastic bag from the defendant's pocket. It contained three smaller bags with cocaine inside. (1) Distinguishing Delaware v. Prouse, 440 U.S. 648, 99 S. Ct. 1391, 59 L. Ed. 2d 660 (1979), the court ruled that the stop of the defendant's vehicle for the license check was constitutional. The court noted that the troopers followed guidelines of their agency in selecting the location and time for the license check and detained every car that passed through (except for those that came through while they were issuing citations). (2) Following State v. Peck, 305 N.C. 734, 291 S.E.2d 637 (1982), the court ruled that the trooper—based on the facts described above, his testimony that people driving stolen cars often provide officers with false names and insist they have no identification, and his seeing the bulge in the defendant's pocket—had reason to believe that the defendant was armed and dangerous and therefore the trooper could frisk him. (3) The court also ruled, based on Minnesota v. Dickerson, 508 U.S. 366, 113 S. Ct. 2130, 124 L. Ed. 2d 334 (1993), that the trooper acted properly in conducting the frisk by feeling the packet in the bulge in the jacket to determine if it was a weapon. (4) The court remanded the case to the trial court to determine, in light of *Dickerson* (decided after this case was heard in the trial court), whether it was immediately apparent to the trooper—when he determined that the bulge was not a weapon, but felt like "hard flour dough"—that what he felt was illegal drugs. ["Immediately apparent" means that there is probable cause to believe the object was illegal to possess. See the discussion in the second edition on page 112 at note 31 and State v. Wilson, 112 N.C. App. 777, 437 S.E.2d 387 (1993).]

In re *Whitley*
122 N.C. App. 290, 468 S.E.2d 610, *review denied*, 344 N.C. 437, 476 S.E.2d 132 (1996)
Two officers responded to a call that drug sales were occurring between two black males on a certain street. The officers saw the respondent and another person under a tree. The officers approached the two men and told them they were going to search them for weapons. During the search of the respondent, an officer noticed that his lower body and legs were really tight, so he asked him to spread his legs. The officer's hands were outside of the respondent's trousers in the bottom crotch area when an item fell from the respondent's buttocks into his pants. (The officer testified at a hearing that based on his personal experience as a law enforcement officer, he had probable cause to believe that the object was some kind of illegal substance.) When the officer felt the item fall on his hand, he held it in one hand and put his other hand into the pants and retrieved it. It was a plastic bag with a white powdered substance, and the officer placed the respondent under arrest. The court ruled: (1) there was reasonable suspicion that the respondent might be armed, dangerous, and involved in criminal activity, so the officer had the authority to frisk him; and (2) the incriminating character of the object seized was immediately apparent to the officer, noting State v. Wilson, 112 N.C. App. 777, 437 S.E.2d 387 (1993), and Minnesota v. Dickerson, 508 U.S. 366, 113 S. Ct. 2130, 124 L. Ed. 2d 334 (1993). The court noted that there was no evidence that the officer improperly manipulated the object to determine if it was an illegal substance.

State v. *Clyburn*
120 N.C. App. 377, 462 S.E.2d 538 (1995)
Officers were conducting surveillance at night at a place that had a reputation for drug activity and where they had previously made drug arrests. The officers saw three males in front of a vacant duplex. Individuals would approach one of the males, who would disappear behind the duplex with each individual. The other two males remained in front of the duplex as if acting as lookouts. Each time the defendant reappeared, the other two males conferred with him. Based on their training and experience with similar activity, the officers believed that drug transactions were being conducted. After one such activity, one of the males and a female got into a car and drove away. Other officers stopped the car and frisked the male (the defendant) and female. An officer searched the passenger area of the car and found a .357 Magnum in the glove compartment. The male was arrested for carrying a concealed weapon. Following the arrest, the car was searched and crack cocaine was found in an ashtray. The

court ruled: (1) the officers had reasonable suspicion to stop the car to investigate drug activity; (2) the search of the car for weapons was proper under Michigan v. Long, 463 U.S. 1032, 103 S. Ct. 3469, 77 L. Ed. 2d 1201 (1983); after the defendant had been frisked, he had become belligerent, and the officers could reasonably believe that the defendant was potentially dangerous and possibly armed because of his involvement in drug trafficking; the court also cited State v. Butler, 331 N.C. 227, 415 S.E.2d 719 (1992); and (3) the search of the ashtray was permissible as a search incident to the arrest of a vehicle occupant under New York v. Belton, 453 U.S. 454, 101 S. Ct. 2860, 69 L. Ed. 2d 768 (1981).

United States v. Menard
95 F.3d 9 (8th Cir. 1996)

An officer stopped a vehicle with a driver and two passengers (Walker and the defendant) at 2:00 A.M. on a relatively deserted highway. After finding a weapon on Walker while frisking him, the officer arrested Walker for carrying a concealed weapon. Walker was also suspected of being a drug trafficker. The officer then frisked the defendant and found a weapon. The court upheld the frisk of the defendant, noting that the arrest of Walker heightened the threat to officer safety because an armed associate of Walker might use force to free him.

United States v. Baker
78 F.3d 135 (4th Cir. 1996)

An officer lawfully stopped a car that was involved in evasive driving and traffic violations with three other cars. The officer saw a triangular-shaped bulge underneath the front of the driver's shirt, near the waistband of his pants. The officer ordered the defendant to raise his shirt so the officer could see what was underneath it. The court ruled that, based on these facts, the officer had reasonable suspicion to frisk the driver for weapons, and the method of conducting the frisk was reasonable. The court rejected the defendant's argument that the officer was limited to conducting a patdown frisk.

United States v. Michelletti
13 F.3d 838 (5th Cir. 1994) (en banc)

The court ruled that a law enforcement officer had reasonable suspicion of criminal activity to justify the frisk of the defendant when (1) the officer was on routine patrol in a high crime area at the closing time for bars, (2) the officer saw the defendant drinking beer as he was leaving a bar, a possible alcoholic beverage offense, (3) the officer saw the defendant approach a group acting suspiciously outside the bar, and (4) the defendant had his right hand in his pocket at all times, leading the officer to believe that the defendant might have a gun.

Inventory

Vehicles [page 339]

State v. Peaten
110 N.C. App. 749, 431 S.E.2d 237 (1993)

Officers executed a search warrant to search a nightclub to determine if alcoholic beverages were being illegally sold there. An executing officer decided to impound and to conduct an inventory of a BMW parked in the club's parking lot, because he believed it would be vandalized if left there. The court ruled, relying on State v. Phifer, 297 N.C. 216, 254 S.E.2d 586 (1979), that the impoundment and inventory search were unlawful because the stated reason for the impoundment and inventory (that the vehicle would be vandalized) was not a ground authorized by departmental policy. The court noted that the defendant was not present to make a disposition about the car, the car was not a hazard to traffic (because it was parked in the club parking lot), and towing the car was not necessary concerning any arrest.

United States v. Duguay
93 F.3d 346 (7th Cir. 1996)

Although a written impoundment is not required under the Fourth Amendment, the court ruled that the facts in this case showed that the law enforcement agency did not have a standardized impoundment procedure to guide officers as to when they could impound a vehicle. In addition, the officers failed to articulate a legitimate rationale for impounding the defendant's vehicle, and impounding it without regard to whether the defendant could have provided for its removal was unreasonable under the Fourth Amendment.

Search of a Crime Scene [page 342]

State v. Scott
343 N.C. 313, 471 S.E.2d 605 (1996)

An officer, responding to a report of a missing person, went to the defendant's home, where the missing person had lived. Two vehicles were in the driveway, but no one responded to the officer's knock on the front door. The officer noticed large green flies flying under the house through an air vent. He had previously seen this kind of fly on dead animals and people. He then went to the rear of the house, where he saw the flies at the access door to the crawl space under the house. He could smell the odor of decaying flesh. He saw a green carpet lying against the access door. When he moved the carpet, he saw the grass under it was green, indicating that the carpet had been placed there recently. He then opened the access door and shone his flashlight in the crawl space. He saw the body of a dead female there. After a warrantless search of the home for other possible victims or suspects, a search warrant was obtained and a thorough search of the home was made pursuant to the search warrant. The defendant argued that the warrantless search of the crawl space and home was unconstitutional. The court ruled, citing Mincey v. Arizona, 437 U.S. 385, 98 S. Ct. 2408, 57 L. Ed. 2d 290 (1978), that the warrantless search of the crawl space and the home was reasonable under the Fourth Amendment.

State v. Williams
116 N.C. App. 225, 447 S.E.2d 817 (1994), *review denied*, 339 N.C. 741, 454 S.E.2d 660 (1995)
Officers responded to an emergency call directing them to the defendant's residence. They found the defendant pacing in the front yard and another male person lying wounded in the doorway of the residence. The defendant told the officers that a man had shot his wife and was fleeing through the woods. The officers radioed for emergency personnel and then entered the residence to check for other victims or suspects. They found the defendant's wife lying dead on a couch in the den, with a gunshot wound above her left ear. They conducted a sweep of the residence. They found a pistol near the kitchen and ammunition casings and a white, rocklike substance on a stereo in the den. Having conducted a thirty-second sweep,

they then left the house and secured it against intruders. No one was allowed to enter the residence until investigators arrived fifteen minutes after the first officers had arrived. The investigators entered the house without consent or a search warrant and continued to search the premises.

Distinguishing Thompson v. Louisiana, 469 U.S. 17, 105 S. Ct. 409, 83 L. Ed. 2d 246 (1984), the court ruled that the search by investigators was constitutional. Here, the investigators arrived shortly (fifteen minutes) after the initial thirty-second sweep by the first responding officers. Responding to the ongoing emergency, the investigators conducted a more complete search of the premises that could have revealed additional victims or hiding suspects. In *Thompson*, the investigators arrived thirty-five minutes after the first officers on the scene had already searched the home, secured the scene, and sent the defendant to the hospital for medical treatment. The court stated that if it ruled that the search in this case was unconstitutional, it would mean that "once any law enforcement officer makes an initial sweep through a home no matter how hurried or brief it may be, no other officers may search the home until a search warrant is obtained. Such a rule ignores the fact that the first responding officers making a quick initial search of a home may overlook a victim or suspect located in less obvious places."

[Note: Although the warrantless search by the investigators in this case may have been consistent with the Fourth Amendment, cautious law enforcement officers should strongly consider obtaining a search warrant or consent to search before conducting a similar search.]

Part III. Search Warrants

*The following summaries of appellate cases provide the page numbers of the
case summaries section in the second edition where these cases should be added.*

Probable Cause

Generally [page 344]

State v. Dickens
346 N.C. 26, 484 S.E.2d 553 (1997)
The court ruled that an officer's affidavit provided probable cause to take blood samples from the defendant. The affidavit contained: (1) a description of the murder (the female victim was beaten to death with a hammer); (2) an accomplice's statement saying the defendant struck the victim several times although indicating uncertainty about whether the defendant sexually assaulted her; (3) the defendant's assertion that he did not actually see his accomplice sexually assault the victim, although she was on the floor and the mattress was partially off the bed when the defendant entered the bedroom; (4) the accomplice's description of the clothes the defendant was wearing when the murder was committed; (5) confirmation that the defendant's clothes were submitted to the SBI serology laboratory; (6) an officer's advice concerning the advantages of obtaining a DNA profile from a suspect; and (7) the defendant's admission that he struck the victim on the head multiple times with a hammer. The court concluded that the cumulative effect of this information established that the blood samples to be seized from the defendant would provide evidence of the murder and the identity of the person participating in the murder.

State v. Styles
116 N.C. App. 479, 448 S.E.2d 385 (1994), *review denied,* 339 N.C. 620, 454 S.E.2d 265 (1995)
The court ruled that the following affidavit did not support a search warrant (dated September 11, 1992) to search the defendant's home:

> I [name of officer] being first duly sworn, do hereby swear the following to be true to the best of my knowledge and based upon personal knowledge and upon information I received from a confidential informant. That [defendant] is a known felon with a large criminal record. He has been convicted of possession of marijuana in the past two years and [has] been reported to me before on many occasions for selling controlled substances. In addition to this

> I received information today that [defendant] has a large quantity of marijuana in his possession today. This was relayed to me by a confidential reliable informant who stated that two other men had been to the apartment on 9-10-92 and saw large quantities of marijuana in the apartment. This informant has given me reliable information in the past which led to arrests.

The court concluded that the affiant did not adequately explain why the double hearsay was credible: "[t]he deputy only states that the informant has given the deputy reliable information in the past. The magistrate had no way of knowing whether the informant was with the two men, if he observed the two men, or if the two men told the informant what happened."

State v. Waterfield
117 N.C. App. 295, 450 S.E.2d 524 (1994)
On May 13, 1993, officers went to the defendant's residence without a search warrant. The defendant refused to consent to a search of his residence. One officer told the defendant that he would stay with the defendant while the other officers obtained a search warrant. When the officers insisted that the defendant remain in their view at all times, the defendant shut and locked the door. One officer kicked the door down and forced the defendant to sit in a chair. About one-and-one-half hours later, officers returned with a search warrant and conducted a search.

No information obtained during the initial entry was used in the affidavit for the search warrant. The affidavit stated that on April 1, 1993, three people gave an officer about three grams of marijuana that they said the defendant had given them. They stated that the defendant had shown them marijuana kept in a padlocked cabinet in his bedroom at his residence. On April 2, 1993, a confidential informant told an officer that he had seen marijuana in the defendant's residence and stated that the defendant kept the marijuana in a padlocked cabinet in his bedroom. On April 5, 1993, officers visited the defendant's residence and confirmed that he lived there. On May 12, 1993, another confidential informant reported to an officer that within the last twenty-four hours the informant had seen about a half pound of marijuana at the defendant's residence and had seen the defendant sell marijuana from his home; the informant also stated that the defendant kept marijuana in a padlocked cabinet in his bedroom. The court ruled that the affidavit supplied probable cause to support the search warrant. Although the affidavit did not mention the reliability of the officers' sources of information, it did provide information about the presence and sale of marijuana at the defendant's residence within twenty-four hours of the warrant application. It further described the location and manner of the defendant's storage of the marijuana that matched information supplied by other sources. Relying on Segura v. United States, 468 U.S. 796, 104 S. Ct. 3380, 82 L. Ed. 2d 599 (1984), the court also ruled that the search pursuant to the search warrant was valid because the information used to obtain the search warrant was obtained entirely independent of the allegedly illegal initial entry to secure the residence.

Barnett v. Karpinos
119 N.C. App. 719, 460 S.E.2d 208, *review denied*, 342 N.C. 190, 463 S.E.2d 232 (1995)

This case was before the court on the plaintiff's appeal of the trial judge's grant of summary judgment for the civil defendants. (Thus for purposes of this appeal, the plaintiffs' allegations are assumed to be true.) A search warrant authorized a search for cocaine, drug paraphernalia, currency, and drug transaction records in buildings at 107 and 115 Graham Street and of people congregating in the block of Graham Street between West Franklin and West Rosemary streets in Chapel Hill. The court ruled that, based on the facts in this case, the search warrant was invalid because it was a general warrant that was not supported by probable cause. The court also ruled that the defendants' decision to detain and frisk all people found within the block was not supported, based on the facts in this case, by individualized justification under the Fourth Amendment.

State v. Ledbetter
120 N.C. App. 117, 461 S.E.2d 341 (1995)

The affidavit for a search warrant described an informant's controlled buy of cocaine under an officer's supervision from a house at 25 Monmouth Street, Winston-Salem. The controlled buy was made within six days of the application for the search warrant to search the house for cocaine. The court ruled that this information provided a substantial basis for concluding that probable cause existed to search the house for cocaine. The court noted that the reliability of the informant was irrelevant in this case because the focus of the information was the controlled buy made under the officer's supervision. The

court also rejected the defendant's argument that the passage of six days from the controlled buy made the information too stale to establish probable cause. The court noted that drug selling is ordinarily a continuing activity.

United States v. Wilhelm
80 F.3d 116 (4th Cir. 1996)

The court ruled that an anonymous person's information was insufficient to establish probable cause to support a search warrant to search a residence for illegal drugs. Although the person claimed to have seen residents selling marijuana at the house within the last forty-eight hours, there was no specific information in the search warrant's affidavit concerning the person's reliability or truthfulness. In addition, the only corroboration offered by law enforcement was that the person's directions to the residence were correct. *See also* United States v. Clark, 31 F.3d 831 (9th Cir. 1994), *cert. denied*, 115 S. Ct. 920 (1995) (similar ruling); United States v. Leake, 998 F.2d 1359 (1993) (similar ruling).

United States v. Berry
90 F.3d 148 (6th Cir.), *cert. denied*, 117 S. Ct. 497 (1996)

An affidavit for a search warrant to search a car stated that a drug detection dog alerted to the car, indicating the probable presence of drugs in the car. It also stated that the dog was trained and qualified to conduct drug investigations. The court ruled that these statements sufficiently established the dog's training and reliability. The court rejected the defendant's argument that the affidavit had to also describe the details of the dog's training. *See also* United States v. Delaney, 52 F.3d 182 (8th Cir.), *cert. denied*, 116 S. Ct. 209 (1995) (description of drug detection dog in affidavit for search warrant was sufficient).

Timeliness or Staleness of Information [page 348]

State v. Witherspoon
110 N.C. App. 413, 429 S.E.2d 783 (1993)

The court ruled that a search warrant for the defendant's home was based on probable cause. The search warrant included the following information. A concerned citizen told officers that he had been in the defendant's home within the past thirty days and had seen about one hundred marijuana plants growing in the home's crawl space with the use of a lighting system and automatic timers. The concerned citizen had spoken with the defendant often about the defendant's growing these plants, and the concerned citizen had used marijuana and had seen it growing in the past. Officers corroborated the concerned citizen's information about the defendant's car that was parked in the defendant's driveway, and officers also checked the power company's records that showed that the defendant had been paying the power bill for the house in the past six months. The court, relying on several cases, including State v. Beam, 325 N.C. 217, 381 S.E.2d 327 (1989), rejected the defendant's argument that the information was stale, because the concerned citizen had seen marijuana plants in the defendant's home within the last thirty days. The court noted that, based on the facts set out in the affidavit, the magistrate who issued the search warrant could reasonably infer that the marijuana would likely remain in the defendant's home for thirty days.

Anticipatory Search Warrants [new section]

State v. Smith
124 N.C. App. 565, 478 S.E.2d 237 (1996)

Officers planned to use a cooperating informant to sell cocaine to the defendant and his accomplice on February 15, 1993. On February 14, 1993, the day before the anticipated sale, they obtained a search warrant to search the defendant's home for cocaine (apparently anticipating that the cocaine would be sold the next day and would then be located in the defendant's home). The affidavit for the search warrant stated, among other things, that on February 15, 1993 (a date that had not occurred yet), the affiant received information from a confidential informant who, within the past seventy-two hours, had seen cocaine in the defendant's residence. The court ruled that this search warrant was not a valid anticipatory search warrant, based on the requirements for such a warrant as set out in its opinion (see below). The court noted that the search warrant's most glaring deficiency was the absence of any language denoting it as anticipatory.

The court ruled that the Constitution of North Carolina does not require that the object of a search be in the place searched when a search warrant is issued; it requires only probable cause to believe that contraband currently in transit will be at the place to be searched when the search warrant is executed. Thus an anticipatory search warrant is permitted, as long as a judicial official who issues such a warrant carefully eliminates the opportunity for officers to exercise unfettered discretion in executing the warrant. The state constitution requires the following conditions: (1) An anticipatory search warrant must set out explicit, clear, and narrowly drawn triggering events that must occur before execution of the warrant may take place. (2) These triggering events, from which probable cause arises, must be (i) ascertainable and (ii) preordained (that is, the property is on a sure and irreversible course to its destination; for example, an undercover officer will deliver the cocaine to the house to be searched).

(3) A search may not occur unless and until the property does, in fact, arrive at that destination. The court stated that these three conditions ensure that the required nexus between the criminal act, the evidence to be seized, and the identity of the place to be searched is achieved.

[Note: An example of what might be contained in an affidavit for an anticipatory search warrant to search premises, in addition to the statement establishing probable cause, is as follows:

> I request that a search warrant for the premises described above be issued with its execution contingent on the following procedures having occurred: On August 14, 1996, an officer with the Smithville Police Department will pose as a Super Express employee and will deliver the package described above to the premises described above. The package—which is addressed to the premises described above—will contain a powdery substance containing a small amount of cocaine, with most of the cocaine having been removed when the package was previously intercepted as described in this affidavit. After the package is delivered to the above-described premises and is taken inside, this search warrant will be executed.

Federal court decisions have ruled that anticipatory search warrants are sufficient when the affidavit instead of the warrant itself contains the contingency language. See, e.g., United States v. Moetamedi, 46 F.3d 225 (2d Cir. 1995). It is unclear whether North Carolina appellate courts would approve such a procedure. The more cautious approach would be to include the contingency language in the affidavit and add a statement on the face of the warrant, such as "This warrant may be executed only if the contingencies set out in the affidavit to this warrant are satisfied."]

Descriptions in a Search Warrant

Description of the Property to Be Seized [page 355]

United States v. Peters
92 F.3d 768 (8th Cir. 1996)

A drug search warrant authorized the seizure of, among other things, "records . . . associated with cocaine distribution. . . ." The court, distinguishing Walter v. United States, 447 U.S. 649, 100 S. Ct. 2395, 65 L. Ed. 2d 410 (1980), ruled that the search warrant authorized the seizure of three unmarked audiocassettes that were intermingled with notes and letters from a drug co-conspirator who was incarcerated. Thus the seizing officer was authorized to listen to the audiotapes before deciding whether to seize them.

A Neutral and Detached Magistrate

[page 357]

United States v. Ramirez
63 F.3d 937 (10th Cir. 1995)
An issuing judge's common-sense alterations of an affidavit for a search warrant and the search warrant itself did not violate the judge's duty to be a neutral and detached magistrate, based on the facts in this case. The judge altered the person and items to be seized, but the alteration was based on the narrative portion of the affidavit that provided probable cause to do so.

Execution of a Search Warrant

Notice and Entry [page 357]

Wilson v. Arkansas
514 U.S. 927, 115 S.Ct. 1914, 131 L. Ed. 2d 976 (1995)
Officers made an unannounced entry into a home to execute a search warrant. The Arkansas Supreme Court ruled that the Fourth Amendment does not require officers to knock and announce before entering a home. The Court, rejecting the state court's ruling, ruled that an officer's unannounced entry into a home must be reasonable under the Fourth Amendment. Whether an officer announced his or her presence and authority before entering a home is among the factors (along with the threat of physical harm to the officer, pursuit of a recently escaped arrestee, and the likely destruction of evidence if advance notice was given) to be considered in determining whether the entry was reasonable. The Court specifically stated that it will leave to lower courts the task of determining whether an unannounced entry was reasonable and remanded this case to the Arkansas Supreme Court for that purpose. *See also* United States v. Conley, 92 F.3d 157 (3d Cir. 1996) (execution of search warrant was reasonable when the officers entered during daylight and business hours: they entered through an unlocked door, an occupant witnessed the officers' approach, they announced their presence soon after entry, and the entry occurred at a commercial establishment); United States v. Moore, 91 F.3d 96 (10th Cir. 1996) (mere statement by officers that firearms were present inside the dwelling to be searched was insufficient to excuse notice when executing search warrant); United States v. Bates, 84 F.3d 790 (6th Cir. 1996) (mere presence of firearm in apartment and barricaded door were insufficient to excuse notice when executing search warrant).

[Note: G.S. 15A-249 sets standards for entering private premises to execute a search warrant, and G.S. 15A-401(e) sets standards for entering private premises to arrest.]

Richards v. Wisconsin
520 U.S. ___, 117 S. Ct. 1416, 137 L. Ed. 2d 615 (1997)
Officers obtained a search warrant to search a hotel room for drugs. Several officers went to the hotel room to execute the warrant. One officer, dressed as a maintenance man, was the lead officer. Among the other officers was at least one uniformed officer. The lead officer knocked on the hotel room door and, responding to a query from inside the room, stated that he was a maintenance man. The defendant cracked open the door with the chain still on it. The defendant saw a uniformed officer among the officers outside the door. The defendant quickly slammed the door shut. After waiting two or three seconds, the officers began kicking and ramming the door to gain entry. The officers identified themselves as officers while they were kicking the door in. (1) The Court rejected a lower court ruling in this case that officers executing a search warrant involving felony drug crimes are never required to comply with the knock-and-announce rule under the Fourth Amendment. The Court stated that Wilson v. Arkansas, 514 U.S. 927, 115 S. Ct. 1914, 131 L. Ed. 2d 976 (1995) did not support the lower court's ruling. (2) The Court ruled that officers are not required to knock and announce their presence before entering a home if they have *reasonable suspicion* that doing so would be dangerous or futile, or that it would inhibit the effective investigation of crime by, for example, allowing the destruction of evidence. The Court stated that this standard—as opposed to the *probable cause* requirement—strikes the appropriate balance between legitimate law enforcement concerns in executing a search warrant and the individual privacy interests affected by no-knock entries. (3) The Court ruled that, based on the facts in this case (the defendant's apparent recognition of the officers and the easily disposable nature of drugs), the officers were justified in entering the hotel room without first announcing their presence and authority.

[Note: G.S. 15A-251 requires an officer, before executing a search warrant and entering premises without giving notice, to have *probable cause* to believe that giving notice would *endanger the life or safety of any person*. Thus this statute imposes a more stringent standard on officers than the Fourth Amendment. *See also* G.S. 15A-401(e)c, which requires an officer, before entering premises to make an arrest without giving notice of the officer's authority and purpose, to have *reasonable cause* to believe that the giving of such notice would present a *clear danger to human life*.]

State v. Lyons
340 N.C. 646, 459 S.E.2d 770 (1995)

Officers executing a search warrant of an apartment to search for drugs announced their identity and purpose while using a battering ram to enter the apartment, even though—based on the facts in this case—they did not need to make such an announcement under G.S. 15A-251(2) (forcible breaking and entering to execute warrant is authorized if officer has probable cause to believe that giving of notice would endanger life). The court ruled that the fact that officers announced their identity and purpose did not mean that entry by force could not be justified under G.S. 15A-251(2). In this case, the court noted that the following evidence supported a forcible entry under G.S. 15A-251(2): the officers believed that a firearm was inside the defendant's apartment; the defendant would not cooperate; the area outside the defendant's door was so small that even though officers felt the situation was dangerous, their weapons were not drawn because of the fear of harming other officers and bystanders; and one officer heard two arguing voices within the apartment.

State v. Knight
340 N.C. 531, 459 S.E.2d 481 (1995)

The murder victim was stabbed twenty-seven times, castrated, and his penis inserted in his mouth. Officers went to the defendant's home to execute arrest and search warrants for this murder. They knocked on the front door several times and announced, "Police! Search warrant!" at least two or three times. After waiting thirty to sixty seconds and hearing no response from inside the residence, the officers used a battering ram to open the door. They entered the residence, conducted a quick sweep for weapons, and arrested the defendant. The defendant was taken to the police station, where he confessed to his participation in the murder and also told the officers where one of the knives used in the murder was located in his house.

The court ruled that the officers' forcible entry into the premises was reasonable under the Fourth Amendment [see Wilson v. Arkansas, 514 U.S. 927, 115 S. Ct. 1914, 131 L. Ed. 2d 976 (1995)] and complied with the provisions of G.S. Chapter 15A. They had probable cause to believe that further delay in entering the residence or the giving of more specific notice would endanger their own safety or that of other occupants of the residence. They knew that the defendant was dangerous, armed

with a hunting knife and possibly firearms; there was at least one other suspect who had not been arrested; they were concerned about the safety of a woman and her children inside the residence, who might become hostages; and if the entry was not forced, it would not be safe.

People Present during the Execution of a Search Warrant

Detaining People Present [page 358]

United States v. Edwards
103 F.3d 90 (10th Cir. 1996)

The defendant, a nonresident of a house to be searched with a search warrant, left that house in a car. He was stopped in his car three blocks from the house. The court ruled that the detention of the defendant was not supported by Michigan v. Summers, 452 U.S. 692, 101 S. Ct. 2587, 69 L. Ed. 2d 340 (1981), because his detention did not play any part in facilitating the execution of the search warrant.

United States v. Fountain
2 F.3d 656 (6th Cir.), *cert. denied*, 510 U.S. 1014 (1993)

The detention of a nonresident occupant during officers' execution of a search warrant to search a home for drugs was reasonable and justified by legitimate interests in preventing flight on discovery of any incriminating evidence and in minimizing the risk of harm to the officers. The officers entered a confined, unfamiliar environment that was likely to be dangerous in light of the nature of the drug investigation and the fact that weapons had been seized from the home one month before the search.

Service of a Search Warrant and Completion of an Inventory [page 360]

State v. Knight
340 N.C. 531, 459 S.E.2d 481 (1995)

The murder victim was stabbed twenty-seven times, castrated, and his penis inserted in his mouth. Officers went to the defendant's home to execute arrest and search warrants for this murder. They knocked on the front door several times and announced, "Police! Search warrant!" at least two or three times. After waiting thirty to sixty seconds and hearing no response from inside the residence, the officers used a battering ram to open the door. They entered the residence, conducted a quick sweep for weapons, and arrested the defendant. The search warrant was read to the defendant about ten minutes after the entry into the residence and the initial sweep, but before any search was undertaken. The court ruled that the execution of the search warrant complied with the provisions of G.S. Chapter 15A.

Using Force to Execute a Search Warrant for Taking Blood [new section]

United States v. Bullock
71 F.3d 171 (5th Cir. 1995), *cert. denied*, 116 S. Ct. 1365 (1996)
Officers obtained a search warrant to take blood from the defendant. Knowing that the defendant had threatened to resist the execution of the search warrant, the officers sought and received judicial approval to use physical force. A seven-member "control team" was used to subdue him. He was handcuffed and shackled between two cots that were strapped together. He physically resisted by kicking, hitting, and attempting to bite the officers. A towel was placed on his face because he was spitting on the officers. A nurse took blood from the defendant's hand. The court ruled, based on these facts, the use of force to execute the search warrant was reasonable under the Fourth Amendment. The court, citing United States v. Wade, 388 U.S. 218, 87 S. Ct. 1926, 18 L. Ed. 2d 1149 (1967), also rejected the defendant's argument that his Sixth Amendment right to counsel was violated because his attorney was not present during the procedures.

Scope of the Search and Seizure with a Search Warrant

Seizing Items in Plain View [page 361]

State v. Cummings
113 N.C. App. 368, 438 S.E.2d 453, *appeal dismissed and review denied*, 336 N.C. 75, 445 S.E.2d 39 (1994)
Officers executing a search warrant for drugs, drug records, and so forth, discovered and seized ninety-four photographs of various nude women. The court ruled that the seizure was proper under plain-view justification because the photographs could have been evidence of an obscenity offense.

United States v. Soussi
29 F.3d 565 (10th Cir. 1994)
The court ruled that even if part of a search warrant is invalid, law enforcement officers may properly seize evidence in plain view that is listed in the invalid part of the warrant, if the redacted warrant justifies the officers' presence in the place to be searched.

United States v. Simpson
10 F.3d 645 (9th Cir. 1993), *vacated on other grounds*, 513 U.S. 983 (1994)
The seizure of a rifle during the execution of a search warrant to search for illegal drugs was proper under the plain view doctrine because of the close relationship between drugs and firearms in the narcotics business.

Challenging the Validity of a Search Warrant

Truthfulness of the Information [page 364]

State v. Barnes
333 N.C. 666, 430 S.E.2d 223, *cert. denied*, 510 U.S. 946 (1993)
The court examined the officer's statements in a search warrant affidavit and determined, based on the facts in this case, that they were not deliberately false or made in reckless disregard of the truth under Franks v. Delaware, 438 U.S. 154, 98 S. Ct. 2674, 57 L. Ed. 2d 667 (1978). *See also* State v. Fernandez, 346 N.C. 1, 484 S.E.2d 350 (1997) (similar ruling); to the extent that State v. Montserrate, 125 N.C. App. 22, 479 S.E.2d 494 (1997), is inconsistent with *Fernandez*, it is no longer valid.

Simmons v. Poe
47 F.3d 1370 (4th Cir. 1995)
The court ruled, based on prior case law, that a defendant must show that omissions from an affidavit to a search warrant, to entitle the defendant to a hearing under Franks v. Delaware, 438 U.S. 154, 98 S. Ct. 2674, 57 L. Ed. 2d 667 (1978), must be (1) designed to mislead or made with reckless disregard of whether they mislead the issuing judicial official, and (2) material to the determination of probable cause. The court reviewed the facts in this case and ruled that the defendant failed to meet his burden on either of the two issues.

Revelation of a Confidential Informant's Identity at a Suppression Hearing or Trial [page 364]

State v. McEachern
114 N.C. App. 218, 441 S.E.2d 574 (1994)
The state's evidence at a pretrial hearing showed that on March 7, 1991, a confidential informant told an officer that he saw cocaine in the defendant's trailer home and that there was a man selling it identified as Toney (defendant's first name). On March 8, 1991, the informant made a controlled buy, set up by the officer, from the same person at the trailer home. Later that day, the officer obtained a search warrant for the trailer home.

The defendant was backing out of his yard when the officers arrived. The officers entered the trailer home and found marijuana and cocaine. The defendant testified that he gave permission to his nephew to use his trailer home for a party and was out of town from March 7, 1991, until just before the officers arrived on March 8, 1991. He said that there were no illegal drugs in his home when he left on March 7, 1991, and that he did not know who was in his home during his absence. The defendant argued that the informant, if called as a witness, could testify that the defendant was not in fact the person who was selling drugs and who sold him drugs; the informant could also testify that the drugs belonged to a third party.

The trial judge found that the defendant's testimony established that the informant was a material and necessary witness for the defense to corroborate his alibi, pointed to the guilt of a third party, and showed the nonexclusivity of the defendant's premises. The judge granted the defendant's motion to require the state to disclose the informant's identity. The state refused to do so, and the judge then dismissed all the charges against the defendant. The court, relying on Brady v. Maryland, 373 U.S. 83, 83 S. Ct. 1194, 10 L. Ed. 2d 215 (1963), Roviaro v. United States, 353 U.S. 53, 77 S. Ct. 623, 1 L. Ed. 2d 639 (1957), and G.S. 15A-910(3b), upheld the trial judge's rulings that required disclosure of the informant's identity and the dismissal of all charges when the state failed to disclose.

Possible Defects in a Search Warrant or the Procedure in Issuing a Search Warrant

Generally [page 366]

State v. Ledbetter
120 N.C. App. 117, 461 S.E.2d 341 (1995)
The affidavit for a search warrant described an informant's controlled buy of cocaine under an officer's supervision from a house at 25 Monmouth Street, Winston-Salem. The application for the search warrant referred to the seizure of the "Schedule II controlled substance marijuana" when it should have stated "cocaine." The court noted that the affidavit referred to cocaine and ruled that this error was not fatal to the validity of the search warrant.

Part IV. Administrative Inspections

The following summaries of appellate cases provide the page numbers of the case summaries section in the second edition where these cases should be added.

Warrantless Administrative Inspections

Generally [page 372]

United States v. Argent Chemical Laboratories, Inc.
93 F.3d 572 (9th Cir. 1996)
A manufacturer of veterinary drugs is a closely regulated industry under United States v. Biswell, 406 U.S. 311, 92 S. Ct. 1593, 32 L. Ed. 2d 87 (1972), and therefore is subject to warrantless administrative inspections under the Fourth Amendment. *See also* Lesser v. Espy, 34 F.3d 1301 (7th Cir. 1994) (similar ruling involving regulation of rabbitry–selling rabbits for research).

United States v. V-1 Oil Co.
63 F.3d 909 (9th Cir. 1995), *cert. denied*, 116 S. Ct. 1824 (1996)
Warrantless, unannounced inspections (authorized by federal law) of a company involved in the transportation and sale of hazardous materials did not violate the Fourth Amendment. The court cited New York v. Burger, 482 U.S. 691, 107 S. Ct. 2636, 96 L. Ed. 2d 601 (1987).

Procedure in Issuing or Executing Administrative Inspection Warrants
[page 374]

In re *Glavan Industries, Inc.*
122 N.C. App. 628, 471 S.E.2d 132 (1996)
A superior court judge issued an administrative inspection warrant to conduct an inspection authorized by the Occupational Safety and Health Act of North Carolina. On the same day the warrant was issued, Glavan Industries made a motion to quash the warrant. The motion was denied. Glavan Industries then gave notice of appeal to the North Carolina Court of Appeals. The court ruled that the appeal is dismissed as interlocutory because no final order had been entered and Glavan did not show that any substantial right was affected.

Part V. Interrogation and Confessions

The following summaries of appellate cases provide the page numbers of the case summaries section in the second edition where these cases should be added.

Voluntariness of the Defendant's Statement

Generally [page 374]

State v. Chapman
343 N.C. 495, 471 S.E.2d 354 (1996)

On August 23, 1993, about 9:30 A.M., the defendant was arrested at a bank for attempting to cash a forged check. He waived his *Miranda* rights and admitted that he had attempted to cash a check that he had forged after taking it in a robbery. Officers took the defendant to a school to search for a purse that had been taken in the robbery. They then returned the defendant to the police station, where he confessed to forgery and uttering charges. A detective procured arrest warrants for these charges at 12:15 P.M. and served them on the defendant. The defendant then was questioned by another detective who was investigating the robbery in which the checks were taken, and the defendant confessed to the robbery at 1:27 P.M. Officers prepared an arrest warrant to charge the robbery, but it was not presented to the magistrate then. The defendant then was interviewed by another detective about a robbery and murder (not related to the crimes discussed previously). The detective put nine photos of the murder victim on the walls of the interrogation room and one photo of the victim on the floor directly in front of the chair in which the defendant sat during the interrogation. Thus the defendant saw a photo of the victim in every direction he turned. During the interview, the detective falsely implied to the defendant that a note found next to the victim's body had been the subject of handwriting analysis that showed it was the defendant's handwriting and that the defendant's fingerprints were on the note. The defendant confessed to the murder at about 7:05 P.M. and was taken to the magistrate about 8:00 P.M.

The court ruled that the defendant's confession was not involuntary. The placement of photos did not cause his free will to be overcome. Relying on State v. Jackson, 308 N.C. 549, 304 S.E.2d 134 (1983), the court stated that the detective's deceit about the defendant's handwriting and fingerprints on the note did not require the trial judge to find that the confession was not of the defendant's own free will, that it was the product of fear or hope of reward, or that the deceit was calculated to produce an untrue statement.

State v. McCullers
341 N.C. 19, 460 S.E.2d 163 (1995)

Officers were investigating a murder in which several people beat, killed, and robbed the victim. The defendant, who was eighteen years old and was working toward his GED, agreed to come to the police station for questioning. He was given his *Miranda* warnings and waived them. The defendant was alert and not under the influence of drugs or alcohol. One officer stated to the defendant that it would be better for the defendant if he said that he did not mean to kill the man than for him to keep denying that he did it. He also swore at the defendant on two occasions. Two other officers then took a statement from the defendant, who stated that no one had threatened him or made him say anything he did not want to say. The trial judge found that no officer made any threats or promises or created any coercive atmosphere near the defendant. No physical or verbal activity by the officers induced the defendant to make his statements. (The defendant did not testify at the suppression hearing.) The trial judge ruled that the confession was voluntarily made.

The court, distinguishing State v. Pruitt, 286 N.C. 442, 212 S.E.2d 92 (1975), State v. Fuqua, 269 N.C. 223, 152 S.E.2d 68 (1967), and State v. Stevenson, 212 N.C. 648, 194 S.E. 81 (1937), and relying on State v. Smith, 328 N.C. 99, 400 S.E.2d 712 (1991), and State v. Jackson, 308 N.C. 549, 304 S.E.2d 134 (1983), upheld the trial judge's ruling. The court noted that the officer did not accuse the defendant of lying but rather informed him of the crime and urged him to tell the truth and think about what would be better for him. The court also noted that the defendant's contention that he was intimidated or coerced by the officer's profanity was not persuasive in light of the defendant's own use of profanity during the interrogation. Under the totality of circumstances, the officer's isolated statements did not support the defendant's contention that his statement was made involuntarily based on fear or hope.

State v. Sturgill
121 N.C. App. 629, 469 S.E.2d 557 (1996)
Officers arrested the defendant for a felony break-in and larceny. During custodial interrogation a detective told the defendant that he would be charged with several other break-ins. The defendant then indicated that the only statement he wanted to make was that he did not commit any of the break-ins. The detective stopped the questioning and began to leave the interrogation room. The defendant then asked "what would be in it" for him if he provided information about the break-ins. The detective told him that he would not seek to indict him for habitual felon status. The defendant then confessed. The court ruled that the officer's statement about the charge of habitual felon status violated the defendant's substantive due process rights (that is, the defendant detrimentally relied on the officer's promise) and statutory rights under G.S. 15A-1021 (which bars improper pressure to induce a defendant to plead guilty) and G.S. 15A-974 (the statutory exclusionary rule), and thus the confession was inadmissible.

United States v. Walton
10 F.3d 1024 (3d Cir. 1993)
The court ruled that an officer's promise to a defendant that what he told the officer would not be used against him coerced the defendant to give a statement, based on the totality of circumstances in this case. Thus the defendant's statement was involuntary and inadmissible.

Use of Deception [page 376]

State v. Hardy
339 N.C. 207, 451 S.E.2d 600 (1994)
The court examined all the evidence surrounding the defendant's confession to law enforcement officers and ruled that the confession was voluntary, even though one officer lied about a witness having identified the defendant and some of that officer's statements, in isolation, could be interpreted to contain implicit promises or threats. The court concluded, citing State v. Jackson, 308 N.C. 549, 304 S.E.2d 134 (1983), that the defendant's independent will was not overcome by mental or psychological coercion or pressure to induce a confession that he was not otherwise disposed to make. *See also* State v. Chapman, 343 N.C. 495, 471 S.E.2d 354 (1996), discussed above on page 94.

Statements to Non–Law Enforcement Officers [page 377]

State v. Powell
340 N.C. 674, 459 S.E.2d 219 (1995), *cert. denied*, 116 S. Ct. 739 (1996)
The defendant was arrested for murder and asserted his right to counsel during custodial interrogation. He was placed in jail. Later, the defendant made telephone calls to two people (Weathers and Yelton), who recorded the conversations and gave the recording to the police. Weathers testified that he recorded the conversation for "personal reasons." He also testified that no officer had asked them to record conversations with the defendant, although they had been told that any information they had concerning the murder would help the police. The court ruled that the defendant's Fifth Amendment rights were not violated because Weathers and Yelton did not make the recording as agents of the police.

Defendant's Statements: *Miranda* Warnings and Waiver

Generally [page 377]

State v. Leary
344 N.C. 109, 472 S.E.2d 753 (1996)
The court rejected the defendant's argument on appeal that the court should rule that the North Carolina Constitution requires law enforcement officers to give *Miranda*-style warnings to defendants even though they are not in custody.

State v. Morrell
108 N.C. App. 465, 424 S.E.2d 147, *appeal dismissed, review denied, and cert. denied*, 333 N.C. 465, 427 S.E.2d 626 (1993)
The defendant was arrested on a federal charge of child abduction and was committed to the county jail. A social worker in the county child protective services unit identified herself to the defendant and told the defendant that she was conducting an investigation of alleged sexual abuse and neglect of a boy with whom the defendant had had a relationship. The defendant confessed to the social worker. Two days later a detective talked with the defendant in the jail after giving her *Miranda* warnings and obtaining a proper waiver. The defendant again confessed. Based on evidence that the social worker was working with the sheriff's department on the case before interviewing the defendant in jail, the court ruled that the social worker was an agent of the state and thus was required to give *Miranda* warnings before her interview with the defendant. [Note, however, that the court did

not discuss Illinois v. Perkins, 496 U.S. 292, 110 S. Ct. 2394, 110 L. Ed. 2d 243 (1990), which ruled that when a person does not know that he or she is talking to a government agent (the court appeared to indicate that a government agent is one who is interrogating a person about criminal activity), there is no reason to assume the possibility of coercion, which is the underlying principle of the *Miranda* decision; thus *Miranda* warnings are not required. If the defendant did not know that the social worker was a government agent, then the ruling in *Illinois v. Perkins* did not require the social worker to give *Miranda* warnings.] The court upheld the admissibility of the defendant's confession to the detective because the confession to the social worker was not coerced; *see* Oregon v. Elstad, 470 U.S. 298, 105 S. Ct. 1285, 84 L. Ed. 2d 222 (1985), and State v. Barlow, 330 N.C. 133, 409 S.E.2d 906 (1991).

The Public-Safety Exception [page 379]

State v. Brooks
337 N.C. 132, 446 S.E.2d 579 (1994)
An SBI agent accompanied other law enforcement officers in executing a search warrant for a nightclub to search for illegal drugs. On arriving at the nightclub, the agent saw a vehicle parked in the parking lot with the defendant sitting in the driver's seat. The agent walked over to the driver's side of the vehicle and shone his flashlight into the car's interior. He saw on the passenger side of the bucket seats an empty unsnapped holster within the defendant's reach. The agent asked the defendant, "Where is your gun?" The defendant replied, "I'm sitting on it." The agent was unable to see the gun although he shone his light all about the vehicle. He asked the defendant to get out of the vehicle; the defendant reached under his right thigh and handed the gun to the agent. The agent did not place the defendant under arrest for carrying a concealed weapon, but he eventually obtained permission to search the vehicle and found cocaine in a nylon pouch there. The court ruled that the defendant was not in custody when the agent asked the defendant, "Where is your gun?" and therefore *Miranda* warnings were not required. In any event—even if the defendant was in custody—*Miranda* warnings were not required because the agent was permitted to ask that question for his own safety; *see* New York v. Quarles, 467 U.S. 649, 104 S. Ct. 2626, 81 L. Ed. 2d 550 (1984).

State v. Garcia-Lorenzo
110 N.C. App. 319, 430 S.E.2d 290 (1993)
The defendant was involved in a vehicular accident with bystanders, ran off the road, and was injured. Officers transported the defendant to a hospital, where officers and doctors had to restrain him because he became violent. Because an officer wanted to know whether to look for other victims of the accident, the officer and then the doctor asked the defendant whether he was alone in the car. The defendant responded several times, "No, alone." The court affirmed the trial judge's conclusions of law that this questioning was permissible because (1) it was within *Miranda*'s public-safety exception, recognized in New York v. Quarles, 467 U.S. 649, 104 S. Ct. 2626, 81 L. Ed. 2d 550 (1984), because officers were concerned that someone else may have been injured and lying undiscovered at the scene, and (2) the defendant was not subjected to *interrogation* as defined in Rhode Island v. Innis, 446 U.S. 291, 100 S. Ct. 1682, 64 L. Ed. 2d 297 (1980).

United States v. Mobley
40 F.3d 688 (4th Cir. 1994), *cert. denied*, 115 S. Ct. 2005 (1995)
Officers began the execution of a search warrant for drugs at the defendant's apartment by arresting the defendant and by conducting a security sweep that revealed that no one else was there. They gave *Miranda* warnings to the defendant, and he asserted his right to counsel. One officer then asked him if there was anything in the apartment that could be of danger to the officers while they executed the search warrant. The court recognized that the public-safety exception under New York v. Quarles, 467 U.S. 649, 104 S. Ct. 2626, 81 L. Ed. 2d 550 (1984), applied even after a defendant's assertion of the right to counsel, but ruled that the officer's question did not qualify under the exception because there was no apparent danger to the officers. The officers had the defendant in custody and had already conducted a security sweep before an officer had asked the question.

The Meaning of "Custody" under *Miranda* [page 380]

Stansbury v. California
511 U.S. 318, 114 S. Ct. 1526, 128 L. Ed. 2d 293 (1994)
In determining whether a suspect was in custody so that an officer must give *Miranda* warnings before conducting an interrogation, the California Supreme Court considered as a factor whether the officer's investigation had focused on the suspect. Relying on its prior rulings—including Beckwith v. United States, 425 U.S. 341, 96 S. Ct. 1612, 48 L. Ed. 2d 1 (1976), Berkemer v. McCarty, 468 U.S. 420, 104 S. Ct. 3138, 82 L. Ed. 2d 317 (1984), California v. Beheler, 463 U.S. 1121, 103 S. Ct. 3517, 77 L. Ed. 2d 1275 (1983), and Minnesota v. Murphy, 465 U.S. 420, 104 S. Ct. 1136, 79 L. Ed. 2d 409 (1984)—the Court rejected that factor in determining custody. The Court noted that the determination of custody depends on the

objective circumstances of the interview, not on the subjective views of the interrogating officers or the person being questioned. An officer's views concerning the nature of an interrogation or beliefs concerning the potential culpability of the person being questioned may be one of many factors in determining the custody issue, but only if the officer's views or beliefs are somehow manifested to the person and would have affected how a reasonable person in that position would perceive one's freedom to leave. See generally the discussion on page 213 of the second edition.

The Court noted that even a clear statement from an officer that the person is a prime suspect is not, in itself, dispositive of the custody issue, since some suspects are free to come and go until an officer decides to make an arrest. The Court also noted that an officer's undisclosed views may be relevant in testing the credibility of the officer's account of what happened during an interrogation; but it is the objective surroundings, not any undisclosed views, that control the custody issue.

Thompson v. Keohane
516 U.S. 99, 116 S. Ct. 457, 133 L. Ed. 2d 383 (1995)
The Court ruled that a state court's ruling on whether a defendant was in "custody" under *Miranda* is not entitled to a presumption of correctness under federal habeas corpus review. Such a ruling resolves mixed questions of law and fact and therefore warrants independent review by a federal habeas court.

State v. Daughtry
340 N.C. 488, 459 S.E.2d 747 (1995), *cert. denied*, 116 S. Ct. 789 (1996)
The defendant voluntarily went with two officers to the police station to be questioned about a murder. The officers advised the defendant that he was not under arrest and could leave at any time. One officer advised the defendant of his *Miranda* rights as a precaution. The defendant waived those rights. After some conversation between the officers and the defendant, the defendant said, "I think I need to speak to a lawyer." One officer handed the defendant the telephone directory opened to the yellow pages with attorney listings. As he did so, the officer told the defendant that he could talk to a lawyer and continue to talk to the officers if he wished. The defendant briefly looked at the yellow pages and then told the officers that he was willing to talk to the officers. One officer reminded the defendant of his rights to remain silent and to an attorney; the defendant indicated that he understood his rights. The defendant had not been placed under arrest. He then confessed. The court ruled that because the defendant was not in custody when he

requested an attorney, his rights under *Miranda* and Edwards v. Arizona, 451 U.S. 477, 101 S. Ct. 1880, 68 L. Ed. 2d 378 (1981), were inapplicable. Therefore the court did not need to decide whether the trial judge had erred in concluding that the defendant had voluntarily reinitiated interrogation after requesting an attorney.

State v. Medlin
333 N.C. 280, 426 S.E.2d 402 (1993)
Atlantic Beach officers arrested the defendant in a breezeway outside a motel room in Atlantic Beach for a murder and robbery committed in Wake County, based on the mistaken belief that an arrest warrant had been issued in Wake County for these offenses. The court determined, however, that the Atlantic Beach officers had sufficient information to establish probable cause to arrest, based on the facts in this case. Therefore the warrantless arrest was proper. When the Atlantic Beach officers learned that there were no arrest warrants for the defendant after they had brought him to the police station, they told him that he was not under arrest and was free to leave. They also told him that investigators were coming from Wake County and wanted to talk to him, that he could stay and move around the police station at will, and that he should let them know if he needed anything. The defendant indicated that he wanted to stay, and in fact he remained there and later gave statements to the officers. Based on these and other facts, the court concluded that the defendant was no longer in custody, and therefore he was not entitled to *Miranda* rights, including the right to counsel under Edwards v. Arizona, 451 U.S. 477, 101 S. Ct. 1880, 68 L. Ed. 2d 378 (1981). Therefore the court ruled that it was unnecessary to decide whether the defendant properly waived his right to counsel.

State v. Corbett
339 N.C. 313, 451 S.E.2d 252 (1994)
The court ruled that the defendant was not in custody to require officers to give *Miranda* warnings for three interviews on three separate days. The first two interviews took place in an officer's car at the defendant's home. The third interview took place in the yard of the defendant's home. The defendant then offered to take the officers to the crime scene. An officer told the defendant's wife that the defendant was not under arrest at this time. At the crime scene the defendant fully confessed to the murder. The defendant repeatedly had been told he was not under arrest and would be taken home anytime he so requested. *See also* State v. Gaines, 345 N.C. 647, 483 S.E.2d 396 (1997) (defendants were not in custody during interrogation at law enforcement facility).

State v. Sweatt
333 N.C. 407, 427 S.E.2d 112 (1993)

The defendant was at the hospital being treated for injuries sustained in an automobile accident. An officer who had responded to the accident (but who had not yet talked with the defendant) came to the hospital. After a doctor alerted the officer (who by then had been informed that the defendant may have been involved in a homicide before the accident had occurred) that the defendant was saying things the officer might be interested in, the officer walked to where the defendant was being treated and asked him questions. The court ruled that the defendant was not in custody, so the officer was not required to give the defendant *Miranda* warnings before questioning him.

State v. Hicks
333 N.C. 467, 428 S.E.2d 167 (1993)

Officers asked the defendant—who had been told by an officer that he was a suspect in a murder because he and the victim had just broken up before she was murdered—to take a polygraph test to "clear his name." They transported the defendant with his consent over an hour's drive away from his home in Mocksville to the SBI office in Hickory for the purpose of taking the test. Although he refused to take the polygraph test three separate times during two hours of questioning, the defendant was never taken home or offered transportation home. Although the polygraph operator informed the defendant during his explanation of the polygraph procedure that he was not under arrest, the defendant never was told that he was free to leave. After his third refusal to take the test, the defendant told the polygraph operator that he wanted to go outside with him. During a conversation in the parking lot, the defendant told the operator that he wanted to take responsibility for the murder. They went back into the building, and the operator informed two investigating officers that the defendant wanted to confess. When the defendant refused to elaborate on the details of the crime, the officers told him that he would have to tell them what had happened, including any details. The defendant then gave them the details and demonstrated how he had shot the victim. After the defendant explained the details of the murder, the officers advised the defendant of his *Miranda* rights and obtained a valid waiver. The defendant then gave a second confession.

The court ruled that a reasonable person in the defendant's position, knowing that he was a suspect in a murder case and having just stated to an officer that he wanted to take responsibility for a murder, would feel that he was compelled to stay and therefore was in custody under *Miranda* immediately following that statement.

Thus the first confession that was taken without *Miranda* warnings should have been ruled inadmissible. However, the court ruled that the second confession, taken after *Miranda* warnings had been properly given and waived, was admissible under the ruling in Oregon v. Elstad, 470 U.S. 298, 105 S. Ct. 1285, 84 L. Ed. 2d 222 (1985) (fact that voluntary confession is inadmissible because of *Miranda* violation does not prohibit admission of later voluntary confession given after proper *Miranda* warnings and waiver). And the court adopted the *Oregon v. Elstad* ruling to determine alleged constitutional violations under Article I, sections 19 and 23, of the North Carolina Constitution.

State v. Benjamin
124 N.C. App. 734, 478 S.E.2d 651 (1996)

An officer conducted a frisk of the defendant after an investigative stop for a traffic violation. As the officer was patting the defendant down, he felt two hard plastic containers in a breast pocket of the defendant's winter jacket. Based on his narcotics training, it was immediately apparent to the officer that these containers were vials of the type that is customarily used to hold illegal drugs. When the officer felt the container through the jacket, he asked the defendant, "What is that?" The defendant responded that it was "crack." The officer removed two vials from the coat pocket and found cocaine. (1) The court ruled that the defendant was not in "custody" to require *Miranda* warnings when the officer asked the question while conducting the frisk. The court noted that the fact that a defendant is not free to leave does not necessarily constitute custody under *Miranda*. Instead, the inquiry is whether a reasonable person in the defendant's position would believe that he or she was under arrest or the functional equivalent of arrest; the court cited and discussed Stansbury v. California, 511 U.S. 318, 114 S. Ct. 1526, 128 L. Ed. 2d 293 (1994), and Berkemer v. McCarty, 468 U.S. 420, 104 S. Ct. 3138, 82 L. Ed. 2d 317 (1984). The court concluded that a reasonable person would not have believed he was in custody, based on these facts. (2) The court ruled that the seizure of the cocaine was proper under the plain-feel theory set out in Minnesota v. Dickerson, 508 U.S. 366, 113 S. Ct. 2130, 124 L. Ed. 2d 334 (1993). The court stated that the officer had probable cause to believe (or to state it a different way, it became immediately apparent to the officer) that the object was contraband, based on the officer's experience and narcotics training; the size, shape, and mass of the objects; and the defendant's response to the officer's question. The court also ruled that an officer may ask a suspect the nature of an object in the suspect's pocket during a lawful frisk even after the officer has determined that the object is not a weapon.

State v. Sanders
122 N.C. App. 691, 471 S.E.2d 641 (1996)

The court ruled that the following evidence supported the trial judge's ruling that the defendant was not in custody to require officers to give *Miranda* warnings. The defendant agreed to accompany the officers to the police station. Two officers were in the interview room with the defendant during the entire period of the interview, which lasted about two hours, and were joined briefly by a third officer. The defendant was never threatened or promised that he would not be prosecuted or would obtain a lesser sentence by cooperating with the officers. He was allowed to go to the bathroom on request and allowed a twenty-minute smoking break outside the room. The defendant was told he was free to leave. He asked to call his wife and was told he could do so later. The officers confronted him with physical evidence that in fact had been found at the crime scene. The officers falsely told him that the victim had identified him as the person who beat and robbed him. The defendant admitted robbing and beating the victim but consistently denied that he had used a weapon.

State v. Dukes
110 N.C. App. 695, 431 S.E.2d 209 (1993)

Officer Moore arrived at a trailer park to investigate the murder of the defendant's wife. Both the defendant and a baby he was holding (outside the trailer where the body was located) had blood on their clothing. The defendant gave an exculpatory statement to the officer. Officer Moore accompanied the defendant and the baby to the defendant's trailer (the defendant lived in a different trailer from his wife). Officer Moore instructed Officer Thompson to guard the defendant, not allow him to leave his trailer, not allow any other person to enter the trailer, and not allow the defendant to wash or to change his clothes. Officer Thompson allowed the defendant to make telephone calls after he asked permission from the officer to do so. Officer Thompson accompanied the defendant to the bathroom to ensure that the defendant did not wash or change his clothes. Officer Thompson later asked the defendant, "Do you know what happened?" (1) The court ruled that, while at his trailer with Officer Thompson, the defendant was in custody to require *Miranda* warnings—a reasonable person, knowing that his wife had just been killed, kept under constant police supervision, told not to wash or change his clothing, and never informed that he was free to leave his own home, would not feel free to get up and go. The court also ruled that the officer's question constituted interrogation under the *Miranda* ruling. (2) The defendant was later arrested and taken to a law

enforcement center. While the officer was advising the defendant of his *Miranda* rights, the defendant said, "I stabbed her." The court ruled that this statement was voluntary and not the result of custodial interrogation.

State v. Soles
119 N.C. App. 375, 459 S.E.2d 4, *appeal dismissed and review denied,* 341 N.C. 655, 462 S.E.2d 523 (1995)

Officers took the defendant, with his consent, to Gastonia for questioning. The defendant was not handcuffed during a four-hour interview, was left alone, and was allowed to use the vending machines. The defendant conceded on appeal that he was free to leave and voluntarily gave a statement to the officers. The court ruled that the defendant was not in custody to require *Miranda* warnings. At a second interview, a polygraph examiner confronted the defendant about patterns of deception and questioned him in addition to the polygraph testing. The operator had given *Miranda* warnings to the defendant and obtained a waiver before the testing. In any event, the court ruled that the defendant was not in custody to require *Miranda* warnings, since the defendant had voluntarily come to the police station for the polygraph and was free to leave at any time. The court also ruled, based on the facts in this case, that the defendant's statement was voluntarily given.

United States v. Murray
89 F.3d 459 (7th Cir. 1996)

Officers stopped a vehicle for a traffic violation but also suspected that the driver was involved in a drug transaction. The driver had appeared to be hiding something before he stopped his car. Officers ordered him out of the car, and after he became verbally combative, they placed him in the back of a police car. After finding a loaded gun under the front passenger seat of the defendant's car, one of the officers showed the defendant the gun and asked him if he knew who owned it. The court ruled that, based on these facts, the defendant was not in custody to require the officers to give *Miranda* warnings before asking that question. The court relied on Berkemer v. McCarty, 468 U.S. 420, 104 S. Ct. 3138, 82 L. Ed. 2d 317 (1984), and United States v. Kelly, 991 F.2d 1308 (7th Cir. 1993). The fact that the defendant was questioned while seated in the back of the patrol car did not by itself place the defendant in custody under *Miranda.*

Booker v. Ward
94 F.3d 1052 (7th Cir. 1996)

The court ruled that the mere giving of *Miranda* warnings when they are not required does not change noncustodial questioning into nonconsensual custodial interrogation.

United States v. Ritchie
35 F.3d 1477 (10th Cir. 1994)

The court ruled that the defendant was not in custody to require officers to give him *Miranda* warnings when he was being detained during the execution of a search warrant of his residence. Officers did not draw their guns, use handcuffs, or otherwise use force or the threat of force during questioning.

United States v. Perdue
8 F.3d 1455 (10th Cir. 1993)

Based on the facts in this case, the court ruled that the intrusiveness of the investigative stop required officers to give the defendant *Miranda* warnings before questioning him. Officers had forced the defendant out of his car at gunpoint, required him to lie on the ground, and interrogated him without giving *Miranda* warnings.

The Meaning of "Interrogation" under *Miranda*

Generally [page 384]

State v. Vick
341 N.C. 569, 461 S.E.2d 655 (1995)

The defendant was arrested for murder. Before *Miranda* warnings had been given and while the defendant was being fingerprinted, an officer approached the defendant and told him he would like to talk to him after the fingerprinting was complete and would answer any of the defendant's questions then. The defendant indicated that he needed to talk to someone. The defendant then said, "I don't understand. Why isn't Collette here? She was there that night with me." The court ruled that the officer's comments were not interrogation under Rhode Island v. Innis, 446 U.S. 291, 100 S. Ct. 1682, 64 L. Ed. 2d 297 (1980).

State v. DeCastro
342 N.C. 667, 467 S.E.2d 653, *cert. denied*, 117 S. Ct. 241 (1996)

The defendant was arrested for two murders and for a robbery committed during the murders in which money was taken. He requested a lawyer during custodial interrogation. He was taken to the jail area to have his clothing collected as evidence. When instructed to empty his pockets, the defendant placed thirteen dollars on a bench. Officer A asked Officer B "if it was okay for [the defendant] to keep the money." Officer B turned toward the defendant and saw some money in the defendant's top pocket. Before Officer B could say anything, the defendant said, "I had some of my own money, too, now." The court ruled, relying on Rhode Island v. Innis, 446 U.S. 291, 100 S. Ct. 1682, 64 L. Ed. 2d 297 (1980), that the defendant's

answer was not the result of interrogation. The question by Officer A was directed toward Officer B. Furthermore, the defendant made his statement during a general conversation while turning over his clothing and property in exchange for an inmate jumpsuit. The officer's question was not an initiation of questioning in violation of the defendant's assertion of the right to counsel, because the question was not reasonably likely to elicit an incriminating response from the defendant.

State v. Coffey
345 N.C. 389, 480 S.E.2d 664 (1997)

The defendant was arrested for murder, and two attorneys were appointed to represent him. The attorneys asked the district attorney that a polygraph examination be conducted on the defendant. The attorneys did not express any desire to accompany their client to the polygraph site. When the defendant was being removed from his cell to be taken to the polygraph examination, he told a deputy sheriff that he wanted to call his attorney. The deputy declined to allow the defendant to do so, because the policy of the sheriff's office did not permit a prisoner to make a telephone call while being transported from one facility to another. Later, when the polygraph operator was explaining the polygraph procedures to the defendant, the defendant stated that he did not tell the investigating officers the truth about the money taken from the murder victim. The operator asked him what he did not tell the truth about. The defendant said that his accomplice handed him the money and "went off." The operator did not ask any questions; instead, he conducted the polygraph examination. After the examination, the operator informed the defendant that he had not passed the polygraph about the murder and robbery. The defendant then made an incriminating statement. The operator then asked the defendant if he would be willing to talk to one of the investigating officers. The defendant named a particular officer and later repeated the same incriminating statement to that officer. The court ruled that the defendant was not being interrogated in violation of Edwards v. Arizona, 451 U.S. 477, 101 S. Ct. 1880, 68 L. Ed. 2d 378 (1981) (interrogation is not permitted after defendant has asserted right to counsel), when he made his statements to the polygraph operator and the investigating officer. These statements were volunteered by the defendant. Thus neither his Fifth nor Sixth Amendment rights to counsel were violated. The court alternatively ruled, assuming that the defendant was being interrogated, that the defendant initiated the communication with the polygraph operator and investigating officer. *See, e.g.*, Oregon v. Bradshaw, 462 U.S. 1039, 103 S. Ct. 2830, 77 L. Ed. 2d 405 (1983).

State v. Jones
112 N.C. App. 337, 435 S.E.2d 574 (1993)

The defendant was arrested for breaking and entering and larceny about 1:05 P.M. and taken to the police department. He waived his *Miranda* rights and talked to officers for a while and then asserted his right to counsel. The officers stopped the interrogation and left the defendant in the interrogation room until about 7:00 P.M., when they obtained a search warrant for his apartment. The officers took the defendant with them to execute the search warrant. The defendant and an officer had a general conversation there, including the officer's responding to the defendant's request for a cigarette (the trial judge found that the conversation was not calculated to induce the defendant to make incriminating statements, and the defendant made none). The defendant's live-in girlfriend became upset during the officers' questioning of her about which items in the apartment were hers. The defendant decided then to initiate a conversation with the officers, so they would not bother her about these items. The defendant then showed the officers which items were stolen. When the officers took him back to the police station, the defendant was advised of his *Miranda* rights; he waived those rights and confessed. The court ruled, following Rhode Island v. Innis, 446 U.S. 291, 100 S. Ct. 1682, 64 L. Ed. 2d 297 (1980), that the evidence did not show that the officers should have known that their actions (taking the defendant for execution of the search warrant, the reaction of his girlfriend to the officers' questioning, the defendant's reaction, etc.) would elicit an incriminating response.

State v. Garcia-Lorenzo
110 N.C. App. 319, 430 S.E.2d 290 (1993)

The defendant was involved in a vehicular accident with bystanders, ran off the road, and was injured. Officers transported the defendant to a hospital, where the officers and doctors had to restrain him because he became violent. Because an officer wanted to know whether to look for other victims of the accident, the officer and then the doctor asked the defendant whether he was alone in the car. The defendant responded several times, "No, alone." The court affirmed the trial judge's conclusions of law that this questioning was permissible because (1) it was within *Miranda*'s public-safety exception, recognized in New York v. Quarles, 467 U.S. 649, 104 S. Ct. 2626, 81 L. Ed. 2d 550 (1984), because officers were concerned that someone else may have been injured and lying undiscovered at the scene, and (2) defendant was not subjected to *interrogation* as defined in Rhode Island v. Innis, 446 U.S. 291, 100 S. Ct. 1682, 64 L. Ed. 2d 297 (1980).

Volunteered Statements [page 386]

State v. Lambert
341 N.C. 36, 460 S.E.2d 123 (1995)

The defendant was in jail and requested that an officer come to speak to her. After the defendant spoke with her father, she approached the officer and told him that she had "blacked out" and could not remember anything. The court ruled that her statement was admissible under *Miranda* because (1) it was not made as a result of interrogation, and (2) it was not an invocation of the right to silence (her specific request to speak to the officer and this statement indicated a desire *not* to remain silent).

State v. Walls
342 N.C. 1, 463 S.E.2d 738 (1995), *cert. denied*, 116 S. Ct. 1694 (1996)

The defendant was arrested, orally informed of his *Miranda* rights, and orally waived them. At the sheriff's department, a detective took the defendant to the fingerprinting room and asked him if he remembered his rights; the defendant said he did. Nevertheless, the detective read him his *Miranda* rights again, provided him with a written copy, and obtained a written waiver. After being told of the crimes (two assaults) with which he was charged, he denied any knowledge of them and signed a writing that he no longer wished to make a statement. The detective did not ask any questions and began to fingerprint him. When he took the defendant's right hand, the defendant exclaimed, "Ouch, take it easy." The detective noticed that the defendant's hand was badly swollen and cut, so he asked him, "What happened to your hand?" The defendant answered, "I hit an oak tree." The detective asked, "[W]hat did you hit a tree for? A tree had never hurt anybody." The defendant replied, "I should have hit her a little harder so I could really hurt my hand." The court ruled that the defendant's remarks were volunteered statements, and the detective's questions did not convert the conversation into an interrogation under *Miranda*.

State v. Coffey
345 N.C. 389, 480 S.E.2d 664 (1997)

The defendant was arrested for murder, and two attorneys were appointed to represent him. The attorneys asked the district attorney that a polygraph examination be conducted on the defendant. The attorneys did not express any desire to accompany their client to the polygraph site. When the defendant was being removed from his cell to be taken to the polygraph examination, he told a deputy sheriff that he wanted to call his attorney. The deputy declined to allow the defendant to do so, because the policy of the sheriff's office did not permit a prisoner to make a telephone call while being transported from one facility to another. Later, when the polygraph operator was explaining the polygraph procedures to the defendant, the defendant stated that he did not tell the investigating officers the truth about the money taken from the murder victim. The operator asked him what he did not tell the truth about. The defendant said that his accomplice handed him the money and "went off." The operator did not ask any questions; instead he conducted the polygraph examination. After the examination, the operator informed the defendant that he had not passed the polygraph about the murder and robbery. The defendant then made an incriminating statement. The operator then asked the defendant if he would be willing to talk to one of the investigating officers. The defendant named a particular officer and later repeated the same incriminating statement to that officer. The court ruled that the defendant was not being interrogated in violation of Edwards v. Arizona, 451 U.S. 477, 101 S. Ct. 1880, 68 L. Ed. 2d 378 (1981) (interrogation is not permitted after defendant has asserted right to counsel), when he made his statements to the polygraph operator and the investigating officer. These statements were volunteered by the defendant. Thus neither his Fifth nor Sixth Amendment rights to counsel were violated. The court alternatively ruled, assuming that the defendant was being interrogated, that the defendant initiated the communication with the polygraph operator and investigating officer. See, e.g., Oregon v. Bradshaw, 462 U.S. 1039, 103 S. Ct. 2830, 77 L. Ed. 2d 405 (1983).

State v. Dukes
110 N.C. App. 695, 431 S.E.2d 209 (1993)

Officer Moore arrived at a trailer park to investigate the murder of the defendant's wife. Both the defendant and a baby he was holding (outside the trailer where the body was located) had blood on their clothing. The defendant gave an exculpatory statement to the officer. Officer Moore accompanied the defendant and the baby to the defendant's trailer (the defendant lived in a different trailer from his wife). Officer Moore instructed Officer Thompson to guard the defendant, not allow him to leave his trailer, not allow any other person to enter the trailer, and not allow the defendant to wash or change his clothes. Officer Thompson allowed the defendant to make telephone calls after he asked permission from the officer to do so. Officer Thompson accompanied the defendant to the bathroom to ensure that the defendant did not wash or change his clothes. Officer Thompson later asked the defendant, "Do you know what happened?" (1) The court ruled that, while at his trailer with Officer Thompson, the defendant was

in custody to require *Miranda* warnings—a reasonable person, knowing that his wife had just been killed, kept under constant police supervision, told not to wash or change his clothing, and never informed that he was free to leave his own home, would not feel free to get up and go. The court also ruled that the officer's question constituted interrogation under the *Miranda* ruling. (2) The defendant was later arrested and taken to a law enforcement center. While the officer was advising the defendant of his *Miranda* rights, the defendant said, "I stabbed her." The court ruled that this statement was voluntary and not the result of custodial interrogation.

Adequacy of *Miranda* Warnings

Necessity to Repeat Warnings [page 387]

State v. Harris
338 N.C. 129, 449 S.E.2d 371 (1994), *cert. denied*, 115 S. Ct. 1833 (1995)

North Carolina law enforcement officers went to Georgia to return the defendant to North Carolina for a first-degree murder charge pending in North Carolina. After properly being advised of his *Miranda* rights, the defendant asserted his right to counsel. No interrogation was conducted. After his return to North Carolina twelve hours later, the defendant asked, through his brother (who was visiting the defendant in jail), to talk to the sheriff. The court ruled that (1) the defendant initiated communication with the sheriff by telling his brother to inform the sheriff that he wanted to speak with him; and (2) the sheriff was not required to give *Miranda* warnings again before interrogating the defendant, based on the facts in this case; *see generally* State v. McZorn, 288 N.C. 417, 219 S.E.2d 201 (1975). The court stated that there was no reason to believe that the defendant, having been properly advised of his *Miranda* rights twelve hours earlier, had forgotten them. For example, he should have known of his right to an attorney, because he had exercised that right twelve hours earlier.

State v. Flowers
121 N.C. App. 299, 465 S.E.2d 70, *appeal dismissed and review denied*, 343 N.C. 125, 468 S.E.2d 788 (1996)

The defendant was not entitled to a repetition of *Miranda* warnings when the evidence showed that (1) she was properly advised of and waived her *Miranda* rights at about 7:38 P.M., (2) she repeated her confession while being tape-recorded at 8:30 P.M. that same night while affirming she had been advised of her constitutional rights, and (3) the next morning at 10:02 A.M. she read and signed a transcript of her recorded statement, affirming her transcript to be her entire statement. The court ruled that initial *Miranda* warnings were not stale at the time of her later confession the same evening or the affirmation of the transcript the next morning.

Guam v. Dela Pena
72 F.3d 767 (9th Cir. 1995)

The court ruled that statements made by a defendant during custodial interrogation are not inadmissible simply because officers failed to repeat *Miranda* warnings previously given to the defendant when he was not in custody. In this case, officers gave *Miranda* warnings to the defendant when he was not in custody. Fifteen hours later, the officers reminded him of their earlier *Miranda* warnings before questioning him while he was in custody. Based on these and other facts, the court ruled that the defendant had properly received his *Miranda* warnings.

Assertion and Waiver of *Miranda* Rights

Generally [page 388]

State v. McKoy
332 N.C. 639, 422 S.E.2d 713 (1992)

An in-custody defendant indicated to officers that he wanted to waive his *Miranda* rights. The defendant was given a waiver form, but he signed at the place on the form that indicated that he did *not* waive his rights. The officers then asked the defendant whether he had made a mistake. The defendant indicated that he still desired to answer questions and did not want a lawyer, and he scratched his signature from the form and signed in the appropriate place to waive his rights. The court ruled that officers properly may ask questions to clarify the apparently mistaken way in which the defendant answered their questions.

State v. Williams
334 N.C. 440, 434 S.E.2d 588 (1993), *vacated on other grounds*, 511 U.S. 1001 (1994)

An officer gave *Miranda* warnings to the defendant. The defendant responded, "Yes," when the officer asked him if he understood his rights. The defendant remained silent when the officer asked the defendant, first, whether he wished to waive his right to remain silent and, second, whether he wished to waive his right to have counsel present during questioning. Soon thereafter, someone else asked the defendant whether anything in the room belonged to him. The defendant responded that he owned the boxes. An officer then asked if he would consent to a search of the boxes, to which the defendant responded, "Yes." Relying on North Carolina v. Butler, 441

U.S. 369, 99 S. Ct. 1755, 60 L. Ed. 2d 286 (1979), the court ruled that the defendant properly waived his rights. The court noted that although the defendant remained silent when asked if he would waive his rights, he had previously affirmatively stated that he understood his rights. He appeared coherent then and capable of understanding his rights. Also, the officers did not pressure him in any way to answer their questions. Thus the defendant impliedly waived his rights to remain silent and to counsel by answering the officers' questions after expressly acknowledging that he understood his right not to do so in the absence of counsel.

State v. Mlo
335 N.C. 353, 440 S.E.2d 98, *cert. denied*, 512 U.S. 1224 (1994)

A detective anticipated potential language difficulties in questioning the defendant. Believing that the defendant spoke Vietnamese, the detective obtained a Vietnamese interpreter. However, the defendant, a native of Vietnam's Montagnard region, spoke Dega as well as some English and Vietnamese. On those occasions when the interpreter assisted the defendant, the defendant was able to continue the interview in English and gave logical responses to the questions asked. During the interview, the defendant appeared to understand the questions and responded most of the time in English without the interpreter's assistance. The court upheld the trial judge's ruling that the defendant knowingly, intelligently, and voluntarily waived his *Miranda* rights.

State v. Brown
339 N.C. 606, 453 S.E.2d 165 (1995)

The court affirmed, per curiam and without an opinion, a ruling by the court of appeals, 112 N.C. App. 390, 436 S.E.2d 163 (1993), that a mentally retarded fifteen-year-old defendant knowingly and intelligently waived his *Miranda* and juvenile rights. The court of appeals' opinion followed the ruling in State v. Fincher, 309 N.C. 1, 305 S.E.2d 665 (1983).

State v. Daniels
337 N.C. 243, 446 S.E.2d 298 (1994), *cert. denied*, 115 S. Ct. 953 (1995)

During a suppression hearing challenging the defendant's mental capacity to waive his *Miranda* rights, the defense called a law enforcement officer who observed the defendant immediately after the defendant's interrogation by other officers. The defense asked the officer whether the defendant "could have waived" his *Miranda* rights and whether the defendant understood the *Miranda* waiver form. The court ruled that the trial judge properly sustained the state's objections to these questions, since they called for a legal conclusion whether the defendant had the capacity to waive his rights. The court noted that the defense did not ask whether the defendant had the capacity to understand keys words used, such as "right," "attorney," "waiver," and so forth (implying that such questions would be permissible).

Assertion of the Right to Remain Silent [page 389]

State v. Lambert
341 N.C. 36, 460 S.E.2d 123 (1995)

The defendant was in jail and requested that an officer come to speak to her. After the defendant spoke with her father, she approached the officer and told him that she had "blacked out" and could not remember anything. The court ruled that her statement was admissible under *Miranda* because (1) it was not made as a result of interrogation, and (2) it was not an invocation of the right to silence (her specific request to speak to the officer and this statement indicated a desire *not* to remain silent).

State v. Murphy
342 N.C. 813, 467 S.E.2d 428 (1996)

The defendant, a murder suspect, was in custody on other charges. Officers gave him *Miranda* warnings, and he waived his rights. After he talked about some other matters, the officers informed him he was going to be charged with murder. The defendant twice denied any knowledge of the killing. When one officer indicated a willingness to stay and continue talking, the defendant stood up and said, "I got nothing to say." The officers stopped their interrogation, charged him with murder, and began the booking process. During the booking process, an officer (without readvising the defendant of his *Miranda* rights) encouraged the defendant to "tell the truth" about the murder so the "bad feeling in his stomach" would go away. The defendant responded, "Man, you know the position I'm in, I can't tell you about it." This statement was made about fifteen minutes after the initial interrogation, which had ended when the defendant had advised the officers that he had nothing to say. The court ruled: (1) the defendant's conduct, in abruptly standing up, combined with his unambiguous statement, "I got nothing to say," was an invocation of the right to remain silent, based on the facts in this case; (2) relying on Michigan v. Mosley, 423 U.S. 96, 96 S. Ct. 321, 46 L. Ed. 2d 313 (1975), a defendant's assertion of the right to remain silent permits reinterrogation (unlike the assertion of the right to counsel) if officers "scrupulously honor" the assertion—that is, the officers immediately stop questioning and do not attempt reinterrogation until a significant period of time has elapsed; (3) distinguishing *Mosley*, the officer in this case did not scrupulously honor the

defendant's assertion of the right to remain silent because the officer initiated conversation with the defendant about the same subject matter fifteen minutes after the assertion; and (4) a readvisement of *Miranda* rights is not a prerequisite to reinterrogation under the *Mosley* ruling—it is but one factor in determining if the defendant's rights had been "scrupulously honored." The defendant's statement was ordered suppressed because of the ruling in (3) above.

State v. Walls
342 N.C. 1, 463 S.E.2d 738 (1995), *cert. denied*, 116 S. Ct. 1694 (1996)

The defendant was arrested, was orally informed of his *Miranda* rights, and orally waived them. At the sheriff's department, a detective took the defendant to the fingerprinting room and asked him if he remembered his rights; the defendant said he did. Nevertheless, the detective read him his *Miranda* rights again, provided him with a written copy, and obtained a written waiver. After being told of the crimes (two assaults) for which he was charged, he denied any knowledge of them and signed a statement saying that he no longer wished to make a statement. The detective did not ask any questions and began to fingerprint him. When he took the defendant's right hand, the defendant exclaimed, "Ouch, take it easy." The detective noticed that the defendant's hand was badly swollen and cut, so he asked him, "What happened to your hand?" The defendant answered, "I hit an oak tree." The detective asked, "[W]hat did you hit a tree for? A tree had never hurt anybody." The defendant replied, "I should have hit her a little harder so I could really hurt my hand." The court ruled that the defendant's remarks were volunteered statements, and the detective's questions did not convert the conversation into an interrogation under *Miranda*.

Coleman v. Singletary
30 F.3d 1420 (11th Cir. 1994), *cert. denied*, 115 S. Ct. 1801 (1995)

Relying on the ruling in Davis v. United States, 512 U.S. 452, 114 S. Ct. 2350, 129 L. Ed. 2d 362 (1994), discussed below on page 105, the court ruled that the defendant made an equivocal assertion of the right to remain silent and therefore the officers had no duty to clarify the defendant's intent and could proceed with their interrogation. The court stated that a reasonable officer could interpret the defendant's words to mean that he did not know whether he wanted to stop talking. *See also* United States v. Mikell, 102 F.3d 470 (11th Cir. 1996) (refusal to answer some questions was not unequivocal assertion of right to remain silent).

Hatley v. Lockhart
990 F.2d 1070 (8th Cir. 1993)
The court ruled, based on the facts in this case, that an officer's questioning of the defendant about two hours after his assertion of the right to remain silent was permissible.

Assertion of the Right to Counsel [page 390]

Davis v. United States
512 U.S. 452, 114 S. Ct. 2350, 129 L. Ed. 2d 362 (1994)
Investigators gave the in-custody defendant *Miranda* warnings and received a proper waiver of his rights. About an hour and a half into the interrogation, the defendant said, "Maybe I should talk to a lawyer." The investigators told the defendant that they did not want to violate his rights, that if he wanted a lawyer then they would stop questioning him, and that they would not pursue the matter unless it was clarified whether he was asking for a lawyer or was just making a comment about a lawyer. The defendant said, "No, I'm not asking for a lawyer," and continued on, and said, "No, I don't want a lawyer." After a short break, the investigators reminded the defendant of his rights to remain silent and to counsel. The defendant then made incriminating statements that he later sought to suppress at trial, arguing that the investigators violated the ruling in Edwards v. Arizona, 384 U.S. 436, 101 S. Ct. 1880, 68 L. Ed. 2d 378 (1981) (officers must immediately stop interrogation if the suspect has clearly asserted the right to counsel).

The Court reviewed its prior rulings and stated that the determination of whether a defendant actually invoked the right to counsel is an objective one. That is, the invocation of the right to counsel requires some statement that can reasonably be construed to be an expression of the desire for the assistance of counsel. The Court ruled that if a defendant makes a reference to an attorney that is ambiguous or equivocal so a reasonable officer under the circumstances would have understood only that the defendant *might* be invoking the right to counsel, the officer is not required to stop the interrogation—rather, the defendant must unambiguously request counsel. The Court specifically rejected a requirement that an officer must stop interrogation immediately when a defendant makes an ambiguous or equivocal request for counsel. [Note: It is unclear whether the Court's ruling applies only when a defendant makes an ambiguous or equivocal request for counsel during custodial interrogation *after* proper *Miranda* warnings have been given and a waiver of rights has been obtained. If a defendant makes an ambiguous or equivocal request for counsel when the officer is giving *Miranda* warnings or obtaining a waiver of rights, the officer should clarify whether or not the defen-

dant wants a lawyer, because the state has the burden of proving that the defendant waived his or her rights, including the right to counsel.]

The Court noted that when a defendant makes an ambiguous or equivocal request for counsel, it often will be good law enforcement practice for officers to clarify whether or not the defendant wants a lawyer. Clarifying questions protect the rights of the defendant by ensuring that the defendant gets a lawyer if he or she wants one and will minimize the risk of a confession being suppressed by later judicial second-guessing of the meaning of the defendant's statement about counsel. But the Court reiterated that if the defendant's statement is not an unambiguous or unequivocal request for counsel, officers are not obligated to stop questioning the defendant.

The Court upheld the lower court ruling that the defendant's remark to the officers in this case, "Maybe I should talk to a lawyer," was not a request for counsel. Therefore the officers were not required to stop questioning the defendant.

[Note: The Court's ruling now casts doubt on the validity of a ruling in State v. Torres, 330 N.C. 517, 412 S.E.2d 20 (1992), discussed in the second edition on pages 392–93, that the defendant unequivocally invoked her right to counsel when she asked law enforcement officers whether she needed a lawyer.]

State v. Morris
332 N.C. 600, 422 S.E.2d 578 (1992)
An officer advised an in-custody defendant of his *Miranda* rights and asked him if he would like to waive his right to counsel. The defendant responded, "I don't know." The officer then asked him if he would sign a waiver-of-counsel form. The defendant responded, "No, because I don't know how much I want to tell you." The court ruled that the defendant invoked his right to counsel when he refused to sign the waiver form. The court stated that the defendant's statement was negative because, without the assistance of counsel, he did not know his legal rights and—until he did—he could not know how much he was willing to say.

State v. Pope
333 N.C. 106, 423 S.E.2d 740 (1992)
The defendant invoked his right to counsel on two occasions: (1) on September 17, 1987, when he told a detective that he did not want to answer any questions then but that he might be willing to make a statement after he talked with a lawyer; and (2) on October 2, 1987, when he told a detective that he did not want to talk until he conferred with an attorney. The court ruled that, based on the facts in this case, the detectives later improperly

initiated interrogation about unrelated crimes (the defendant had remained in continuous custody after his assertions for counsel) in violation of the ruling in Arizona v. Roberson, 486 U.S. 675, 108 S. Ct. 2093, 100 L. Ed. 2d 704 (1988).

State v. Daughtry

340 N.C. 488, 459 S.E.2d 747 (1995), *cert. denied*, 116 S. Ct. 789 (1996)

The defendant voluntarily went with two officers to the police station to be questioned about a murder. The officers advised the defendant that he was not under arrest and could leave at any time. One officer advised the defendant of his *Miranda* rights as a precaution. The defendant waived those rights. After some conversation between the officers and the defendant, the defendant said, "I think I need to speak to a lawyer." One officer handed the defendant the telephone directory opened to the yellow pages with attorney listings. As he did so, the officer told the defendant that he could talk to a lawyer and continue to talk to the officers if he wished. The defendant briefly looked at the yellow pages and then told the officers that he was willing to talk to the officers. One officer reminded the defendant of his rights to remain silent and to an attorney; the defendant indicated that he understood his rights. The defendant had not been placed under arrest. He then confessed. The court ruled that because the defendant was not in custody when he requested an attorney, his rights under *Miranda* and Edwards v. Arizona, 451 U.S. 477, 101 S. Ct. 1880, 68 L. Ed. 2d 378 (1981), were inapplicable. Therefore the court did not need to decide whether the trial judge had erred in concluding that the defendant had voluntarily reinitiated interrogation after requesting an attorney.

State v. Medlin

333 N.C. 280, 426 S.E.2d 402 (1993)

Atlantic Beach officers arrested the defendant in a breezeway outside a motel room in Atlantic Beach for a murder and robbery committed in Wake County, based on the mistaken belief that an arrest warrant had been issued in Wake County for these offenses. The court determined, however, that the Atlantic Beach officers had sufficient information to establish probable cause to arrest, based on the facts in this case. Therefore the warrantless arrest was proper. When the Atlantic Beach officers learned that there were no arrest warrants for the defendant after they had brought him to the police station, they told him that he was not under arrest and was free to leave. They also told him that investigators were coming from Wake County and wanted to talk to him, that he could stay and move around the police station at

will, and that he should let them know if he needed anything. The defendant indicated that he wanted to stay, and in fact remained there and later gave statements to the officers. Based on these and other facts, the court concluded that the defendant was no longer in custody and thus was not entitled to *Miranda* rights, including the right to counsel under Edwards v. Arizona, 451 U.S. 477, 101 S. Ct. 1880, 68 L. Ed. 2d 378 (1981). Therefore the court ruled that it was unnecessary to decide whether the defendant properly waived his right to counsel.

State v. Barber

335 N.C. 120, 436 S.E.2d 106 (1993), *cert. denied*, 512 U.S. 1239 (1994)

A fire occurred at a home in which the fifteen-year-old defendant and her grandparents lived. Both grandparents died as a result of the fire. The court assumed without deciding that the defendant was in custody when she was given *Miranda* and juvenile warnings in the sheriff's office hours after the fire, then ruled—distinguishing State v. Torres, 330 N.C. 517, 412 S.E.2d 20 (1992)—that the defendant did not assert her Fifth Amendment right to counsel when she asked an officer (during his recitation of the warnings) if she needed a lawyer. The defendant's inquiry constituted an ambiguous or equivocal invocation of her right to counsel. The officer's response—that he could not advise her whether she needed a lawyer or not, but that he was merely advising her about her right to a lawyer—was a proper narrow response to clarify her intent. Immediately thereafter, her specific affirmative waiver of her rights (including whether she wished to answer questions without a lawyer, parents, guardian, or custodian present) demonstrated that she had not invoked her right to counsel when she asked the officer if she needed a lawyer. *See also* State v. Marion, 126 N.C. App. 58, 483 S.E.2d 447 (1997) (defendant did not assert right to counsel when he told officer that his attorney had told him not to turn himself in).

State v. Davis

124 N.C. App. 93, 476 S.E.2d 453 (1996)

The defendant was given his *Miranda* warnings and properly waived them. Before questioning began, the defendant requested and was allowed to make a phone call. After the phone call, the defendant told a law enforcement officer that "somebody at [his] office told [him he] needed a lawyer." The officer responded, "Well, that's your decision." The defendant then asked, "Do I need a lawyer?" and the officer replied, "That is your decision; I can't make that decision for you." The defendant did not respond and followed the officer into an office to be questioned. He eventually confessed. The court ruled, relying on State v. Barber, 335 N.C. 120, 436 S.E.2d 106 (1993), *cert. denied*, 114 S. Ct. 2747 (1994), discussed above, that the defendant did not invoke his right to counsel based on the facts in this case. *See also* Diaz v. Senkowski, 76 F.3d 61 (2d Cir. 1996) ("Do you think I need a lawyer?" was not clear assertion of right to counsel).

State v. Gibbs
335 N.C. 1, 436 S.E.2d 321 (1993), *cert. denied*, 512 U.S. 1246 (1994)

On May 31, 1990, the defendant was in custody at a police department as a murder suspect. He had not yet been given *Miranda* warnings or interrogated. About fifteen minutes before being taken to the magistrate's office for service of arrest warrants charging him with murder and other offenses, the defendant asked Officer Batchelor if he had to get an attorney (the defendant's inquiry was not in response to questions by the officer). Batchelor told the defendant that the question of a lawyer had to be his decision and asked the defendant if he could afford to hire an attorney. The defendant said he could not, and Batchelor then told him that the court would appoint an attorney to represent him if he asked for one. About an hour later, Batchelor and another officer gave the defendant *Miranda* warnings, properly obtained a waiver, and took a statement from the defendant. The officers obtained another statement from the defendant on June 3, 1990. The defendant had a first appearance in district court on June 4, 1990, which was within 96 hours of his arrest [as required under G.S. 15A-601(c)]. (1) Distinguishing State v. Torres, 330 N.C. 517, 412 S.E.2d 20 (1992), the court ruled that the defendant did not assert his Fifth Amendment right to counsel when he asked Officer Batchelor if he had to get an attorney. In this case, unlike *Torres*, interrogation was not impending and the defendant had not been told he would be questioned. Batchelor's responses to the defendant's question about an attorney constituted narrow clarification, and the defendant did not ask for an attorney afterwards. Moreover, Batchelor did not attempt to dissuade the defendant from exercising his right to an attorney. Based on the entire context in which the defendant's inquiry was made, the defendant did not assert his right to counsel. (2) The court, following State v. Detter, 298 N.C. 604, 260 S.E.2d 567 (1979), State v. Nations, 319 N.C. 318, 354 S.E.2d 510 (1987), and State v. Tucker, 331 N.C. 12, 414 S.E.2d 548 (1992), ruled that the defendant's Sixth Amendment right to counsel did not attach when the defendant was arrested. It did not attach until the defendant's first appearance in district court. Therefore the defendant did not have a Sixth Amendment right to counsel during the interrogations on May 31, 1990, and June 3, 1990.

State v. Harris
338 N.C. 129, 449 S.E.2d 371 (1994), *cert. denied*, 115 S. Ct. 1833 (1995)

North Carolina law enforcement officers went to Georgia to return the defendant to North Carolina for a first-degree murder charge pending in North Carolina. After properly being advised of his *Miranda* rights, the defendant asserted his right to counsel. No interrogation was conducted. After his return to North Carolina twelve hours later, the defendant asked, through his brother (who was visiting the defendant in jail), to talk to the sheriff. The court ruled that (1) the defendant initiated communication with the sheriff by telling his brother to inform the sheriff that he wanted to speak with him; and (2) the sheriff was not required to give *Miranda* warnings again before interrogating the defendant, based on the facts in this case; *see generally* State v. McZorn, 288 N.C. 417, 219 S.E.2d 201 (1975). The court stated that there was no reason to believe that the defendant, having been properly advised of his *Miranda* rights twelve hours earlier, had forgotten them. For example, he should have known of his right to an attorney, because he had exercised that right twelve hours earlier.

State v. Munsey
342 N.C. 882, 467 S.E.2d 425 (1996)

After the defendant had been arrested and given *Miranda* warnings, he told officers that he would like to have a lawyer. At the defendant's request, an officer called a particular lawyer but was unable to reach him. The defendant then asked the officer to call his brother and said "that would do instead of" the lawyer. In response to an officer's telephone call, the defendant's brother came to the law enforcement office where the defendant was located and conferred in private with him for about fifteen to twenty minutes. After the defendant's brother left, the officers went into the office and asked the defendant if he was ready to talk to them now. The defendant answered affirmatively. The officers then questioned the defendant and obtained a statement. The court ruled that this evidence showed that the defendant did not initiate the conversation with officers after his brother left, and therefore the officers' questioning violated the ruling in Edwards v. Arizona, 451 U.S. 477, 101 S. Ct. 1880, 68 L. Ed. 2d 378 (1981).

State v. Coffey
345 N.C. 389, 480 S.E.2d 664 (1997)

The defendant was arrested for murder, and two attorneys were appointed to represent him. The attorneys asked the district attorney that a polygraph examination be conducted on the defendant. The attorneys did not express any desire to accompany their client to the polygraph site. When the defendant was being removed from his cell to be taken to the polygraph examination, he told a deputy sheriff that he wanted to call his attorney. The deputy declined to allow the defendant to do so, because the policy of the sheriff's office did not permit a prisoner to make a telephone call while being transported from one facility to another. Later, when the polygraph operator was explaining the polygraph procedures to the defendant, the defendant stated that he did not tell the investigating officers the truth about the money taken from the murder victim. The operator asked him what he did not tell the truth about. The defendant said that his accomplice handed him the money and "went off." The operator did not ask any questions; instead, he conducted the polygraph examination. After the examination, the operator informed the defendant that he had not passed the polygraph about the murder and robbery. The defendant then made an incriminating statement. The operator then asked the defendant if he would be willing to talk to one of the investigating officers. The defendant named a particular officer and later repeated the same incriminating statement to that officer. The court ruled that the defendant was not being interrogated in violation of Edwards v. Arizona, 451 U.S. 477, 101 S. Ct. 1880, 68 L. Ed. 2d 378 (1981) (interrogation is not permitted after defendant has asserted right to counsel) when he made his statements to the polygraph operator and the investigating officer. These statements were volunteered by the defendant. Thus neither his Fifth nor Sixth Amendment rights to counsel were violated. The court alternatively ruled, assuming that the defendant was being interrogated, that the defendant initiated the communication with the polygraph operator and investigating officer. *See, e.g.,* Oregon v. Bradshaw, 462 U.S. 1039, 103 S. Ct. 2830, 77 L. Ed. 2d 405 (1983).

State v. Gibson
342 N.C. 142, 463 S.E.2d 193 (1995)

Officers who were investigating a homicide properly gave a fifteen-year-old his juvenile custodial interrogation rights under G.S. 7A-595(a) and obtained a waiver of those rights. The juvenile argued on appeal that his waiver of rights was involuntary as a matter of law because the officers did not inform the juvenile that his parents and attorney were at the police station during the time of the interrogation. The court, relying on Moran v. Burbine, 475 U.S. 412, 106 S. Ct. 1135, 89 L. Ed. 2d 410 (1986), and State v. Reese, 319 N.C. 110, 353 S.E.2d 352 (1987), rejected the defendant's argument. The court stated that law enforcement officers are not required to inform a juvenile that his parents or attorney are present

before taking a voluntary confession, and the failure to do so does not make the juvenile's confession involuntary as a matter of law or otherwise inadmissible. [Note: This ruling would not apply to a juvenile under fourteen, because such a juvenile's parent, guardian, custodian, or attorney must be present during custodial interrogation.]

State v. Willis
109 N.C. App. 184, 426 S.E.2d 471, *review denied*, 333 N.C. 795, 431 S.E.2d 29 (1993)

The defendant did not validly assert a Fifth Amendment violation when he requested counsel during an interview with law enforcement officers, because he was not in custody when he requested counsel.

State v. Easterling
119 N.C. App. 22, 457 S.E.2d 913, *review denied*, 341 N.C. 422, 461 S.E.2d 762 (1995)

(Note: To better understand the summary of this appellate case, be aware that the defendant was tried and convicted of multiple counts of rape and sexual offense that he committed with his accomplice, Sherman White.) After a detective gave the defendant his *Miranda* warnings, the defendant asserted his right to counsel. The detective later informed the defendant that he would be taken to the magistrate's office to be served with arrest warrants. The detective then asked, "Who was Sherman?" The defendant said, "White." Just a few moments later the defendant indicated that he wanted to talk about the case. The detective then gave him *Miranda* warnings and obtained a waiver, and the defendant gave an incriminating statement that was introduced in the state's case-in-chief at trial. The court ruled that the detective's question constituted interrogation because it was designed to elicit an incriminating response. Therefore the question was improper under Edwards v. Arizona, 384 U.S. 436, 101 S. Ct. 1880, 68 L. Ed. 2d 378 (1981), because it was made after the defendant's assertion of his right to counsel. In addition, the defendant's statement a few moments later that he was willing to talk about the case was a continuation of the improper interrogation (that is, it was not simply the defendant's initiation of communication with the detective). Thus the trial judge erred in admitting the defendant's confession. The court also ruled that, based on the state's overwhelming evidence against the defendant in this case, the defendant was not induced to testify on his behalf because of the introduction in the state's case-in-chief of this illegally obtained confession; *see generally* Harrison v. United States, 392 U.S. 219, 88 S. Ct. 2008, 20 L. Ed. 2d 1047 (1968). The court also ruled that the introduction of the confession was harmless error beyond a reasonable doubt.

United States v. Cheely

36 F.3d 1439 (9th Cir. 1994)

The defendant unequivocally asserted his right to counsel when he refused to sign a written waiver of *Miranda* rights, explaining to the officers that his attorney did not want him to talk to them.

Ledbetter v. Edwards

35 F.3d 1062 (6th Cir. 1994), *cert. denied*, 115 S. Ct. 2584 (1995)

When the defendant was informed of his *Miranda* warnings for a third time, immediately before giving a recorded confession, he indicated that "it would be nice" to have an attorney present. The court ruled that his statement was not an unequivocal assertion of his right to counsel. *See also* Lord v. Duckworth, 29 F.3d 1216 (7th Cir. 1994) (defendant's statement during questioning that "I can't afford a lawyer but is there any way I can get one?" was not an unequivocal assertion of his right to counsel).

Alston v. Redman

34 F.3d 1237 (3d Cir. 1994), *cert. denied*, 115 S. Ct. 1122 (1995)

The defendant was arrested for several robberies, waived his *Miranda* rights and confessed to the robberies, and was committed to a detention facility. He signed a letter, prepared by the public defender's office, that he did not want to speak with law enforcement officers without a public defender being present. Several days later officers questioned him again about the robberies. The court ruled that the defendant's signed letter was an insufficient invocation of his right to counsel because it was not made during custodial interrogation; that is, he was not being interrogated and interrogation was not imminent when he signed the letter. The court's ruling relied on dicta in note three of the majority opinion in McNeil v. Wisconsin, 501 U.S. 171, 111 S. Ct. 2204, 115 L. Ed. 2d 158 (1991). *See also* United States v. LaGrone, 43 F.3d 332 (7th Cir. 1994).

Use of a Defendant's Silence as Evidence

[page 396]

State v. Carter

335 N.C. 422, 440 S.E.2d 268 (1994)

A detective was permitted to testify that, in the police department's interrogation room, he advised the defendant of his *Miranda* rights and the defendant indicated he understood those rights. The court ruled that the testimony (1) did not violate Doyle v. Ohio, 426 U.S. 610, 96 S. Ct. 2240, 49 L. Ed. 2d 91 (1976), because no evidence was introduced showing that the defendant exercised his right to remain silent; and (2) was relevant in this case

because defense counsel consistently throughout the trial had attacked the professionalism of the investigating officers, and the testimony tended to refute the characterization of the officers' conduct as unprofessional.

State v. Quick

337 N.C. 359, 446 S.E.2d 535 (1994)

Five law enforcement officers were questioning the defendant about a murder. They informed him that he was not under arrest and was free to leave at any time. The officers gave him *Miranda* warnings and obtained a waiver. The defendant denied his involvement in the murder. During the interview an officer received a telephone call from the SBI lab that the defendant's fingerprints had been found in an ashtray in the victim's home. Another officer told the defendant that he was under arrest for first-degree murder. The officer then made accusatory remarks to the defendant, including asking him how it felt to have killed a seventy-eight-year-old helpless man. The trial judge permitted the officer to testify how the defendant reacted to these accusatory remarks: "He had no reaction. He acted like I was talking about the weather." Relying on State v. Hoyle, 325 N.C. 232, 382 S.E.2d 752 (1989), and Doyle v. Ohio, 426 U.S. 610, 96 S. Ct. 2240, 49 L. Ed. 2d 91 (1976), the court ruled that this evidence impermissibly referred to the defendant's exercise of his right to remain silent. The court also ruled that the state's cross-examination of the defendant (which again elicited the defendant's silence in response to the officer's accusation) was improper.

State v. Buckner

342 N.C. 198, 464 S.E.2d 414 (1995), *cert. denied*, 117 S. Ct. 91 (1996)

The court ruled that the prosecutor's jury argument recounting the defendant's failure to tell officers at his interrogation that another person had shot the murder victim did not violate the ruling in Doyle v. Ohio, 426 U.S. 610, 96 S. Ct. 2240, 49 L. Ed. 2d 91 (1976), because there was no evidence that the defendant had been given his *Miranda* warnings during the interrogation. The court relied on the ruling in Jenkins v. Anderson, 447 U.S. 231, 100 S. Ct. 2124, 65 L. Ed. 2d 86 (1980).

State v. Alkano

119 N.C. App. 256, 458 S.E.2d 258, *appeal dismissed*, 341 N.C. 653, 465 S.E.2d 533 (1995)

The defendant, who had not been given *Miranda* warnings, volunteered several inculpatory statements after his arrest. At trial, the prosecutor asked officers about the defendant's failure to explain several matters surrounding the crime. The court ruled that the state did not impermissibly comment on the defendant's silence in violation of Doyle v. Ohio, 426 U.S. 610, 96 S. Ct. 2240, 49 L. Ed. 2d 91 (1976), because the defendant in this case was not silent about the facts of the crime when he was arrested.

Use of Evidence Obtained as the Result of a Miranda Violation [page 397]

State v. Hicks

333 N.C. 467, 428 S.E.2d 167 (1993)

(1) Officers asked the defendant—who had been told by an officer that he was a suspect in a murder because he and the victim had just broken up before she was murdered—to take a polygraph test to "clear his name." They transported the defendant with his consent over an hour's drive away from his home in Mocksville to the SBI office in Hickory for the purpose of taking the test. Although he refused to take the polygraph test three separate times during two hours of questioning, the defendant was never taken home or offered transportation home. Although the polygraph operator informed the defendant during his explanation of the polygraph procedure that he was not under arrest, the defendant never was told that he was free to leave. After a third refusal to take the test, the defendant told the polygraph operator that he wanted to go outside with him. During a conversation in the parking lot, the defendant told the operator that he wanted to take responsibility for the murder. They went back into the building, and the operator informed two investigating officers that the defendant wanted to confess. When the defendant refused to elaborate on the details of the crime, the officers told him that he would have to tell them what had happened, including any details. The defendant then gave them the details and demonstrated how he had shot the victim. After the defendant explained the details of the murder, the officers advised the defendant of his Miranda rights and obtained a valid waiver. The defendant then gave a second confession.

The court ruled that a reasonable person in the defendant's position, knowing that he was a suspect in a murder case and having just stated to an officer that he wanted to take responsibility for a murder, would feel that he was compelled to stay and therefore was in custody under Miranda immediately following that statement. Thus the first confession that was taken without Miranda warnings should have been ruled inadmissible. (2) The court ruled that the second confession, taken after Miranda warnings had been properly given and waived, was admissible under the ruling in Oregon v. Elstad, 470 U.S. 298, 105 S. Ct. 1285, 84 L. Ed. 2d 222 (1985) (fact that voluntary confession is inadmissible because of

Miranda violation does not prohibit admission of later voluntary confession given after proper Miranda warnings and waiver). And the court adopted the Oregon v. Elstad ruling to determine alleged constitutional violations under Article I, sections 19 and 23, of the North Carolina Constitution. (3) The court ruled that the state must prove that evidence admitted in violation of Miranda (in this case, the first confession) must be proven harmless beyond a reasonable doubt under G.S. 15A-1443(b); the court concluded that the state did so in this case.

State v. May

334 N.C. 609, 434 S.E.2d 180 (1993), cert. denied, 510 U.S. 1198 (1994)

The court ruled that physical evidence found as a result of a Miranda violation (in this case, the defendant's statement led officers to a knife, a pair of gloves, and a rag in the defendant's backyard) is admissible when the defendant was not coerced into giving the statement (that is, the statement was voluntarily given). The court relied on Michigan v. Tucker, 417 U.S. 433, 94 S. Ct. 2357, 41 L. Ed. 2d 182 (1974), and Oregon v. Elstad, 470 U.S. 298, 105 S. Ct. 1285, 84 L. Ed. 2d 222 (1985), in ruling that although the officers violated the prophylactic rules of Miranda and Edwards v. Arizona, they did not violate the defendant's right against compelled self-incrimination. The rule's deterrent value is satisfied by excluding the defendant's statement, but not the physical evidence.

State v. Morrell

108 N.C. App. 465, 424 S.E.2d 147, appeal dismissed, review denied, and cert. denied, 333 N.C. 465, 427 S.E.2d 626 (1993)

The defendant was arrested for a federal charge of child abduction and was committed to the county jail. A social worker in the county child protective services unit identified herself to the defendant and told the defendant that she was conducting an investigation of alleged sexual abuse and neglect of a boy with whom the defendant had had a relationship. The defendant confessed to the social worker. Two days later, a detective talked with the defendant in the jail after giving her Miranda warnings and obtaining a proper waiver. The defendant again confessed. Based on evidence that the social worker was working with the sheriff's department on the case before interviewing the defendant in jail, the court ruled that the social worker was an agent of the state and thus was required to give Miranda warnings before her interview with the defendant. [Note, however, that the court did not discuss Illinois v. Perkins, 496 U.S. 292, 110 S. Ct. 2394, 110 L. Ed. 2d 243 (1990), which ruled that when a person does not know that he or she is talking to a law enforcement officer (or agent of a law enforcement officer), there is no reason to assume the possibility of coercion, which is the underlying principle of the *Miranda* decision; thus *Miranda* warnings are not required. If the defendant did not know that the social worker was a law enforcement officer (or agent of a law enforcement officer), then the ruling in *Illinois v. Perkins* did not require the social worker to give *Miranda* warnings.]

The court upheld the admissibility of the defendant's confession to the detective because the confession to the social worker was not coerced; *see* Oregon v. Elstad, 470 U.S. 298, 105 S. Ct. 1285, 84 L. Ed. 2d 222 (1985), and State v. Barlow, 330 N.C. 133, 409 S.E.2d 906 (1991).

North Carolina Statutory Warnings for Young Arrestees [page 398]

State v. Miller
344 N.C. 658, 477 S.E.2d 915 (1996)

Officers arrested a seventeen-year-old for murder. The officers could not find a juvenile rights form so they used an adult *Miranda* form and inserted an additional question, "Do you wish to answer questions without your parents/parent present?" The defendant waived all of his rights except that he stated that he wanted his mother present. No questioning was conducted until his mother was present. During the questioning, the defendant appeared embarrassed and ill at ease. An officer asked the defendant if he was comfortable talking in front of his mom or would he want her to step out of the room. He replied, "She might as well leave." His mother left the interrogation room and sat on a bench outside the open doorway where the defendant could see her if he leaned forward. She was told she could come back into the room at any time. The defendant then confessed to the murder. The court ruled that the additional language added to the adult *Miranda* form adequately conveyed the substance of the defendant's right to have his parent(s) present during questioning. It was clear that the defendant understood his rights because he asked that his mother be present, he did not give any statement until she arrived, and he answered questions in her presence. The court also ruled that the defendant's statements and conduct that resulted in his mother leaving the interrogation room were a knowing and intelligent waiver of his right to have her present during the custodial interrogation.

The Defendant's Sixth Amendment Right to Counsel

Generally [page 399]

State v. Palmer
334 N.C. 104, 431 S.E.2d 172 (1993)

The court ruled that an officer who gave *Miranda* warnings sufficiently established the defendant's waiver of his Sixth Amendment and state constitutional right to counsel. To constitute a valid waiver, the officer was not required to explain specifically to the defendant that he was waiving his right to counsel under these constitutional provisions. *See also* United States v. Chadwick, 999 F.2d 1282 (8th Cir. 1993) (*Miranda* warnings sufficient to waive Sixth Amendment right to counsel; officer is not required to inform defendant that he or she has been indicted).

State v. Gibbs
335 N.C. 1, 436 S.E.2d 321 (1993), *cert. denied*, 114 S. Ct. 2767 (1994)

On May 31, 1990, the defendant was in custody at a police department as a murder suspect. He had not yet been given *Miranda* warnings or interrogated. About fifteen minutes before being taken to the magistrate's office for service of arrest warrants charging him with murder and other offenses, the defendant asked Officer Batchelor if he had to get an attorney (the defendant's inquiry was not in response to questions by the officer). Batchelor told the defendant that the question of a lawyer had to be his decision and asked the defendant if he could afford to hire an attorney. The defendant said he could not, and Batchelor then told him that the court would appoint an attorney to represent him if he asked for one. About an hour later, Batchelor and another officer gave the defendant *Miranda* warnings, properly obtained a waiver, and took a statement from the defendant. The officers obtained another statement from the defendant on June 3, 1990. The defendant had a first appearance in district court on June 4, 1990, which was within 96 hours of his arrest [as required under G.S. 15A-601(c)]. (1) Distinguishing State v. Torres, 330 N.C. 517, 412 S.E.2d 20 (1992), the court ruled that the defendant did not assert his Fifth Amendment right to counsel when he asked Officer Batchelor if he had to get an attorney. In this case, unlike *Torres*, interrogation was not impending and the defendant had not been told he would be questioned. Batchelor's responses to the defendant's question about an attorney constituted narrow clarification, and the defendant did not ask for an attorney afterwards. Moreover, Batchelor did not attempt to dissuade the defendant from exercising his right to an attorney. Based on the entire context in which the defendant's inquiry was made, the defendant did not assert his right to counsel. (2) The court, following State v. Detter, 298 N.C. 604, 260 S.E.2d 567 (1979), State v. Nations, 319 N.C. 318, 354 S.E.2d 510 (1987), and State v. Tucker, 331 N.C. 12, 414 S.E.2d 548 (1992), ruled that the defendant's Sixth Amendment right to counsel did not attach when the defendant was arrested. It did not attach until the defendant's first appearance in district court. Therefore the defendant did not have a Sixth Amendment right to counsel during the interrogations on May 31, 1990, and June 3, 1990. *See also* State v. Adams, 345 N.C. 745, 483 S.E.2d 156 (1997) (defendant did not have Sixth Amendment right to counsel when state brought civil petition for child abuse and neglect against her; Sixth Amendment right to counsel applies only to criminal charges).

State v. Harris
111 N.C. App. 58, 431 S.E.2d 792 (1993)

The defendant was arrested for an armed robbery of a Fast Fare store, committed to jail, and given his first appearance in district court, where he declined appointed counsel (he stated he would hire his own attorney). He remained in jail for that charge. The next day he changed his mind and asked for and was appointed counsel. Later that day, a detective who was investigating an unrelated armed robbery of a Circle K store interrogated the defendant after properly giving him *Miranda* warnings and obtaining a waiver of rights. Relying on McNeil v. Wisconsin, 501 U.S. 171, 111 S. Ct. 2204, 115 L. Ed. 2d 158 (1991), the court ruled that the defendant, when he invoked his Sixth Amendment right to counsel for the Fast Fare robbery, did not invoke his Fifth Amendment right to counsel concerning the interrogation of the Circle K robbery (and he did not have a Sixth Amendment right to counsel because he had not even been charged yet for that offense). The court also rejected the defendant's arguments under Article I, Section 23, of the North Carolina Constitution.

Chewning v. Rogerson
29 F.3d 418 (8th Cir. 1994)

The court ruled that the defendant's representation by an attorney at an extradition hearing was not an invocation of his Sixth Amendment right to counsel for the murder charge for which he was being extradited.

Defendant's Statements after an Alleged Unconstitutional Arrest

When an Unconstitutional Arrest Occurred
[page 406]

State v. Knight
340 N.C. 531, 459 S.E.2d 481 (1995)

The murder victim was stabbed twenty-seven times, castrated, and his penis inserted in his mouth. Officers went to the defendant's home to execute arrest and search warrants for this murder. They knocked on the front door several times and announced, "Police! Search warrant!" at least two or three times. After waiting thirty to sixty seconds and hearing no response from inside the residence, the officers used a battering ram to open the door. They entered the residence, conducted a quick sweep for weapons, and arrested the defendant. The defendant was taken to the police station, where he confessed to his participation in the murder and also told the officers where one of the knives used in the murder was located in his house.

The court ruled that the officers' forcible entry into the premises was reasonable under the Fourth Amendment [*see* Wilson v. Arkansas, 514 U.S. 927, 115 S. Ct. 1914, 131 L. Ed. 2d 976 (1995)] and complied with the provisions of Chapter 15A. They had probable cause to believe that further delay in entering the residence or the giving of more specific notice would endanger their own safety or that of other occupants of the residence. They knew that the defendant was dangerous, armed with a hunting knife and possibly firearms; there was at least one other suspect who had not been arrested; they were concerned about the safety of a woman and her children inside the residence, who might become hostages; and if the entry was not forced, it would not be safe. The court ruled, citing New York v. Harris, 495 U.S. 14, 110 S. Ct. 1640, 109 L. Ed. 2d 13 (1990) (confession is not to be suppressed even though officers made unconstitutional entry into home to arrest defendant, when officers had probable cause to arrest and the confession was taken outside the home), that even assuming the forcible entry was unconstitutional, the defendant's confession at the police station was still admissible. The confession was not the fruit of the alleged illegal entry into the home, when the confession was taken at another location and the officers had probable cause to arrest him in any event.

Defendant's Statements after a North Carolina Statutory Violation [page 406]

State v. Chapman
343 N.C. 495, 471 S.E.2d 354 (1996)

On August 23, 1993, about 9:30 A.M., the defendant was arrested at a bank for attempting to cash a forged check. He waived his *Miranda* rights and admitted that he had attempted to cash a check that he had forged after taking it in a robbery. Officers took the defendant to a school to search for a purse that had been taken in the robbery. They then returned the defendant to the police station, where he confessed to forgery and uttering charges. A detective procured arrest warrants for these charges at 12:15 P.M. and served them on the defendant. The defendant was questioned by another detective who was investigating the robbery in which the checks were taken, and the defendant confessed to the robbery at 1:27 P.M. Officers prepared an arrest warrant to charge the robbery but it was not presented to the magistrate. The defendant then was interviewed by another detective about a robbery and murder (not related to the crimes discussed previously). The detective put nine photos of the murder victim on the walls of the interrogation room and one photo of the victim on the floor directly in front of the chair in which the defendant sat during the interrogation. Thus the defendant saw a photo of the victim in every direction he turned. During the interview, the detective falsely implied to the defendant that a note found next to the victim's body had been the subject of handwriting analysis that showed it was the defendant's handwriting and that the defendant's fingerprints were on the note. The defendant confessed to the murder at about 7:05 P.M. and was taken to the magistrate about 8:00 P.M.

(1) The court ruled that there was no unreasonable delay in a magistrate's determination of whether there was probable cause to issue an arrest warrant. Distinguishing County of Riverside v. McLaughlin, 500 U.S. 44, 111 S. Ct. 1661, 114 L. Ed. 2d 49 (1991), and Gerstein v. Pugh, 420 U.S. 103, 95 S. Ct. 854, 43 L. Ed. 2d 54 (1975), the court noted that the defendant was arrested at 9:30 A.M. without a warrant and a magistrate issued an arrest warrant based on probable cause at 12:30 P.M. This procedure satisfied the rulings in these cases that a magistrate promptly determine probable cause. The court noted that the defendant was then in lawful custody and could be interrogated about other crimes. (2) The court ruled that the defendant's statutory right under G.S. 15A-501(2) to be taken to a magistrate without unnecessary delay was not violated. The court noted that much of the time from the defendant's arrest at 9:30 A.M. until he was taken before a magistrate at 8:00 P.M. was spent interrogating the defendant about several crimes. The court stated

that the officers had the right to conduct these interrogations and they did not cause an unnecessary delay by doing so. (3) The officers failed to advise the defendant of his right to communicate with friends, in violation of G.S. 15A-501(5). The court ruled that, based on State v. Curmon, 295 N.C. 453, 245 S.E.2d 503 (1978), the defendant was not prejudiced by this violation, based on the facts in this case.

State v. Jones
112 N.C. App. 337, 435 S.E.2d 574 (1993)

The defendant was arrested for breaking and entering and larceny about 1:05 P.M. and taken to the police department. He waived his *Miranda* rights and talked to officers for a while and then asserted his right to counsel. The officers stopped the interrogation and left the defendant in the interrogation room until about 7:00 P.M., when they obtained a search warrant for his apartment. The officers took the defendant with them to execute the search warrant. The defendant and an officer had a general conversation there, including the officer's responding to the defendant's request for a cigarette (the trial judge found that the conversation was not calculated to induce the defendant to make incriminating statements, and the defendant made none). The defendant's live-in girlfriend became upset during the officers' questioning of her about which items in the apartment were hers. The defendant decided then to initiate a conversation with the officers, so they would not bother her about these items. The defendant then showed the officers which items were stolen.

When the officers took him back to the police station, the defendant was advised of his *Miranda* rights; he waived those rights and confessed. (1) The court ruled, following Rhode Island v. Innis, 446 U.S. 291, 100 S. Ct. 1682, 64 L. Ed. 2d 297 (1980), that the evidence did not show that the officers should have known that their actions (taking the defendant for execution of the search warrant, the reaction of his girlfriend to the officers' questioning, the defendant's reaction, and so on) would elicit an incriminating response. (2) The trial judge had ruled that officers violated G.S. 15A-501(2) (taking the defendant to magistrate without unnecessary delay) and G.S. 15A-501(5) (advising the defendant without unnecessary delay of right to communicate with counsel and friends), but these violations had not proximately caused the defendant's incriminating statements. The court affirmed the trial judge's ruling, following State v. Richardson, 295 N.C. 309, 245 S.E.2d 754 (1978) (statutory exclusionary rule requires, at a minimum, a "but for" causal relationship between statutory violation and confession), and noted that the defendant did not argue a causal connection before the trial judge.

Defendant's Trial Testimony Allegedly Induced by Introduction of Illegally Obtained Statement [new section]

State v. Easterling
119 N.C. App. 22, 457 S.E.2d 913, *review denied*, 341 N.C. 422, 461 S.E.2d 762 (1995)

(Note: To better understand the summary of this appellate case, be aware that the defendant was tried and convicted of multiple counts of rape and sexual offense that he committed with his accomplice, Sherman White.) After a detective gave the defendant his *Miranda* warnings, the defendant asserted his right to counsel. The detective later informed the defendant that he would be taken to the magistrate's office to be served with arrest warrants. The detective then asked, "Who was Sherman?" The defendant said "White." Just a few moments later the defendant indicated that he wanted to talk about the case. The detective then gave him *Miranda* warnings and obtained a waiver, and the defendant gave an incriminating statement that was introduced in the state's case-in-chief at trial. The court ruled that the detective's question constituted interrogation because it was designed to elicit an incriminating response. Therefore the question was improper under Edwards v. Arizona, 384 U.S. 436, 101 S. Ct. 1880, 68 L. Ed. 2d 378 (1981), because it was made after the defendant's assertion of his right to counsel. In addition, the defendant's statement a few moments later that he was willing to talk about the case was a continuation of the improper interrogation (that is, it was not simply the defendant's initiation of communication with the detective). Thus the trial judge erred in admitting the defendant's confession. The court also ruled that, based on the state's overwhelming evidence against the defendant in this case, the defendant was not induced to testify on his behalf because of the introduction in the state's case-in-chief of this illegally obtained confession; *see generally* Harrison v. United States, 392 U.S. 219, 88 S. Ct. 2008, 20 L. Ed. 2d 1047 (1968). The court also ruled that the introduction of the confession was harmless error beyond a reasonable doubt.

Scope of the Witness's Fifth Amendment Privilege [page 407]

Debnam v. Department of Correction
334 N.C. 380, 432 S.E.2d 324 (1993)

The court ruled that the state did not violate a public employee's Fifth Amendment right against compelled self-incrimination by firing the employee for refusing to answer questions relating to his employment (questions about an incident involving a ring allegedly stolen from an inmate). The employee had been informed that his failure to answer might result in his dismissal, but the state did not seek the employee's waiver of his immunity from the state's use of any of his answers in a criminal action against him. The court rejected the employee's argument that the Fifth Amendment prohibited the state from firing him for refusing to answer questions during its internal investigation, because the employee was not advised that his responses could not be used against him in any criminal prosecution and that the questions would relate specifically and narrowly to his performance of official duties.

State v. Ray
336 N.C. 463, 444 S.E.2d 918 (1994)

The defendant was convicted of first-degree murder that was drug-related. During direct examination of a state's witness—an eyewitness to the murder—the state asked the witness about his and the murder victim's involvement with drug dealing. On cross-examination, the witness refused to answer some questions about drug dealing, asserting his Fifth Amendment privilege against compelled self-incrimination. The trial judge found that some of the answers to the cross-examination questions could be incriminating and that the witness had a right to refuse to answer those questions. After the witness had completed his testimony, the defendant asked the trial judge to direct the witness to answer the questions to which he had invoked the privilege or to strike the witness's entire testimony. The court noted that the issue of whether the witness was properly allowed to assert the privilege was not raised on appeal. However, the court ruled that the defendant's right to confront witnesses through cross-examination was unreasonably limited by the witness's assertion of the testimonial privilege. The court discussed several cases, particularly United States v. Cardillo, 316 F.2d 606 (2d Cir.), *cert. denied*, 375 U.S. 822 (1963), and noted that courts have distinguished between the assertion of the privilege preventing inquiry into *matters about which the witness testified on direct examination* (in which case the defendant's motion to strike the testimony should be granted) and the assertion of the privilege preventing inquiry into *collateral matters, such as the credibility of the witness* (in which case the defendant's motion to strike the testimony should be denied). The court examined the facts in this case and ruled that the trial judge erred in not striking the testimony of the witness because the prohibited inquiry on cross-examination involved matters discussed on direct examination—drug dealing that was the basis of the relationship between the victim, the defendant, and the witness. (However, the court found that the error was harmless beyond a reasonable doubt.)

Qurneh v. Colie
122 N.C. App. 553, 471 S.E.2d 433 (1996)

The plaintiff (natural father) filed a civil lawsuit against the defendant (natural mother) seeking custody of his child. The defendant and intervenors (the child's maternal grandparents) alleged that the plaintiff was unfit to have custody. When the plaintiff was cross-examined about his alleged illegal drug use, he asserted his Fifth Amendment privilege against compelled self-incrimination. The court ruled that when the plaintiff failed to make a prima facie showing that he was fit to have custody and the trial judge could not determine the plaintiff's fitness because he had asserted his Fifth Amendment privilege, the trial judge properly dismissed the plaintiff's claim for custody and awarded custody to the intervenors. The court noted a similar ruling in Cantwell v. Cantwell, 109 N.C. App. 395, 427 S.E.2d 129 (1993).

State v. Locklear
117 N.C. App. 255, 450 S.E.2d 516 (1994)

The trial judge during the trial ordered the defendant to speak the exact words of the robber so a state's witness could attempt to make a voice identification. The court ruled, relying on State v. Perry, 291 N.C. 284, 230 S.E.2d 141 (1976), and other cases, that the defendant's Fifth Amendment privilege against compelled self-incrimination was not violated by the judge's order.

In re Jones
116 N.C. App. 695, 449 S.E.2d 221 (1994)

Jones, who had a pending murder charge against him, was called as a defense witness in a related murder trial of another person. Jones refused, by asserting his Fifth Amendment privilege against compelled self-incrimination, to answer two questions asked by the prosecutor on cross-examination. The trial judge held Jones in contempt of court for refusing to answer the questions. The court re-

versed. One question—whether the defendant owed money for drugs to some specified people—was a matter that the state was seeking to prove at Jones's upcoming murder trial. Thus the answer to this question could incriminate Jones. The other question—did Jones have a reputation for robbing drug dealers—could be used to undermine Jones's credibility if he were charged with some crime in the future. Thus, the court stated, it was possible that the answer to this question could incriminate Jones.

Admissibility of Written Confession
[new section]

State v. Wagner
343 N.C. 250, 470 S.E.2d 33 (1996)

The state sought to introduce the detective's handwritten notes of the defendant's confession. The notes were not read to the defendant, signed by him, or otherwise admitted to be correct. The court ruled that State v. Walker, 269 N.C. 135, 152 S.E.2d 133 (1967) (setting out the rules for the admission of a written confession), does not bar the admissibility of an unsigned statement taken in longhand of a defendant's actual responses to recorded questions. The court noted that the evidence showed that the notes were an exact, word-for-word rendition of the interview of the defendant.

State v. Bartlett
121 N.C. App. 521, 466 S.E.2d 302 (1996)

While the defendant spoke to law enforcement officers, one of the officers attempted to write down the defendant's answers to the questions asked by another officer. The officer's questions were not written down. When the paper writing was given to the defendant, he refused to sign it. The court ruled that the trial judge erroneously permitted the state to introduce the paper writing into evidence. The court noted the general rule that a defendant's written statement may not be introduced into evidence unless (1) it was read to or by the defendant and signed or otherwise admitted to being correct or (2) it was a verbatim record of the questions asked and answers given by the defendant. In this case, the officer did not write down the questions asked and never testified that the answers given by the defendant were correctly reflected on the paper writing. In addition, there was no evidence that the defendant acquiesced in the correctness of the paper writing. [Note: This ruling applies only to the admissibility of the paper writing, not to the admissibility of oral testimony of the conversation between the officers and the defendant.]

Part VI. Lineups and Other Identification Procedures

The following summaries of appellate cases provide the page number of the case summaries section in the second edition where these cases should be added.

Due–Process Review of Identification Procedures

Generally [page 409]

State v. Hunt
339 N.C. 622, 457 S.E.2d 276 (1995)
The witness's identification of the defendant was independent of an illegal lineup, based on the facts in this case.

State v. Capps
114 N.C. App. 156, 441 S.E.2d 621 (1994)
Although one-on-one showups were unnecessarily suggestive, they were not impermissibly suggestive to result in a substantial likelihood of irreparable misidentification, based on the facts in this case. Therefore the trial judge did not err in admitting evidence of the witnesses' out-of-court identifications of the defendant that occurred during the showups. Also, the in-court identifications by the witnesses were properly admitted.

Part VII. Nontestimonial Identification Orders

The following summary of an appellate case provides the page number of the case summaries section in the second edition where this case should be added.

Authority to Conduct Nontestimonial Identification Procedures [page 413]

State v. Green
124 N.C. App. 269, 477 S.E.2d 182 (1996)
A law enforcement officer took a photograph of a thirteen-year-old juvenile suspect with his consent but without a nontestimonial identification order. The court noted that the detective's action violated G.S. 7A-596 because a nontestimonial identification order had not been obtained (that is, the juvenile's consent did not alleviate the obligation to obtain the order).

Part VIII. Motions to Suppress, Suppression Hearings, and Exclusionary Rules

The following summaries of appellate cases provide the page numbers of the case summaries section in the second edition where these cases should be added.

Motions to Suppress; Appellate Review
[page 415]

State v. Palmer
334 N.C. 104, 431 S.E.2d 172 (1993)

An order denying a motion to suppress was valid even though the written order was filed after the superior court term had concluded and fifty-seven days after the notice of appeal had been entered, when the judge had verbally denied the motion in open court after the suppression hearing was held. *See, e.g.,* State v. Smith, 320 N.C. 404, 358 S.E.2d 329 (1987), and State v. Horner, 310 N.C. 274, 311 S.E.2d 281 (1984).

State v. Brooks
337 N.C. 132, 446 S.E.2d 579 (1994)

The defendant had previously been prosecuted in federal court on federal drug charges arising from the same search. A federal judge had ruled that the search violated the Fourth Amendment and suppressed the cocaine that had been seized. The court ruled that the federal court suppression of the cocaine did not collaterally estop the state from introducing the same evidence in state court. Collateral estoppel does not apply, under either federal or state constitutions, to criminal cases in which separate sovereigns are involved in separate proceedings and there is no privity between the two sovereigns in the first proceeding. The state was not in privity with the federal government concerning federal charges simply because it may have deferred to having federal prosecution begin first.

State v. Bunnell
340 N.C. 74, 455 S.E.2d 426 (1995)

The defendant's motion to suppress at trial challenged the voluntariness of his statement to a law enforcement officer. The court ruled that the defendant could not assert, for the first time on appeal, a challenge to his statement on the ground that it was obtained in violation of his Sixth Amendment right to counsel, because he did not assert this ground in his suppression motion at trial. The court cited State v. Benson, 323 N.C. 318, 372 S.E.2d 517 (1988).

State v. Jaynes
342 N.C. 249, 464 S.E.2d 448 (1995), *cert. denied,* 116 S. Ct. 2563 (1996)

Before trial, a suppression hearing was held on the issue of the defendant's motion to suppress two letters written by the defendant. The judge denied the motion. During trial, the defendant moved to suppress a third letter written by the defendant based on the same legal grounds as the pretrial motion. The trial judge refused to conduct another suppression hearing. The court ruled that the trial judge did not err because, based on these facts, there was no reason for another hearing.

State v. Watkins
120 N.C. App. 804, 463 S.E.2d 802 (1995)

An officer stopped a vehicle for impaired driving. A prior appeal of this case determined that anonymous information and the officer's observations provided reasonable suspicion for the stop; *see* State v. Watkins, 337 N.C. 437, 446 S.E.2d 67 (1994). The defendant then filed a supplemental suppression motion based on newly discovered evidence that the anonymous information had been supplied to the stopping officer by another officer and that this other officer had fabricated the information (there was no evidence that the stopping officer knew that the information was fabricated). The court ruled that the defendant had the authority to file a supplemental suppression motion based on newly discovered evidence; *see* G.S. 15A-975(c).

State v. McBride
120 N.C. App. 623, 463 S.E.2d 403 (1995), *affirmed,* 344 N.C. 623, 476 S.E.2d 106 (1996)

The defendant negotiated a guilty plea with the state, and the judge accepted the guilty plea. The defendant then filed a notice of appeal of the judge's denial of his suppression motion; *see* G.S. 15A-979(b). The court dismissed the appeal without reaching the merits of the suppression motion because the defendant failed, under State v. Reynolds, 298 N.C. 380, 259 S.E.2d 843 (1979), to preserve the right to appeal by giving notice to the judge and prosecutor of his intent to appeal before entering the guilty plea.

Suppression Hearings [page 417]

State v. Cohen
117 N.C. App. 265, 450 S.E.2d 503 (1994)

Officers obtained the consent of the defendant's wife to search her car. The officers searched its contents, including an unlocked briefcase. The defendant made a motion to suppress the search of the briefcase on the ground that his wife did not have the authority to consent to its search by the officers. The trial judge refused to accept the wife's affidavit at the suppression hearing because she was available as a witness; the defendant declined the judge's offer of additional time to produce his wife as a witness. The court ruled that the judge properly refused to admit the affidavit, based on these facts. The court also ruled that the defendant's suppression motion was properly denied because the defendant failed to present evidence that he had ownership of or a possessory interest in the briefcase.

Standing to Contest Fourth Amendment Violations [page 418]

United States v. Padilla
508 U.S. 77, 113 S. Ct. 1936, 123 L. Ed. 2d 635 (1993)

An Arizona law enforcement officer stopped a vehicle driven by Arciniega, the sole occupant. Arciniega consented to a search of the vehicle, and the officer found cocaine. The Ninth Circuit Court of Appeals ruled that various drug co-defendants had standing to contest the search of the vehicle, because a co-conspirator has a legitimate expectation of privacy under Fourth Amendment if a co-conspirator's participation in an operation or arrangement indicates joint control and supervision of the place searched. The Court rejected the Ninth Circuit's ruling, and remanded the case for consideration of standing under principles set out in Alderman v. United States, 394 U.S. 165, 89 S. Ct. 961, 22 L. Ed. 2d 176 (1969), Rakas v. Illinois, 439 U.S. 128, 99 S. Ct. 421, 58 L. Ed. 2d 387 (1978), Rawlings v. Kentucky, 448 U.S. 98, 100 S. Ct. 2556, 65 L. Ed. 2d 633 (1980), and Soldal v. Cook County, 506 U.S. 56, 113 S. Ct. 538, 121 L. Ed. 2d 450 (1992).

State v. Mlo
335 N.C. 353, 440 S.E.2d 98, *cert. denied*, 512 U.S. 1224 (1994)

The defendant was on trial for first-degree murder. The defendant sought to suppress evidence obtained from a search of the murder victim's car. The court ruled that the defendant's unsubstantiated and self-serving statements that the victim had loaned his car to him were insufficient to satisfy his burden of showing a legitimate possessory interest in the car; thus the defendant did not have standing to contest the search of the car. There was evidence from the victim's best friend that he had never known the victim to loan his car to anyone.

State v. Howell
343 N.C. 229, 470 S.E.2d 38 (1996)

The defendant lived in a converted school bus located in a used car junkyard. The defendant owed money to an employee and the owner of the junkyard. Before leaving North Carolina, the defendant told the employee that he could have the bus and contents. The employee sold the bus to the junkyard owner. The court ruled, based on these facts, that the defendant did not have standing under the Fourth Amendment to contest a search of the bus.

State v. Cohen
117 N.C. App. 265, 450 S.E.2d 503 (1994)

Officers obtained the consent of the defendant's wife to search her car. The officers searched its contents, including an unlocked briefcase. The defendant made a motion to suppress the search of the briefcase on the ground that his wife did not have the authority to consent to its search by the officers. The trial judge refused to accept the wife's affidavit at the suppression hearing because she was available as a witness; the defendant declined the judge's offer of additional time to produce his wife as a witness. The court ruled that the judge properly refused to admit the affidavit, based on these facts. The court also ruled that the defendant's suppression motion was properly denied because the defendant failed to present evidence that he had ownership of or a possessory interest in the briefcase.

State v. Smith
117 N.C. App. 671, 452 S.E.2d 827 (1995)

[Note: There was a dissenting opinion in this case, but the defendant declined to seek further review.] Officers stopped a cab in which the defendant and Campbell were passengers. The defendant consented to a search of his luggage, and Campbell consented to the search of his luggage; cocaine was found in both. The defendant was charged with a trafficking offense. A judge granted the defendant's motion to suppress evidence seized from the defendant's luggage, because the stop of the cab was unconstitutional. The defendant then was charged with a drug trafficking conspiracy offense. The defendant then moved to suppress the cocaine found in Campbell's luggage and to suppress proposed testimony by Campbell. The court ruled that a judge (a different judge from the one who had ruled on the first motion) properly denied that motion, because the defendant did not have a reasonable expectation of privacy in Campbell's luggage and did not have standing to object to the proposed testimony of Campbell, even if it was the fruit of the illegal stop of the cab.

United States v. Dumas
94 F.3d 286 (7th Cir. 1996)

Whether or not a driver or passenger of a vehicle would have standing to contest a search of the vehicle, such a person has standing to challenge the seizure of his or her own person that occurred when the officers stopped the vehicle and detained the vehicle's occupants. *See also* United States v. Eylicio-Montoya, 70 F.3d 1158 (10th Cir. 1993) (similar ruling); United States v. Kimball, 25 F.3d 1 (1st Cir. 1994) (similar ruling, but passenger lacked standing to challenge seizure of vehicle and later inventory search).

United States v. Riazco
91 F.3d 752 (5th Cir.), *cert. denied*, 117 S. Ct. 497 (1996)

The court ruled that the driver of a rental car did not have standing to contest the search of the car (in this case, the stereo speaker cavities where drugs were found), when he was not authorized by the rental agreement to drive it and did not have the permission to drive it from the renter of the car. It also was irrelevant that the driver had the permission of the passenger to drive the car, because the passenger was not authorized to drive the car either. *See also* United States v. Muhammad, 58 F.3d 353 (8th Cir. 1995) (similar ruling).

Bonner v. Anderson
81 F.3d 472 (4th Cir. 1996)

Officers executed a search warrant at a residence while the plaintiff was inside. The plaintiff asserted in a civil lawsuit against the officers that they violated the Fourth Amendment in failing to appropriately knock and announce before entering the residence. The plaintiff did not live in the residence. However, the court, noting Minnesota v. Olson, 495 U.S. 91, 110 S. Ct. 1684, 109 L. Ed. 2d 85 (1990), ruled that the plaintiff had a reasonable expectation of privacy in the residence because she frequently visited there and often ran errands for an elderly person who lived there.

Bond v. United States
77 F.3d 1009 (7th Cir.), *cert. denied*, 117 S. Ct. 270 (1996)

The defendant told an officer that he did not own a suitcase that was in a hotel room (even though the officer noticed that the suitcase had the defendant's name on it). The officer searched the suitcase and found $128,000 in-

side. The defendant then admitted that the suitcase was his but denied owning the money inside. The court ruled that the defendant's denial of ownership of the suitcase and his leaving the suitcase in another person's hotel room (the defendant did not have a key to the room and was not registered there) was an abandonment of the suitcase. The defendant therefore did not have a reasonable expectation of privacy in the suitcase to contest its search.

United States v. Austin
66 F.3d 1115 (10th Cir. 1995), *cert. denied*, 116 S. Ct. 799 (1996)

A person (the defendant) who entrusted his bag to a stranger at an airport, by asking him if he would watch the bag while he was gone for "a few minutes," did not retain a reasonable expectation of privacy in the bag. By leaving the bag in the stranger's possession and control, the defendant assumed the risk that the stranger would allow airport authorities access to the bag.

United States v. King
55 F.3d 1193 (6th Cir. 1995)

The defendant mailed some letters to his wife, who later gave them to another person. Law enforcement officers later seized the letters from this person. The court ruled that the defendant had no standing to contest the seizure of the letters. If a letter is sent to another, the sender's expectation of privacy ordinarily terminates on delivery, even if the sender instructs the recipient to keep the letters private.

United States v. Kopp
45 F.3d 1450 (10th Cir.), *cert. denied*, 115 S. Ct. 1721 (1995)

The defendant was driving a pickup truck that was pulling a U-Haul trailer. The court noted that it must consider separately the defendant's reasonable expectation of privacy in the pickup truck and in the trailer. Although the defendant owned the pickup truck, he neither owned nor rented the trailer. Rather, a passenger in his pickup truck rented the trailer and carried the key to it. Based on these facts, the court ruled that the defendant did not have a reasonable expectation of privacy in the trailer and could not contest the legality of the officer's search of the trailer.

United States v. Poulsen
41 F.3d 1330 (9th Cir. 1994)

A person did not have a reasonable expectation of privacy in the contents of his storage locker when the manager of the self-service storage locker had seized the contents pursuant to a valid state law lien after the person failed to pay overdue rent.

United States v. Wellons
32 F.3d 117 (4th Cir. 1994), *cert. denied*, 115 S. Ct. 1115 (1995)

The defendant did not have a reasonable expectation of privacy to contest the search of a rental car and the defendant's luggage inside the car when the rental agreement did not authorize the defendant to drive the car, even if the authorized driver gave the defendant permission to drive the car.

United States v. Stallings
28 F.3d 58 (8th Cir. 1994)

The defendant did not have a reasonable expectation of privacy in a tote bag he left in an open field owned by another person. There was no indication of ownership on the bag.

United States v. Perea
986 F.2d 633 (2d Cir. 1993)

A bailee of a duffel bag had a reasonable expectation of privacy in the bag to contest its search by law enforcement officers.

General Exclusionary Rules

The Independent-Source Exception [page 423]

State v. Wallace
111 N.C. App. 581, 433 S.E.2d 238, *review denied*, 335 N.C. 242, 439 S.E.2d 161 (1993)

Officers received information that marijuana was being grown in the basement of a residence. However, the officers were unable to corroborate the informant's information. Therefore they went to the residence to confirm or to refute the information. After the officers knocked on the door, Jolly came out and closed the door behind him. The officers told him why they were there and asked him if there were others in the residence. Jolly told the officers that one of his roommates was asleep inside. The officers then asked for consent to search the residence. Before Jolly could answer, Wallace came out of the residence. The officers then asked for consent to search, which Wallace and Jolly denied. According to the court's opinion, "Jolly then stated that '*there might be some drug paraphernalia and marijuana seeds in the house*,' and that he would not consent to a search until he had time to get rid of the contraband." After the officers were denied consent to search, they heard footsteps in the residence and a door shut on the inside. The officers asked Wallace and Jolly about who was in the residence, and they said they did not know because they had just arrived. The officers then went inside to execute a protective sweep before leaving the residence to obtain a search warrant. The officers saw what appeared to be marijuana plants while inside. The defendants were detained in the residence while other officers obtained a search warrant, which included information about their observation of marijuana in the house.

The court ruled: (1) Uncorroborated information initially given to the officers was insufficient to establish probable cause to search the residence. (2) The officers did not violate the defendants' rights by going to the residence to investigate the information they had received. (3) Probable cause existed to search the residence when Jolly made the statement noted in italics above. (4) The officers did not have exigent circumstances to enter the residence without a search warrant. The court stated that the "record is devoid of any evidence that the officers entered the residence with a reasonably objective belief that evidence was about to be removed or destroyed." The court noted that the only purpose of the officers' entry into the residence was to conduct a protective sweep until a search warrant could be obtained, and the officers did not believe they were in danger at any time. (5) The state could not justify the search of the residence under the independent-source exception to the exclusionary rule; Murray v. United States, 487 U.S. 533, 108 S. Ct. 2529, 101 L. Ed. 2d 472 (1988), and Segura v. United States, 468 U.S. 796, 104 S. Ct. 3380, 82 L. Ed. 2d 599 (1984). In this case, the search warrant was prompted by what the officers saw in their unlawful entry, and the information obtained during the illegal entry was presented to the magistrate and affected the decision to issue the search warrant.

State v. Waterfield
117 N.C. App. 295, 450 S.E.2d 524 (1994)

On May 13, 1993, officers went to the defendant's residence without a search warrant. The defendant refused to consent to a search of his residence. One officer told the defendant that he would stay with the defendant while the other officers obtained a search warrant. When the officers insisted that the defendant remain in their view at all times, the defendant shut and locked the door. One officer kicked the door down and forced the defendant to sit in a chair. About one-and-one-half hours later, officers returned with a search warrant and conducted a search.

No information obtained during the initial entry was used in the affidavit for the search warrant. The affidavit stated that on April 1, 1993, three people gave an officer about three grams of marijuana that they said the defendant had given them. They stated that the defendant had shown them marijuana kept in a padlocked cabinet in his bedroom at his residence. On April 2,

1993, a confidential informant told an officer he had seen marijuana in the defendant's residence and stated that the defendant kept the marijuana in a padlocked cabinet in his bedroom. On April 5, 1993, officers visited the defendant's residence and confirmed that he lived there. On May 12, 1993, another confidential informant reported to an officer that within the last twenty-four hours the informant had seen about a half pound of marijuana at the defendant's residence and had seen the defendant sell marijuana from his home; the informant also stated that the defendant kept marijuana in a padlocked cabinet in his bedroom. The court ruled that the affidavit supplied probable cause to support the search warrant. Although the affidavit did not mention the reliability of the officers' sources of information, it did provide information about the presence and sale of marijuana at the defendant's residence within twenty-four hours of the warrant application. It further described the location and manner of the defendant's storage of the marijuana that matched information supplied by other sources. Relying on Segura v. United States, 468 U.S. 796, 104 S. Ct. 3380, 82 L. Ed. 2d 599 (1984), the court also ruled that the search pursuant to the search warrant was valid because the information used to apply for the search warrant was obtained entirely independently of the allegedly illegal initial entry to secure the residence.

State v. McLean
120 N.C. App. 838, 463 S.E.2d 826 (1995)
Exterminators and apartment managers discovered marijuana in an apartment as a result of the exterminating work performed there. The apartment managers then contacted a local law enforcement agency. An officer entered the apartment with the managers and saw the marijuana. The officer, without seizing any evidence, left the apartment to await a detective. The detective gathered information from the exterminators, apartment managers, and the law enforcement officer. He provided this information in an affidavit for a search warrant, obtained a search warrant, searched the apartment, and seized the marijuana. [Note: The entry, apparently without the tenant's consent or exigent circumstances, would have been unconstitutional.] The court ruled, assuming without deciding that the officer's entry with the managers was unconstitutional that the seizure of the marijuana should not be suppressed, based on the independent-source exception to the exclusionary rule; see Murray v. United States, 487 U.S. 533, 108 S. Ct. 2529, 101 L. Ed. 2d 472 (1988). There was sufficient probable cause, independent of the illegal entry by the officer and his corroborative observations of the marijuana, to support the search warrant. The finding of probable cause was uncon-

nected with the illegal entry. The court also noted that the detective who applied for the search warrant did not participate in the illegal entry.

United States v. Johnson
994 F.2d 980 (2d Cir.), cert. denied, 510 U.S. 959 (1993)
Officers arrested the defendant for felonious assaults and properly seized audio cassette tapes in his pockets. Six months later the officers listened to the tapes without obtaining a search warrant. The defendant filed a motion to suppress the contents of the tapes, and a judge expressed concern that the officers' warrantless listening to the tapes could not be justified as a search incident to arrest. The government then applied for a search warrant to listen to the tapes again. The court ruled that the affidavit for the search warrant revealed probable cause independent of the information learned from listening to the tapes. Two tapes were labeled with the names of witnesses who had heard that the defendant had taped conversations due to his problems with one of the assault victims. The court also ruled that the officers would have applied for a search warrant had they not listened to the tapes beforehand. Thus the evidence from the tapes was properly admitted under the independent-source exception.

The Inevitable-Discovery Exception [page 424]

State v. Pope
333 N.C. 106, 423 S.E.2d 740 (1992)
Although the defendant's admissions that led to the discovery of the handgun used in a murder were obtained in violation of Arizona v. Roberson, 486 U.S. 675, 108 S. Ct. 2093, 100 L. Ed. 2d 704 (1988), the court ruled that the gun and tests performed on handgun were admissible under the inevitable-discovery exception; see State v. Garner, 331 N.C. 491, 417 S.E.2d 502 (1992). The handgun was found by officers under the seat of a 1953 model Ford truck when it was owned by Alan Estridge. Estridge later sold the truck, and he testified at the suppression hearing that when he sells something, he looks in "every crack and crevice of the truck—car or anything—to make sure there's nothing valuable in there or anything left, or even change." He also testified that if he had found a handgun, he would have delivered it to the detectives. [Note: This evidence would be admissible in any event under the later ruling of State v. May, 334 N.C. 609, 434 S.E.2d 180 (1993), cert. denied, 510 U.S. 1198 (1994).]

United States v. Procopio
88 F.3d 21 (1st Cir. 1996)
A local police department's search of a briefcase exceeded the scope of its inventory search policy and was unconstitutional under the Fourth Amendment. However, based

on the facts in this case, the court ruled that the contents of the briefcase would have been inevitably discovered by federal law enforcement officers. Local officers would have alerted federal officers to the presence of the briefcase because the local officers knew of a pending federal robbery investigation of the defendant, and the federal officers would have obtained a search warrant to search it.

United States v. Eylicio-Montoya
70 F.3d 1158 (10th Cir. 1993)

An officer lawfully stopped a vehicle to investigate marijuana trafficking but then unlawfully arrested the defendant, who was a passenger. The officer then saw burlap bags in the vehicle, which gave him probable cause to search the vehicle for marijuana. The court ruled that the marijuana was admissible because the officer would have inevitably discovered it during the lawful investigative stop, despite the unlawful arrest of the defendant.

United States v. Cabassa
62 F.3d 470 (2d Cir. 1995)

The government failed to prove by a preponderance of evidence that drugs would have inevitably been discovered by means of a search warrant after officers entered an apartment illegally. The officers had prepared a search warrant but never presented it to a judicial official for its issuance.

United States v. Kennedy
61 F.3d 494 (6th Cir. 1995), *cert. denied*, 116 S. Ct. 1351 (1996)

Officers discovered illegal drugs after unlawfully searching lost luggage at the airport without a search warrant. However, the court ruled that the drugs would have inevitably been discovered by lawful means because the airline company, following its policy of opening lost luggage to determine its owner, would have opened it, found the cocaine, and then turned it over to the officers.

Other Exceptions [page 427]

Arizona v. Evans
514 U.S. 1, 115 S. Ct. 1185, 131 L. Ed. 2d 34 (1995)

An officer stopped the defendant for a traffic violation. The officer was informed by a computer message that there was an outstanding arrest warrant for the defendant, which—unknown to the officer—was incorrect be-

cause the warrant had already been dismissed. The officer arrested the defendant based on the information about the warrant, discovered marijuana, and charged the defendant with possession of marijuana. The defendant moved to suppress the marijuana evidence. The Arizona Supreme Court ruled that the evidence should be suppressed regardless of whether the error about the arrest warrant was the fault of court employees or law enforcement personnel. The United States Supreme Court ruled that if the error was the fault of court employees, then the exclusionary rule should not bar the admission of the marijuana evidence. Relying on its rulings in United States v. Leon, 468 U.S. 897, 104 S. Ct. 3405, 82 L. Ed. 2d 677 (1984), Massachusetts v. Sheppard, 468 U.S. 981, 104 S. Ct. 3424, 82 L. Ed. 2d 737 (1984), and Illinois v. Krull, 480 U.S. 340, 107 S. Ct. 1160, 94 L. Ed. 2d 364 (1987), the Court noted that the exclusionary rule was historically designed to deter law enforcement misconduct, not errors by court employees. There was no evidence that court employees were inclined to violate the Fourth Amendment, thus requiring the exclusionary rule to be invoked. Most importantly, there is no basis for believing that the application of the exclusionary rule would have a significant deterrent effect on court employees who are responsible for informing law enforcement when a warrant has been dismissed.

[Note: Since the North Carolina Supreme Court strongly indicated in State v. Carter, 322 N.C. 709, 370 S.E.2d 553 (1988), that a good-faith exception to the exclusionary rule did not exist under the North Carolina Constitution, thereby not adopting the *Leon* and *Sheppard* rulings that were decided under the United States Constitution, it is unclear whether this ruling would apply in North Carolina state courts. However, for a later case that seemed to express different reasoning from that in *Carter*, see State v. Garner, 331 N.C. 491, 417 S.E.2d 502 (1992).]

Withrow v. Williams
507 U.S. 680, 113 S. Ct. 1745, 123 L. Ed. 2d 407 (1993)

The Court ruled that *Miranda* violations must be considered in federal habeas corpus review of state convictions. The Court rejected an extension to *Miranda* violations of the ruling in Stone v. Powell, 428 U.S. 465, 96 S. Ct. 3037, 49 L. Ed. 2d 1067 (1976) (if state provided full and fair review of Fourth Amendment claim, federal habeas corpus review of that claim is unavailable).

Index of Cases in the Case Summaries Section and Descriptive-Word Index

Index of Cases in the Case Summaries Section

United States Supreme Court cases are in bold.

Descriptive-Word Index

Note: This index refers to both the text and the case summaries.